Benefits and Beneficiaries

An Introduction to Estimating Distributional Effects in Cost-Benefit Analysis
(Second Edition)

Elio Londero

Published by the Inter-American Development Bank
Distributed by the Johns Hopkins University Press

Washington, D.C.
1996

The views and opinions expressed in this publication are those of the authors and do not necessarily reflect the official position of the Inter-American Development Bank.

**Benefits and Beneficiaries: An Introduction
to Estimating Distributional Effects in Cost-Benefit Analysis**

© Inter-American Development Bank

First Edition, 1987
Second Edition, 1996

Distributed by
The Johns Hopkins University Press
2715 North Charles Street
Baltimore, Maryland 21218-4319

Library of Congress Catalog Card Number: 96-77939
ISBN: 0-940602-23-7

PREFACE

Since it began operations in 1960, the Inter-American Development Bank has shown particular concern for the income levels of the beneficiaries of the projects it helps to finance. Until 1979, this concern was expressed mainly through the sectorial composition of its portfolio and the importance attributed to projects for low-income beneficiaries.[1] In effect, the Bank played a pioneering role among multilateral finance institutions by supporting "social infrastructure" projects.

Since 1979, in response to a resolution by its Board of Governors (IDB, 1978), Bank economists have been estimating the distribution of income changes brought about by projects for three main categories of beneficiaries: the public sector, low-income people and the remainder of the private sector. In accordance with Bank policy, this distributional effect does not form part of the criteria for taking decisions at the level of individual projects, but it is recorded for all projects and constitutes the main source of information for reporting to the Board of Governors on the overall distributional effect of all operations approved within a particular period. These estimates, which are also innovative among multilateral finance organizations, are carried out for

---

1. See, for example, Herrera et al. (1970) and Dell (1972).

all projects for which a cost-benefit analysis is made, and of which they form an integral part. Current practice at the Bank was developed along with the methodological effort, which the author has endeavored to report on in this study.

Chapter 1 shows that many criteria can be devised to obtain a net "total" benefits figure, corresponding to different distributional value judgments. The most widespread of these criteria, which has come to be known as the "efficiency criterion," corresponds to the following distributional value judgment: one additional unit of income is equally valuable (for the purpose of calculating "total" benefits) whatever the recipient's income level. Consequently, in this approach, the distribution of those income changes among beneficiaries is not a relevant aspect of the analysis and this is why most studies on cost-benefit analysis disregard it. In other approaches, in which the distributional aspects *are* relevant, more emphasis has been placed on deducing and estimating accounting prices incorporating distributional value judgments different from those in the "efficiency" analysis, and less emphasis on estimating the distributional effects proper.

The objective of this study is to present the distributional aspects involved in cost-benefit analysis, to provide guidelines for quantifying the distributional effects of an investment project within such an analysis, and to point out the main difficulties encountered. It is directed towards professionals in the field of applied economic analysis and students interested in a more detailed approach to such topics than that offered in the most widely used textbooks, which it may serve to supplement. An effort has been made to explain topics by giving a summary presentation of the basic principles of cost-benefit analysis, rather than evaluating it as an investment planning tool. The reader will therefore also find numerous references to specialized literature where he or she may find the main topics discussed in more detail.

The first part of this study is devoted to basic principles, their application to deducing expressions for accounting prices, identifying the most important distributional effects and applying them to two examples of investment analysis, all within a framework that has been simplified from various points of view. In the first place, the analysis has been made in a partial equilibrium context which is maintained throughout the text. Secondly, some topics are touched on only indirectly, without being given all the attention they deserve; this is the case for the discount rate. Thirdly, drastic simplifications have been made in regard to the accounting prices of non-traded goods, dealt with in more detail in Part II. Finally, the complications introduced by inter-personal distributional weights and accounting prices of investment have been avoided, these topics being dealt with briefly in Part III.

The three parts in which the subject matter has been organized were intended to be as independent from the other as possible. Therefore, the reader may skip Part II without hindering his comprehension of Part III. While Parts II and III may be perused according to the reader's interest, he may find it difficult to tackle them without previous knowledge of the subjects presented in Part I.

Parts of this study are the result of a joint effort made at the Bank to which the following, among others, contributed: E. Castagnino, J. Fernández, E. Howard, L. Morales Bayro, T. Powers, J. Tejada and the economists of the Project Analysis Department. The author benefited from the experience of E. Howard, C. MacDonald and S. Schmukler, with whom he shared the learning process accompanying the technical supervision of the first stages of application.

The comments of E. Barbieri, J. Coker, X. Comas, R. Fernández, M. Flament and, particularly, A. Thieme helped to improve the presentation of various aspects of the work.

It was T. Powers' suggestion that the section on implementation be added to Chapter 16. E. Mishan made some useful remarks about the first three chapters and A. Harberger commented in detail on several aspects throughout the book. The typing of several drafts was done by S. Zurbarán, L. Romero, N. Lee and P. Wharton. The author sincerely thanks all these people and, since he did not always follow their advice, remains the sole person responsible for the final result.

PREFACE TO THE SECOND EDITION

This second edition is essentially the same as the first. While the original text seems to have withstood the test of time reasonably well, corrections to improve accuracy and to clarify the presentation have been made in response to comments by several attentive readers, especially A. Sciara. In Chapter Six, more substantive changes were made to correct the presentation of the compensating variations of entering into and leaving employment by unskilled workers.

CONTENTS

APPENDICES

PART I

BASIC CONCEPTS

CHAPTER 1

PRINCIPLES AND DISTRIBUTIONAL VALUE JUDGMENTS

1.1 Principles

Any method used to obtain a single measure of the various effects resulting from a particular action requires that the objective of measuring be clearly identified, in order to define how a *measure* of each one of those effects can be obtained, and how such measures *compare* with one another in order to reach the single measure sought. If the objective of measuring is to *judge* the result of the effects as beneficial or harmful, it is also necessary to define *who* does the judging and how relevant the measure chosen and the criterion for comparison are for such purposes.

Cost-benefit analysis is a method for comparing alternative resource allocation and providing answers as to which is "preferable." Since such allocations are the result of "doing" or "not doing," cost-benefit analysis includes the criteria for defining who judges the effects of alternative allocations, how the effects of such actions on the people affected (whether benefiting from or harmed by it) are measured, and how the resulting measures are compared. Each of these criteria colors the final result achieved by using this type of analysis and, consequently, the use made of such results.

The first criterion defines who judges the nature of the effects, and specifies that each person affected is the one who will evaluate the effects on him of the actions being examined. In practice, however, the criterion is used in a social context that determines who is included and in which circumstances. The appointing of "ex officio" defending lawyers and the regulating of narcotics production and marketing are examples of cases where the judgment of effects is not left to individual preferences. Another related problem is whether *all* those affected are taken into account, or only a subset. For example, foreign investment affects the inhabitants of both the investing and recipient countries, and defining the subset of all those affected and considered will depend on the objectives of whoever carries out, or commissions, the analysis.

The second criterion is the measurement criterion, known as the compensating variation (CV). This consists of measuring the effects of an action on a person through the sum of money by which his income needs to be changed so that he is in a situation equivalent to the one he was in before the course of action whose effects we are trying to measure. For example, and by way of a preface to more detailed treatment in Chapter 2, if the result of one allocation of resources in relation to another is an increase in the price of a certain product to a certain person, the CV will be the sum of money which, following that increase, needs to be given to that person so that he is in a situation that he considers equivalent to the previous one. Thus if the CV of the price increase for that person is \$100, that person is said to have incurred a loss of \$100 or a benefit of $-\$100$. Logically, the measurement criterion is critically dependent not only on the above premise regarding who decides whether a person has been affected, but also on a second one, i.e., that the affected person can fully appreciate the effect and convert it into a compensating sum of money.

Once the subset of persons constituting the field of analysis has been defined, and the members of that group affected have been identified, their corresponding CVs need to be known. Since the effects of the actions examined take place over a period of time, a criterion for intertemporal comparisons will be needed. And since a basic principle of cost-benefit analysis is to accept the preferences revealed by individuals, the logically consistent criterion *appears* to be the intertemporal preferences revealed by individuals. The criterion for comparing CVs corresponding to effects at different times, or the criterion for *intertemporal* welfare comparisons, is the one that corresponds to the definition and quantification of the *discount rate* and will be dealt with in more detail in Chapter 8. It is useful, however, to present the basic reasoning underlying the concept of an individual discount rate in summary form. Consider, for example, a course of action A that affects only two persons P and R at two moments in time ($t = 0,1$) and whose CVs are $CV_0^P(A)$ and $CV_1^R(A)$ respectively. Following course of action A implies foregoing course of action B, which also affects only P and R and whose effects are measured by $CV_0^P(B)$

and $CV_1^r(B)$. The welfare change or net benefits (NB) for each person may be expressed as

$$NB^p(A - B) = v_0^p\, CV_0^p(A) - v_0^p\, CV_0^p(B) + v_1^p\, CV_1^p(A) - v_1^p\, CV_1^p(B)$$
$$NB^r(A - B) = v_0^r\, CV_0^r(A) - v_0^r\, CV_0^r(B) + v_1^r\, CV_1^r(A) - v_1^r\, CV_1^r(B)$$

in which v_t^i is the subjective valuation by the individual i of an additional unit of income at time t. The same expressions can be written in shorter form as

$$NB^p(A - B) = v_0^p\, CV_0^p(A - B) + v_1^p\, CV_1^p(A - B)$$
$$NB^r(A - B) = v_0^r\, CV_0^r(A - B) + v_1^r\, CV_1^r(A - B)$$

It is assumed that individuals prefer an additional unit of present consumption to one of future consumption, i.e. that the intertemporal weights v_t^i diminish with time. If for the sake of simplification, the assumption is made that for each individual i these weights decrease at a constant rate d_i, it follows that:

$$v_0^i = v_1^i(1 + d^i) = v_2^i(1 + d^i)^2 = \ldots = v_n^i(1 + d^i)^n$$

This can be expressed in equivalent form as

$$v_n^i = \frac{v_0^i}{(1 + d^i)^n}$$

in which d^i is the so-called individual discount rate. If now the intertemporal valuations of individual i are expressed in accordance with his valuation in year zero, i.e. using the weight at the initial time as a numeraire or unit of account, which is current practice, we have

$$\frac{v_n^i}{v_0^i} = \frac{1}{(1 + d^i)^n}$$

which is the individual discount factor. The expressions for individual net benefits can now be rewritten by dividing both sides by v_0^i, since this will not alter the sign for $NB^i(A - B)$, and replacing the quotients between the weights v_t by the expression just obtained. Thus we arrive at

$$NB^p(A - B) = CV_0^p(A - B) + \left[\frac{1}{(1 + d^p)}\right] CV_1^p(A - B)$$

$$NB^r(A - B) = CV_0^r(A - B) + \left[\frac{1}{(1 + d^r)}\right] CV_1^r(A - B)$$

which is the standard expression for calculating present value, except that up to now the calculation has been made for each person separately and using the discount rate of each individual.

Each of these individual net benefits $NB^i(A - B)$ will be considered the measure of the effect on the respective person, and logically, there will be those who gain and those who lose. But cost-benefit analysis seeks to find an answer for the "total" effect, an answer that would enable us to determine whether the action concerned is "preferable" to another alternative, "preferable" for the group of persons defined. Since the purpose is to answer the question of how "total" welfare varies when that of some of its members changes because of a certain action, it is necessary to have a criterion that relates the measures of the individual's welfare changes (CV) to a change in "total" welfare. This criterion is known as that of *interpersonal* welfare comparisons. Obviously each person will have his own criterion in this respect, which will reflect his judgments on how much the loss of some and the gain of others is "worth" for the total, which is why it comes as no surprise that this is a controversial topic. In practice, the criterion for *comparing* individual measures against one another and obtaining the single measure sought consists of a weighted sum of individual net benefits.

Thus the change in "total" welfare or *total net benefits* (NB) which can be attributed to following course of action A instead of B will be

$$NB(A - B) = w^P NB^P(A - B) + w^r NB^r(A - B)$$

where w^P and w^r are the weights which the CVs of Messrs. P and R receive in the comparison criterion and which reflect the value judgments inherent in it. Thus, if the effect of courses of action A and B is to reduce the prices of the products bread and jewels respectively, using the same resources, and P does not wear jewels and R does not consume bread, course of action $A - B$ will benefit P and be harmful to R, so that $NB^P(A - B)$ will be positive and $CV^r(A - B)$ will be negative. Assuming, for example, that

$$NB^P(A - B) = 50$$
$$NB^r(A - B) = -70$$

"total" net benefits will be

$$NB(A - B) = w^P 50 - w^r 70$$

The result will depend on the weights w^P and w^r, and course of action $(A - B)$ will be considered preferable to $(B - A)$ if $NB(A - B)$ is positive. If the result

6

is negative, $(B - A)$ will be preferred to $(A - B)$. It should be pointed out that until the value judgment implicit in the interpersonal aggregation criterion is introduced, it is not possible to speak of "costs" or "benefits" in a given year beyond the level of each individual. In such cases, speaking of *changes in the income* of people (or CVs) is a more appropriate way of referring to the information available, keeping the expressions "total benefits" or their equivalents for the next step, which involves introducing the interpersonal aggregation criterion.

Almost all the versions of cost-benefit analysis have the same criteria regarding who defines the nature of effects and how they are measured, and any differences concern mainly the criteria for comparison.[1] As an introduction to this topic, it is useful to begin with the most widespread version of cost-benefit analysis known as "efficiency" analysis. This corresponds to the interpersonal comparison criterion, or distributional value judgment as it will also be called later, which is summarized below: the interpersonal comparison weights, representations of an interpersonal distributional value judgment, are the same for all concerned.[2] In terms of the notation used, this means that $w^r = w^p = w$. This value judgment can also be expressed by saying that one additional unit of income is equally "valuable" whatever the beneficiary's income level. In terms of the previous example of Messrs. P and R, the net benefits from course of action $A - B$ would be

$$NB(A - B) = w \, [NB^p(A - B) + NB^r(A - B)]$$

Since w is positive and the same for all concerned, its value will not affect the sign of $NB(A - B)$ and can be ignored. In practice therefore, the interpersonal comparison criterion of efficiency analysis can be expressed simply as the sum of present values of changes in net individual income.

Finally, most operational versions of efficiency analysis assume that it is possible to have a single discount rate d based on individual discount rates, and that the rate of return of marginal investment at efficiency prices is equal to discount rate d, which would be valid if the amount of investment made each period is what is required to include *all* the projects whose sum total of present values of changes in individual incomes is positive at rate d. For the moment, the reader need not be concerned with these assumptions, which will be discussed in more detail in Chapter 8, but it is useful to remember an

---

1. An exception is UNIDO's (1972) "merit wants."

2. Mishan (1981a, p. 317n) has pointed out that interpersonal comparison weights could also be based upon judgments of fact. This can only refer to the relation between individual real income changes and individual welfare changes, but not to that between the latter and total welfare changes. Since no factual information supports the use of equal weights, they can only be regarded as representing a value judgment. See Appendix B and Ray (1984, Ch. 2 and 3).

important consequence stemming from them: since the amount of investment is sufficient to include all projects whose present value of net benefits (at efficiency prices) is greater than zero, the present value of net economic benefits of marginally displaced investment is nil.[3]

If it is possible to have a single discount rate d for all individuals, and recalling that the present value has distributional property as regards the sum, in efficiency analysis, the $NB(A - B)$ can also be written as the present value (PV) of the sum of the CVs corresponding to following course of action A less the present value of the sum of the CVs corresponding to following the alternative course of action:

$$NB(A - B) = PV[CV_t^p(A) + CV_t^r(A)] - PV[CV_t^p(B) + CV_t^r(B)]$$

Note that this expression enables us to calculate the net benefits at efficiency prices from following course of action A, as well as the distribution of the respective changes in net incomes, since it can be rewritten as

$$NB(A - B) = PV[CV_t^p(A) - CV_t^p(B)] - PV[CV_t^r(A) - CV_t^r(B)]$$

Now if B is a marginal course of action, the present value of the corresponding CVs will be equal to zero and net benefits at efficiency prices from following course of action A will be

$$NB(A - B) = PV[CV_t^p(A) + CV_t^r(A)]$$

which is the conventional expression for the present value of net benefits at efficiency prices. However, this latter expression does not enable us to know the distribution of net benefits; for that it is also necessary to know the distribution of changes in income generated by the alternative course of action.

Since the interpersonal comparison criterion of efficiency analysis is only one of many possible, and since it is not always made explicit, the following sections of this chapter deal with those interpersonal comparison criteria that are most widespread in the literature on cost-benefit analysis.

---

3. This implies that it is indifferent (is equally valuable) to use an additional peso for consumption or investment. See Chapters 8 and 15.

1.2 Pareto Optima and Strict Pareto Improvements

The Pareto optimum is a static equilibrium situation in which it is impossible to improve the welfare of one of the persons involved without necessarily reducing the welfare of at least one of the other persons. Classifying a situation as optimum in Pareto's sense does not involve any distributional value judgment *per se.* There are as many Pareto optima as there are distributions of resources between the persons involved, and none of them can be preferred to any other without this automatically implying preference for one distribution of resources compared with another or, in other words, without the introduction of distributional value judgments. These are deliberately excluded from the qualification of optimality, but at the price of making any attempt at practical application impossible, since Pareto optima cannot be compared with one another without introducing such value judgments. If by chance a situation corresponded to a Pareto optimum, it would not be possible within the Paretian rules to propose any change since this would involve harming at least one of the participants.

The above need not be cause for concern *per se,* since nobody ever expects to actually be in an optimum defined in this way. But, what happens if the situation is not a Pareto optimum? In this case the Paretian rules define possible changes that would allow the situation to move closer to an optimum situation, changes that will here be called strict Pareto improvements (SPI). An SPI is an action that improves the welfare of least one of those involved while none of the remainder sees his situation worsen. Thus, a Pareto optimum can be defined as a situation in which it is not possible to effect an SPI. However, although there are infinite Pareto optima that constitute points of arrival, it is not possible to choose any of them without a distributional value judgment; the SPI criterion automatically eliminates those optima that correspond to situations in which one of the persons involved is worse off compared with the sub-optimal situation. It follows then that, given a distribution of resources and an associated sub-optimal situation, the SPI criterion will limit the field of choice to situations that are very close to the existing distribution. This may be clarified with a hypothetical example of two persons, P and R, the various combinations possible for distributing resources between them and the different "welfare levels" brought about by these distributions. Such a situation is set out in Figure 1.1, where each point on the line that goes through I, A and B represents the maximum level of welfare that one of them can reach given the level of welfare of the other, or, in other words, each point on the line is a Pareto optimum. Point S shows the sub-optimum situation which they are in and SAB the area in which it is possible to effect SPIs, illustrating what was pointed out earlier, that is, that the field of action defined

Figure 1.1. Maximum Levels of Welfare Attainable by *P* and *R*

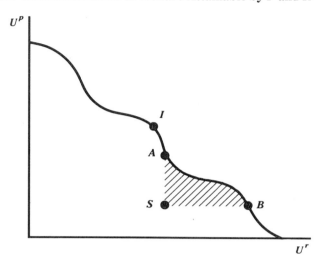

does not allow for substantial changes in distribution. The SPI criterion is conservative and excludes such possibilities as point *I*, which although it allows *P* to improve, requires *R*'s welfare level to be reduced. As a reference point, the reader may consider point *I* as the one corresponding to an equal distribution of resources.[4]

It should be pointed out that although the Paretian rules proper do not allow a particular point such as *I* to be preferred to others such as *A* or *S*, the SPI criterion in fact results in only those optima included between *A* and *B* constituting objectives that can be reached without introducing distributional value judgments. Then however, if the SPI criterion is the one used for taking decisions, the range of possible alternatives tends to perpetuate a distribution similar to the existing one. Any economic policy recommendation based on the SPI criterion can only be based on a value judgment with regard to such distribution, viz: that it is desirable, and so should not be departed from too radically.

Let us now consider four mutually exclusive actions (X_1, X_2, X_3, X_4) which can be carried out to bring about a change in situation *S*. For this purpose, Figure 1.2 shows an enlarged area *SAB* already considered where the arrows SX_1 to SX_4 show the four possible actions.

The rules of play determine that the action must be chosen according to the SPI criterion. As a result, action SX_4 is eliminated since it results in a worsening of the situation for *P* whereas the remaining alternatives are SPIs in

---

4. Which does not necessarily correspond to an equal distribution of monetary income.

Figure 1.2. Four Mutually Exclusive Actions X_i

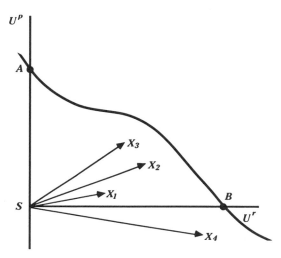

relation to S. If now the same criterion is applied to the remaining three, the result is that SX_2 and SX_3 are SPIs in relation to SX_1 since from a point like X_1 it is possible to improve both P and R by going to points X_2 or X_3. However, it is not possible to choose between SX_2 and SX_3, since adopting either of them always involves someone being better off with the other. The SPI criterion does not enable us to obtain a complete preference order among alternatives. This would only be possible by exercising interpersonal welfare comparisons, for example by stating that what R loses when going from X_2 to X_3 is "worth" less than what P gains. Interpersonal welfare comparisons would not only make it possible to choose between X_2 and X_3, but in addition would not allow X_4 to be excluded, since what P loses could be considered "less valuable" than what R gains. Even more, for the same reason it would be possible to compare any two situations, including Pareto optima such as points I and A in Figure 1.1.

1.3 Strict Pareto Improvements and Project Comparisons

Let us suppose that we are not in a Pareto optimum and that as a result SPIs can be effected. Let X_1, X_2, X_3 and X_4 in Figure 1.1 be the mutually exclusive alternatives for a project whose beneficiaries are persons P and R. The project would be carried out by the Government, which would pay investment costs for a total of 100. Operating and maintenance costs would be borne by the beneficiaries P and R, whose CVs of the "output" of the project exceed such

11

Table 1.1. Mutually Exclusive Alternatives for Project "X"

Alternative	Government	P	R	Total
X_1	-100	20	90	10
X_2	-100	25	95	20
X_3	-100	23	96	19
X_4	-100	10	130	40

costs (what they pay) by the amount shown for each alternative. Henceforth, this distribution will be called *the income changes generated by the project*. If the project were not carried out, the Government would pay back the amount of 100 in taxes to P and R in the proportions 20% and 80% respectively, since it has no other alternative investment. As can be seen in Table 1.1, P and R receive different amounts of income from each alternative. We want to know: a) whether it is desirable to carry out the project in any of its alternatives; and b) if it is carried out, what the best alternative is. In addition, any recommendation must be based on the SPI criterion. To this end, the situations will first be compared with and without the project and then the alternatives compared.

Alternative X_1 is an SPI, since with the project R would gain 90 in comparison with 80 in taxes repaid, whereas P would receive from the project the same as he would get back as a refund. Consequently, R can be better off without P being worse off. The reader will be able to check by using a similar process that X_2 and X_3 are also SPIs in relation to the situation without a project. X_4, on the other hand, is not an SPI since with the project P would gain only 10, less than the 20 he would receive in tax refunds if the project were not carried out.[5] Consequently, it is worth carrying out the project in any of its alternative forms with the exception of X_4. Now we can go on to the problem of choosing the best alternative according to the SPI criterion. For this purpose, the alternatives are compared, from which it is seen that both X_2 and X_3 are SPIs in relation to X_1 since with both of them P and R gain compared with X_1. X_2 now needs to be compared with X_3, from which we conclude that it is not possible to recommend one over the other. If X_3 is carried out (foregoing X_2) P loses 2 for R to gain 1, whereas if X_2 is carried out (foregoing X_3) it is R who loses 1 for P to gain 2. To conclude, the SPI criterion excludes X_1 and X_4, but does not allow a complete preference order to be established for the remaining alternatives.

Let us now compare the above with the result of using the following distributional value judgment: 1 peso more (less) of income is equally valuable for P and for R. The first consequence of the above is that now X_4 is not

---

5. The reader can check that a change in the proportions in which taxes are refunded can turn X_4 into an SPI. Furthermore, X_4 could lead to a Pareto optimum and, nevertheless, not be an SPI.

only acceptable in relation to the situation without a project but is the best alternative, since its net "total" benefits are greater than those of any of the others. In fact, what P loses $(10 - 20 = -10)$ is "worth" less than what R gains $(130 - 80 = 50)$ leaving a net balance of $50 - 10 = 40$, more than the net balance of any other alternative. The distributional value judgment also enables all the alternatives to be compared and put in order, which results in the following: X_4 is preferable to all the others, X_2 is preferable to X_3 and X_1, and X_3 is preferable only to X_1.

1.4 Potential Pareto Improvements

In the real world, SPIs are very unlikely. The execution of a project will normally involve the displacing of other projects with *different* beneficiaries. Moreover, in the section above it was concluded that the SPI criterion might not provide one single solution (alternatives X_2 and X_3). This situation gave rise to the proposal for another criterion related to the Pareto analysis: that of the *potential* Pareto improvement (PPI). This is an action in which it is *possible* for at least one to gain without anybody losing. It should be noted that *possible* does not mean that nobody actually loses. In a PPI there may be winners and losers but the gains of the former must be enough to *compensate* the latter by means of (costless) transfers, which enable them to be brought back to their previous situation, and even leave a surplus. Note that the fact that the gains are sufficient to compensate the losers does not mean that they are actually compensated. In that sense it is a *potential* Pareto improvement, since it is *possible* that some will improve their position without anybody being worse off, even though in fact some may gain and others lose. If a course of action constituting a PPI is supplemented by another that makes compensation effective at no cost, then the situation of some will have improved without anybody being worse off and all the measures together will constitute a strict Pareto improvement. In the view of some authors, the potential Pareto improvement criterion ought to be the basis of cost-benefit analysis, and the choice of a project in contrast to following an alternative course of action ought to be based on it.[6] That is why, in the following pages this criterion will be applied to the choice of projects, which will allow us to make explicit the value judgments incorporated in this analysis.

An example will show how to utilize the potential Pareto improvement criterion in cost-benefit analysis and the distributional value judgments involved in it. In Table 1.2, A_1 and A_2 are the mutually exclusive alternatives for a project to be carried out by the Government, which would be financed with

---

6. Mishan (1982, Part IV)

Table 1.2. Mutually Exclusive Alternatives for Project "A"

Alternative	Government	P	R	Total
A_1	−100	20	90	10
A_2	−100	90	20	10

taxes already paid. It is also assumed that if the project is not carried out, the taxes would be refunded to the beneficiaries of the project (P and R), in the proportions 20% and 80% respectively, which cannot be altered.

Knowing which alternatives it faces, the Government can now ask itself whether it is advisable to carry out the project in either of its two alternative forms. The answer is obtained by comparing the situations with and without the project for each of the alternatives. In the case of A_1, P will receive an additional income of 20 with the project, equal to what he would receive in the situation without the project, and so he neither gains nor loses. In other words the *net* additional income he obtains from the project is nil. R, on the other hand, will receive an additional income of 90 with the project compared with the 80 that he would receive without it, resulting in a net additional income of 10. Alternative A_1 is therefore a strict Pareto improvement: R gains 10 without anybody losing. In the case of A_2, the same reasoning shows us that the net additional income of P is 70 whereas that of R is −60. This alternative is a potential Pareto improvement because there is somebody who loses (R) but his loss can be compensated for (assuming that the cost of compensation is nil) and thus even leave a gain for P of 10. To conclude, based on the potential Pareto improvement criterion, both alternatives are desirable and the Government decides to carry out the project in one of its two alternatives, but it wishes to know which one. In answer to this second question, there is no difference between the two alternatives because neither of them is a PPI in relation to the other. In other words, both projects differ only in the distribution of the additional income they generate. This means that for this "economic" analysis

$$20\ w^p + 90\ w^r = 90\ w^p + 20\ w^r$$

in which w^p and w^r are the valuations (implicit in the answer that there is no difference between A_1 and A_2) that the additional incomes of P and R receive when the PPI criterion is applied. From this it follows that

$$70\ w^p = 70\ w^r$$

$$w^p = w^r$$

or in other words, the additional income is considered equally valuable regardless of who receives it. For this reason, cost-benefit analysis based on the potential Pareto improvement criterion is not concerned with determining who benefits from and who loses from a project, and provides for the purposes of decision-making only the algebraic sum of the income changes generated by the project (10 in the case of the example), the only result required for the application of this criterion.

Clearly there is no change in the result if the same value judgment ($w^p = w^r$) is introduced at an earlier stage of the analysis. That will allow for the net income (in comparison with the without project situation) that each alternative provides for each person to be totalled. Then the ensuing totals for each alternative can be compared. In this way the "net economic benefits" of A_1 and A_2 will be

$$NB(A_1) = (20 - 20) + (90 - 80) = 10$$
$$NB(A_2) = (90 - 20) + (20 - 80) = 10$$

1.5 The Reaction to Efficiency Analysis

Cost-benefit analysis in its "efficiency prices" version uses the PPI as the criterion for quantifying changes in "social welfare". In this section, a summary of the various positions maintained in this regard will pave the way for those topics that are dealt with in later chapters. For that purpose, the example of alternatives A_1 and A_2 of project A, presented above, will be used, together with an additional one summarized in Table 1.3. There, B_1 and B_2 are also mutually exclusive alternatives for a project carried out by the Government, which would be financed by imposing additional taxes on the beneficiaries P and R for amounts of 20 and 80 respectively. In the situation without the project such taxes would not be levied, from which we deduce that B_1 is a strict Pareto improvement and B_2 is a potential Pareto improvement, in both cases compared with the project not being carried out.

The first position, supported only implicitly in most cases, recommends using the distributional value judgment that attaches equal weights to the marginal income variations of all persons.[7] In other words, presenting the results in the form of a single present value figure of net economic benefits valued at efficiency prices (the *Total* column). It is enough to know that the gainers receive more than enough to compensate the losers. In such cases, there is no need to worry about who the beneficiaries (losers) are nor, as a

---

7. The distributional problems would be tackled through fiscal policy. This is the position adopted by Harberger (1971b and 1973). However, see also Harberger (1978).

Table 1.3.   Mutually Exclusive Alternatives for Project "B"

Alternative	Government	P	R	Total
B_1	-100.0	25.0	85.0	10.0
B_2	-100.0	15.0	96.0	11.0
B_2C	-100.0	25.0	85.9	10.9

result, what their net benefit (loss) is. Thus, in the case of project B the analyst would recommend that it be carried out, since both B_1 and B_2 are potential Pareto improvements. He would however go a step further and recommend that alternative B_2 be carried out, since this represents a potential Pareto improvement in relation to B_1. To do this, in his report he would only need to show the present value of the net economic benefits of both alternatives. In the case of project A (Table 1.2) he would recommend that the project be carried out and would say that both alternatives are equal from the "economic" point of view. What is important to point out here is that even if the analyst agreed with Harberger (1971b) that economists are not professionally qualified to pronounce on the distributional aspects, he could not share that author's opinion that the interpersonal sum of the present values of individual CVs should be presented as the result of the analysis, since this would imply precisely what he would be trying to avoid.

A second position suggests that the gainers and the losers be identified and that the figure for the present value of changes in income, calculated the same way as in the previous case, be given together with the respective distribution. In this way, this distributional effect would not remain hidden behind a single figure for the present value of the changes in net income. On the contrary, it would represent additional information for decision makers.[8] Thus, in the case of project A, the analyst would present the results in a form similar to that given in Table 1.2, indicating that the alternatives differ only in the distribution of the changes in income brought about between P and R. In the case of project B, the analyst would restrict himself to submitting the results of Table 1.3 without recommending one alternative over the other, but leaving open the options of the decision maker to exercise distributional value judgments. However, the reader must note that this procedure involves an infringement of

---

8. For example, Meade (1972) and Mishan (1982, Chapters 24 & 27, Section 2). However, making distributional effects explicit does not allow us to concur with Mishan (1982, p. 164) that "the quantitative outcome of a cost-benefit calculation (based on the PPI, author's note) itself carries no distributional significance. It shows that the total of gains exceeds the total of losses, no more." As pointed out at the beginning of the chapter, calculating "*total* gains" requires a value judgment on which the aggregation criterion is based. Furthermore, given two situations without the project, which differ only in income distribution, the total of CVs of a project will depend on which of the two situations without the project is used as a basis for comparison.

the potential Pareto improvement criterion, since B_2 is one of these in relation to B_1.

A derivative of the position above, based on the principle of compensation implied in the concept of potential Pareto improvement, goes a step further by opening up the possibility for the project analyst to propose procedures that make compensation effective in order to convert the project into a strict Pareto improvement.[9] In this way, the losers in both alternatives of project A (A_1 and A_2) can be compensated and the choice will depend probably on the compensation mechanism. In the case of project B, the analyst would recommend carrying out alternative B_2, but at the same time he could propose compensation mechanisms whose implementation costs would be less than 1. In other words, open up the *possibility* that a strict Pareto improvement be carried out. However, once again this means an infringement of the potential Pareto improvement criterion each time that the cost of effecting compensation is positive. In the case of project B, alternative B_2 is recommended as a potential Pareto improvement in relation to B_1.

Let us now suppose that an exact compensation procedure is proposed whose cost is 0.10, with this alternative being indicated by B_2C in Table 1.3. Then it is necessary for R to transfer 10.1, of which 10 is used to compensate P and 0.1 to cover the costs of compensation. Since the potential Pareto improvement criterion does not require compensation to be made, B_2 is one of these improvements in relation to B_2C. In addition, it must be noted that there is no reason why compensation for the losers (P) should be exact (10), since one or more "over-compensation" mechanisms could also be proposed and two or more B_2C_i obtained, each one of which would be an SPI whenever the cost of compensation was less than 1. Once again, it is impossible to avoid bringing distributional value judgments into: a) the definition of the compensation mechanisms; and b) the choice between PPIs and compensated PPIs. In a later work, Hicks (1975, Section 1) appears inclined to restrict the choice set to all the SPI and the compensated PPI which does not, as already mentioned, avoid distributional value judgments either. All this is without even considering the possibility of discussing redistribution mechanisms within SPIs.

In summary, it is not generally possible to effect a single ordering of alternatives without introducing distributional value judgments, among which is included "I don't care what happens with distribution." What has been presented so far has led to the discussion of ways of explicitly including distributional value judgments in, *inter alia*, the field of cost-benefit analysis. Two of the best known ones will be presented here with the discussion being limited to project appraisal.

---

9. Hicks (1939, Section 7) and Mishan (1982, Chapter 27, Section 2).

The first approach within this second group proposes that either of the previous two be used, together with the task of identifying and explaining the value judgments revealed by the political authority in making decisions.[10] If between A_1 and A_2 the second were chosen, it would be inferred that

$$90w^p + 20w^r > 20w^p + 90w^r$$

meaning that $w^p > w^r$ and consequently $w^p/w^r > 1$. If then B_1 and B_2 were considered and B_2 were chosen, it could be inferred that

$$15w^p + 96w^r > 25w^p + 85w^r$$

meaning that $11w^r > 10w^p$ and consequently $w^p/w^r < 1.1$. In other words, and assuming that the decision had been taken for distributional reasons, after considering these two projects, the analyst would know that one additional unit of income for P is more valuable than for R, but not by more than 10%. If the political authority is consistent in its distributional value judgments, after a number of decisions—not too many—the interval in which w^p/w^r would lie would have narrowed enough for all practical purposes to around a certain number u. From then on, the value found in this way could be used by the analyst, who would simply report the value of the net economic benefits calculated for $w^p/w^r = u$.

Finally, a welfare function W could be made explicit, depending on the utility functions of P and R,

$$W = f[U^r(C^r); U^p(C^p)]$$

in which C is the person's level of consumption, or, directly on individual consumption, $W = f(C^r; C^p)$. In this way it would be possible to define how much "social welfare" increases by, when small changes occur in the income of each person or group of persons:

$$w^p = \frac{\Delta W}{\Delta C^p}$$

$$w^r = \frac{\Delta W}{\Delta C^r}$$

From this the values $u = w^p/w^r$ would be extracted, which the analyst would use, then proceeding just as in the previous case.[11]

---

10. See Weisbrod (1968), UNIDO (1972) and critiques by Stewart (1975) and Kornai (1979).
11. For example, Little and Mirrlees (1974), Squire and van der Tak (1977) and Lal (1980).

18

1.6 Summary

At the beginning of this chapter, we suggested that efficiency analysis is based on a distributional value judgment that can be summarized as follows: an additional unit of income is equally valuable whatever the income level of the beneficiary. By using simple examples of the distribution of costs and benefits of hypothetical projects, it has proved possible to demonstrate this, and also to show, though only in outline form, the most widespread alternative criteria. In Part III we shall return to the topic of distributional value judgments that are different from the one that assigns the same weights to the marginal income changes of all persons.

What is of interest to point out, is that all the alternatives to efficiency analysis require that the distribution of the income changes brought about by the project in question be estimated. This estimate is based on the principles of economic valuation used in cost-benefit analysis. In the following chapters the reasoning on which this valuation process is based will be discussed in some detail, with particular attention to those topics that are more often neglected in texts on efficiency analysis.

CHAPTER 2

COMPENSATING VARIATION, CONSUMER SURPLUS CHANGE AND WILLINGNESS TO PAY

2.1 Compensating and Equivalent Variations

Cost-benefit analysis sees investment as a way to increase future consumption, which raises the problem of how to measure changes in the "economic welfare" of individuals as a result of changes in their consumption of goods and services. In this sense, the objective of this chapter is to answer the following questions: (a) how does "welfare economics" go about obtaining a monetary measure of the changes in individual economic welfare; (b) in the case of changes in the prices of goods and services, what is the relation between such a measure and the demand functions for such goods and services; and (c) what is the relationship between the distributional value judgment of efficiency analysis and the use of willingness to pay as a valuation criteria?

From an analytical point of view, changes in the consumption of goods and services by an individual may originate in the following situations or combinations of situations: i) changes in the availability of goods that are received free; ii) changes in monetary income for given prices; or iii) changes in prices for a given monetary income. If we wish to obtain a measure of the changes in a consumer's welfare brought about by any of the three alternatives, we have to have a measuring criterion. For this purpose, "welfare economics" provides two alternative measuring criteria; the compensating variation and the equivalent variation. The first criterion considers the situation resulting *after* the change has taken place in order to ask the following question: how much does the consumer's monetary income need to be changed by for him to be at the same level of welfare as *before* the change whose contribution to his economic welfare we want to measure? The answer to this question is a certain sum of money called the *compensating variation* of the change concerned, and it is used as the monetary measure of the change in his economic welfare. Thus, for example, the consumer will increase his level of welfare by obtaining free access to a park. The compensating variation of such access will be the reduction in his monetary income required to cancel (compensate) the increase in his welfare resulting from access to the park. This reduction in his income will be regarded as the monetary measure of the increase in his economic welfare resulting from free access to the park.

The second criterion, the equivalent variation, considers the situation *before* the change whose contribution to economic welfare we wish to measure in order to ask the following question: how much would the consumer's monetary income need to be altered by in order to bring about a change in his economic welfare equivalent to what would result from the change whose contribution to his economic welfare we want to measure? The sum of money that corresponds to the former question is the so-called *equivalent variation* of the change whose contribution to the welfare of the consumer we want to measure. In the example of access to the park, the equivalent variation of such access will be the sum of money necessary to give the consumer in order for him, starting from an initial situation *without access to the park,* to have the same level of welfare as he would have without that sum but with access to the park.

If the change in question is an increase in monetary income (which does not affect relative prices) the problem is simpler. If a person receives a transfer of $100, the corresponding compensating variation is obviously equal to $100. At the same time, by definition, the equivalent variation of such a transfer is also $100.

The situation is not as simple when price changes are involved. In this case measuring the compensating and equivalent variations is based on the assumptions of the consumer equilibrium theory. Let us consider the consumer's map of indifference curves between good q and all the other goods. If the relative prices between the goods excluding q are not affected by changes in the price p^q of the latter, the remaining goods can be dealt with as a single commodity m.[1] Figure 2.1(a) illustrates this indifference curves map and the initial budgetary constraint

$$Y_0 = m\,p_0^m + q\,p_0^q$$

represented by the line $m_0 A'$, so that his monetary income is

$$Y_0 = m_0\,p_0^m$$

With monetary income Y_0 and the existing relative prices, the consumer will be situated at point A', consuming q_0 units of q at price p_0^q. Consequently, this point is situated on his demand function for q as shown in Figure 2.1(b). If now the price of q is reduced to p_1^q the consumer will be situated at point B', consuming q_1. If we wish to obtain a monetary measure of the increase $U_1 - U_0$ in the consumer's welfare, the following question can be asked: after the reduction in p^q, how much would the consumer's income need to be reduced by to cancel out the increase $U_1 - U_0$ in his welfare? This reduction in his income is his *compensating variation* of the price reduction $p_0^q - p_1^q$. Thus, in Figure 2.1(a), if his income is reduced to

$$Y_c = m_c\,p_0^m$$

the consumer will be at point C' with the same level of welfare as before the price reduction. It can be shown that the compensating variation Y_c is approximately equal to the change in the consumer's surplus measured over the demand function D_y in Figure 2.1(b),[2] that is

$$Y_c = p_0^q A B p_1^q$$

A second possible measure of the increase in welfare $U_1 - U_0$ of the consumer due to the reduction in p^q could be made by asking the following question: if the reduction in p^q were not made, how much would the consumer's income need to be increased by to achieve an *equivalent* effect? This increase is called the *equivalent variation* (Y_e) to the reduction $p_0^q - p_1^q$ and is represented in Figure 2.1(a) by the quantity

$$m_e = \frac{Y_e}{p_0^m}$$

---

1. See Hicks (1946, Chapter II, Section 4).
2. See demonstration in Appendix A.

Figure 2.1. Compensating and Equivalent Variations

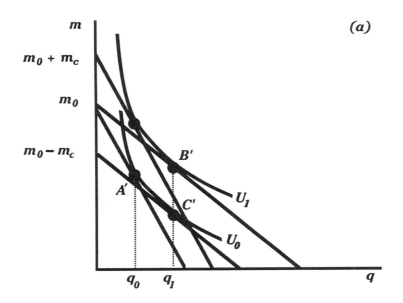

(a)

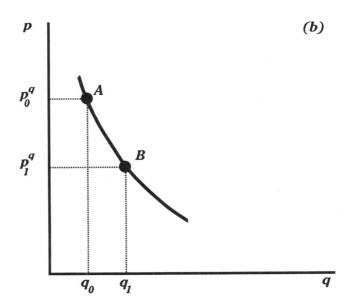

(b)

Table 2.1. Relationship between the Compensating and Equivalent Variations for a Given Change in Price

	$E_{qy} > 0$	$E_{qy} = 0$	$E_{qy} < 0$
Price increase	$Y_e < Y_c$	$Y_e = Y_c$	$Y_e > Y_c$
Price reduction	$Y_e > Y_c$	$Y_e = Y_c$	$Y_e < Y_c$

of basket of goods m, from which

$$Y_e = m_e p_0^m$$

It can be demonstrated that Y_e is also approximately equal to the change in the consumer surplus over the demand function in Figure 2.1(b), that is

$$Y_e = p_0^q A B p_1^q$$

In general, Y_c will be different from Y_e and the sign and the size of the difference will depend on: (a) whether there is a reduction or increase in the price; and (b) the income elasticity of demand E_{qy} of the good whose price varies (see Table 2.1).

To summarize, given a price change $p_0 - p_1$, the CV criterion will in general give a different measure than that of the equivalent variation (EV) and the change in the consumer surplus is only an approximate measure of them. Consequently, two problems arise. The first is which of the two measures, CV or EV, should be used. The second, is what the error involved is in using the change in the consumer surplus as an approximation of the measure chosen. The first problem goes beyond the objectives of this study and consequently will not be discussed. Suffice it to say that the prevailing criterion is the use of the CV as a measure of changes in economic welfare.[3] As for the second problem, Appendix A demonstrates that the change in consumer surplus deriving from a change in the price of a good is, from a practical point of view, a good approximation of the respective CV.

2.2 The Aggregation of Compensating Variations and the Concept of Willingness to Pay

From here on, we will consider that, for all practical purposes, the compensating variation of the change in the price of consumer good q can be measured by the area between the two prices and the respective individual demand

---

3. The interested reader may consult Meade (1972), Mishan (1982, Chapters 23–26) and the references therein.

function (area $p_0^q ABp_1^q$ in Figure 2.1(b)). However, in practice, cost-benefit analysis is carried out in relation to the market demand functions, which are the "horizontal" aggregation of individual demand functions. In Figure 2.2, D^r is the demand function of R for consumer good q and D^{r+p} is the aggregate demand function of R and P. When the price is p_0, R consumes q_0^r and P, by construction of the aggregate demand function, consumes

$$q_0^p = q_0^{r+p} - q_0^r$$

When the price is reduced to p_1, R increases his consumption to q_1^r and P to

$$q_1^p = q_1^{r+p} - q_1^r$$

since by construction of the aggregate demand function, q_1^{r+p} is the sum of the quantities demanded by both consumers at price p_1. The change in the consumers' (of q) surplus can be estimated as

$$\Delta CSs = (p_0 - p_1)\, q_0^{r+p} + \tfrac{1}{2}\,(p_0 - p_1)\,(q_1^{r+p} - q_0^{r+p})$$
$$\Delta CSs = (p_0 - p_1)(q_0^r + q_0^p) + \tfrac{1}{2}\,(p_0 - p_1)(q_1^r + q_1^p - q_0^r - q_0^p)$$

Regrouping the terms in convenient form, we arrive at

$$\Delta CSs = (p_0 - p_1)\, q_0^r + \tfrac{1}{2}\,(p_0 - p_1)(q_1^r - q_0^r) + (p_0 - p_1)\, q_0^p$$
$$+ \tfrac{1}{2}\,(p_0 - p_1)(q_1^p - q_0^p)$$

Figure 2.2. The Aggregate Demand Function

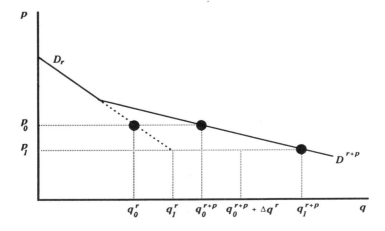

25

But since q^r and q^p are both points on the individual demand functions, the first two terms on the right-hand side of the previous equation correspond to the estimate of the CV of R and the second two, to that of P. As a result, it may be stated that

$$\Delta CSs = CV^r + CV^p$$

The change in the consumers' surplus of q resulting from a price change is (approximately) equal to the sum of the corresponding compensating variations. In other words, if after price reduction $p_0 - p_1$ the income of R is reduced by CV^r and that of P by CV^p, with their new incomes $Y^i - CV^i$ ($i = r,p$) both consumers will be in the same situation as before the price reduction.

However, these are not all the changes that have taken place. As a consequence of the reduction in the price of q, the incomes of other people have also been affected and their respective CVs also have to be considered. Suppose for the sake of simplicity that the supply of consumer good q is completely inelastic (fixed supply)[4] and that the reduction in the price of q is due to the increase in an import quota granted entirely to businessman h, that is, with reference to Figure 2.2

$$\Delta q^h = q_1^{r+p} - q_0^{r+p} = \Delta q^r + \Delta q^p$$

Consequently, businessman h will receive additional income from the sale of Δq^h equal to $\Delta q^h p_1$ whereas each businessman j who sells q (including h) will see his income reduced by $\Delta p\, q_0^j$. Logically,

$$\sum_j q_0^j = q_0^{r+p}$$

the sum of the quantities sold by each businessman is equal to the total quantity sold and, consequently, the reduction in the income of the remaining businessmen will be

$$\sum_j \Delta p\, q_0^j = \Delta p\, q_0^{r+p}$$

Table 2.2 outlines the effects on the only two groups affected in this simplified example: the businessmen and the consumers. The total in the first

---

4. For example, a tax-free import quota that the Government sells at cost price. This avoids taking into consideration changes in income beyond the businessmen who sell q.

Table 2.2. Effects of an Increase in the Quota of q

	Businessman h	Businessman $j \neq h$	Consumer i
Sale of Δq	$\Delta q^h p_1$	—	$\frac{1}{2} \Delta q^i \Delta p$
Price Reduction	$-\Delta p \, q_0^h$	$-\Delta p \, q_0^j$	$\Delta p \, q_0^i$
Total	CV^h	CV^j	CV^i

column shows the change in the income of businessman h (excluding the purchase of Δq) and the total in the second shows the reduction in the income of each of the remaining businessmen. By definition, such totals are also the CVs of the businessmen (CV^j) corresponding to the additional supply Δq. Finally, the total in the last column is the CV of consumer i (CV^i). Now since the CV is the criterion chosen to "measure" the changes in people's economic welfare, the totals in the columns show the changes in the economic welfare of each one of those affected by the sale of Δq units. If now we want to obtain a measure of the change in "total economic welfare" starting from the changes in "economic welfare" of each of those affected, an interpersonal aggregation criterion obviously has to be defined that shows the change in total welfare as a function of changes in the economic welfare of the individuals, so that

$$\text{change in "total welfare"} = f(CV^i; CV^j)$$

If the interpersonal aggregation criterion is the sum of the CVs of those affected, it is obvious that one unit of change in the income of any of them has the same value, which without any doubt constitutes a value judgment by whoever bases the decision on that criterion. Applying this criterion to the example of Table 2.2 yields

$$\sum_i CV^i + \sum_j CV^j = \Delta q^h p_1 + \tfrac{1}{2} \Delta p \sum_i \Delta q^i - \Delta p \, q_0^h$$

$$-\Delta p \sum_{j \neq h} q_0^j + \Delta p \sum_i q_0^i$$

But as the additional sales are equal to the additional purchases

$$\Delta q^h = \sum_i \Delta q^i$$

27

and the original sales are equal to the original purchases

$$q_0^h + \sum_{j \neq h} q_0^j = \sum_i q_0^i$$

it follows that

$$\sum_i CV^i + \sum_j CV^j = \Delta q^h p_1 + \tfrac{1}{2} \Delta p \, \Delta q^h$$

The right-hand side of this equality is the willingness to pay for Δq^h which, according to the criterion chosen, is the contribution to "total welfare" resulting from the sale of Δq^h and is by definition the value at efficiency prices of that quantity.[5]

However, the advocates of the "new welfare economics" would argue that the sum of the CVs does not aim to obtain a measure of the change in "total welfare" but is merely the procedure for bringing into operation the criterion of the potential Pareto improvement (PPI) discussed in Chapter 1. Let us assume that the sum of the CVs from increasing the supply of q is

$$\Sigma \, CV(\Delta q) = \$150$$

and that the same resources can be used to increase the quota of another commodity k, so that

$$\Sigma \, CV(\Delta k) = \$100$$

As a result, it will be *possible* to reduce the income of the beneficiaries from Δq by \$100, transfer this sum to those who no longer benefit from Δk and then even be left with a *net benefit* of

$$\Sigma \, CV(\Delta q) - \Sigma \, CV(\Delta k) = \$50$$

However, the fact that compensation is possible does not mean that it is effected and no conclusion can be drawn from the application of the PPI without introducing a distributional value judgment. It would therefore be necessary to show how much those affected gain and lose, which would only move the point at which the value judgment is made. This in turn could make

---

5. See Appendix B for a demonstration from a "utilitarian" point of view.

desirable, projects that do not meet the PPI criterion, when the weight for the income changes of the losers is greater than that of the gainers. Only if the weights of all those affected are equal, does the indicator of changes in the resulting "total welfare," in the sense given to this expression in Section 1.1, show the same result as the PPI criterion.

CHAPTER 3

THE ACCOUNTING PRICE
OF FOREIGN EXCHANGE

3.1 Accounting Prices and Efficiency Prices

Starting from an equilibrium position or without project situation, the project will generate changes in the supply and demand of goods and services whose effects on people will be measured by means of the corresponding CVs. The value at accounting prices of supply (demand) change Δq at a certain time t, will be equal to $\Sigma_i\, u_t^i\, CV_t^i(\Delta q)$, i.e., the interpersonal aggregation of the CVs attributable to supply change Δq. The accounting price of good q will be the value at accounting prices of a unitary supply (demand) change. Although from a theoretical point of view, the value at accounting prices of a certain supply change Δq expressed per unit of the latter is distinct from the value at accounting prices of a unitary supply change, i.e.,

$$\frac{\sum_i u_t^i\, CV_t^i\,(\Delta q)}{\Delta q} \neq \sum_i u_t^i\, CV_t^i(\Delta q = 1)$$

in practice, for a "small" Δq its value at accounting prices approximates Δq multiplied by its accounting price. In terms of the notation used,

30

$$\Delta q \sum_i u_t^i \, CV_t^i(\Delta q = 1) \approx \sum_i u_t^i \, CV_t^i(\Delta q)$$

When the distributional value judgment permitting interpersonal aggregation assigns the same weight to the marginal income changes of all persons, an accounting price is expressed at efficiency level or, more concisely, is an "efficiency price". Consequently, the concept of accounting price is more general than that of efficiency price. The change in "total economic welfare" per unit of change in the good or service in question is referred to without specifying the interpersonal aggregation criterion used. Since the most widespread operational version of cost-benefit analysis is that of efficiency prices, assuming equality between the discount rate and the rate of return at efficiency prices of marginal investments, the specialists usually use the expression *accounting (or shadow) price of foreign exchange* when they in fact refer to its efficiency price. In this study, this imprecision in the use of language will continue to be used.

This chapter is devoted to deducing the most widespread expression for the accounting (efficiency) price of foreign exchange. For this purpose, the same sequence of steps will be followed as in theoretical reasoning. Thus once supply or demand changes and their immediate effects have been identified, the latter will be followed to the point at which they affect persons so that these effects can then be quantified by means of the corresponding CVs. Only when this process has been completed, will the interpersonal aggregation criterion of efficiency analysis be introduced in order to obtain a quantifiable expression for the accounting (efficiency) price of foreign exchange. This will make it possible to clarify the relation between the concept of compensating variation, the verification that the potential compensation criterion has been fulfilled and the use of willingness to pay as a valuation criterion in efficiency analysis.

equilibrium exchange rate. That is why it is necessary to digress briefly on what is meant by "equilibrium" before going into further detail. An appropriate start would be to consider which market prices should be used when preparing a project's final financial flows: the prevailing prices at a given time (short run), or those that reflect long-run conditions. When a project is prepared, the execution starting date is unknown. Taking that into account and considering that the project's flows will be spread over several years, it is advisable to value the financial flows at long-run prices, separately considering the relevant short-run effects. Consequently, the project's input and output prices will generally reflect the long-run prices of primary inputs such as foreign exchange and labor.

In a cost benefit analysis, it is also interesting to know whether the project represents a "total welfare improvement" under long-run equilibrium conditions and, if necessary, to consider separately short-run conditions that may affect the final results (as, for example, short-run unemployment). Therefore, when any further mention is made of the equilibrium exchange rate, this must be interpreted as a long-run one. However, the exchange rate must be defined for a *given* set of foreign trade incentives and disincentives (and interest rates) because if these change, the long-run equilibrium exchange rate will also change. From here on, the expression "equilibrium exchange rate" refers to the long-run one, for a given set of foreign trade incentives and disincentives (and interest rates), therefore the accounting price of foreign exchange will also refer to these conditions. These considerations are implied in the following chapters.

3.2 A Simple Example

Consider an investment project that increases the supply of foreign exchange by increasing exports, which are not subject to any foreign trade tax. To begin with a simple example, which will gradually become more complicated, let us initially assume that the supply of foreign exchange (exports) is completely inelastic with respect to price, that the exchange rate is determined by the market, that only final consumer goods are imported and that these goods are not produced domestically. The assumption of a fixed supply of foreign exchange will be abandoned in Section 3.5 and imported goods that compete with domestic production will be considered in Section 3.6. Thus, in Figure 3.1, S_0 is the foreign exchange supply in the situation without the project, S_i is that supply in the situation with the project and D is the demand for foreign

Figure 3.1. The Foreign Exchange Market

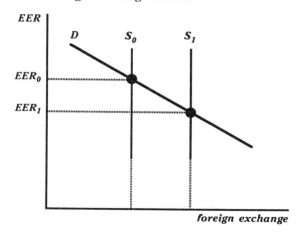

foreign exchange

exchange. This is used to import consumer goods *a* and *b,* which are not produced domestically, at international prices expressed in foreign exchange CIF_a and CIF_b.

Assuming that the domestic transport and trade margins are nil, the domestic prices of such goods in the situation without the project will be

$$p_a^0 = CIF_a \times EER_0 \times (1 + t_a)$$
$$p_b^0 = CIF_b \times EER_0 \times (1 + t_b)$$

[3.1]

in which EER_0 is the equilibrium exchange rate and t_i is the (*ad valorem*) import tariff. Since the adjustment to the additional supply of foreign exchange will be made by means of a reduction in the (long term) equilibrium exchange rate to EER_1, the domestic prices of *a* and *b* will be reduced to:

$$p_a^1 = CIF_a \times EER_1 \times (1 + t_a)$$
$$p_b^1 = CIF_b \times EER_1 \times (1 + t_b)$$

[3.2]

in which it is supposed that the international prices CIF_i are constant in relation to small variations in the domestic demand of a country.

The compensating variation of the reduction in the price of the goods imported can be approximated by the increase in consumers' surplus (ΔCS), equal to the sum of the shaded areas in Figure 3.2(a) and (b). These areas can be approximated linearly as[1]

$$\Delta CS_a = (p_a^0 - p_a^1)\, a_0 + \tfrac{1}{2}\, (p_a^0 + p_a^1)(a_1 - a_0) - p_a^1\, (a_1 - a_0)$$
$$\Delta CS_b = (p_b^0 - p_b^1)\, b_0 + \tfrac{1}{2}\, (p_b^0 + p_b^1)(b_1 - b_0) - p_b^1\, (b_1 - b_0)$$

[3.3]

that is, the reduction in the domestic value of the quantity that they consumed before the reduction in the exchange rate, plus their willingness to pay for additional consumption less what they actually pay for this consumption. It will now be useful to analyze each of the terms ΔCS is comprised of. Substituting the expressions [3.1] and [3.2] in the first term of expressions [3.3] yields the following:

$$(p_a^0 - p_a^1)\, a_0 = CIF_a\, (1 + t_a)\, (EER_0 - EER_1)\, a_0$$
$$(p_b^0 - p_b^1)\, b_0 = CIF_b\, (1 + t_b)\, (EER_0 - EER_1)\, b_0$$

---

1. Henceforth, to simplify the presentation, the areas below demand functions will always be approximated linearly.

Figure 3.2. The Effects of an Increase in the Supply of Foreign Exchange on the Markets of Imported Goods

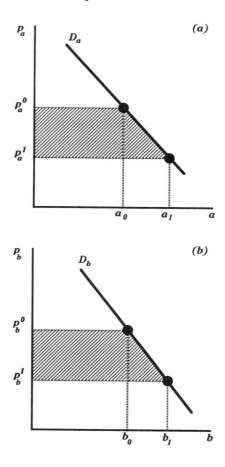

In turn, each of the above expressions can be broken down into two parts. The first is the reduction in Government revenue—by way of receipts from the import tariffs corresponding to imports in the situation without the project—because of the reduction in the EER:

$$CIF_a \ (EER_0 - EER_1) \ t_a \ a_0$$

$$CIF_b \ (EER_0 - EER_1) \ t_b \ b_0$$

The second part is the reduction in the exporters' revenue from the sale of the same quantity of foreign exchange (S_0 in Figure 3.1) at a lower exchange rate:

$$CIF_a (EER_0 - EER_1) a_0 + CIF_b (EER_0 - EER_1) b_0 = (EER_0 - EER_1) S_0$$

The second term of expression [3.3] is willingness to pay for the additional quantity of goods a and b, which expresses the maximum quantity of other goods that the consumers would be prepared to forgo rather than do without such quantities. In this sense, this is not an actual income flow but a measure of income equivalent to such quantities. Finally, what is paid by the consumers for additional consumption

$$p_a^1 (a_1 - a_0)$$
$$p_b^1 (b_1 - b_0)$$

can be broken down by replacing the prices by expressions [3.2]. From this we see that what the consumers pay is equal to what the project receives from the sale of foreign exchange $S_1 - S_0$ generated by exports, equal to the value of the additional imports before taxes

$$CIF_a EER_1(a_1 - a_0) + CIF_b EER_1(b_1 - b_0) = (S_1 - S_0) EER_1$$

plus the increase in receipts from import tariffs by the Government

$$CIF_a EER_1 t_a (a_1 - a_0)$$
$$CIF_b EER_1 t_b (b_1 - b_0)$$

A summary of the direct effects of the additional supply of foreign exchange appears in Table 3.1.

It is now possible to interpret the information contained in this table from two points of view: (a) that of the potential compensation criterion; and (b) that of the distributional value judgment assigning equal weights to all income changes. From the perspective of the potential compensation criterion, what we want to know is whether the additional income (effective or equivalent) received by those who benefit is sufficient to compensate the losers and leave a remainder. To do this, it is necessary to examine the table column by column. The first contains the sum of the CVs of the consumers benefiting from the effect of the greater supply of foreign exchange on consumer goods prices, an effect that, strictly speaking, ought to be subdivided into one

Table 3.1. Direct Effects of the Increase in the Availability of Foreign Exchange

	Consumers	Project	Other Exporters	Government	Total
Change in the market value of the quantity consumed without the project	$CIF_a(EER_0 - EER_1)(1+t_a)a_0$	—	$-CIF_a(EER_0 - EER_1)a_0$	$-CIF_a(EER_0 - EER_1)t_a a_0$	—
Consumers' willingness to pay	$\frac{1}{2}(p_a^0 + p_a^1)(a_1 - a_0)$	—	—	—	$\frac{1}{2}(p_a^0 + p_a^1)(a_1 - a_0)$
Paid by the consumers	$-CIF_a EER_1(1+t_a)(a_1 - a_0)$	$CIF_a EER_1(a_1 - a_0)$	—	$CIF_a EER_1 t_a(a_1 - a_0)$	—
Total	Change in consumers' surplus	+ Income from project +	Change in exporters' income	+ Change in Government revenue =	Consumers' willingness to pay

column for each consumer.[2] In other words, the total in the first column is the reduction in the income of the consumers, which would leave them at the same level of welfare as before the increase in the supply of foreign exchange (fall in the price of consumer goods). The second column records the project's revenue from the sale of exported goods. As the excess supply of foreign exchange causes a reduction in the EER, the remaining exporters see their incomes reduced by the extent shown in the third column. The fourth column shows the changes in tax revenue brought about by the project. Although the sign of the net effect on the Government is not defined, we will assume that it is positive.[3]

Consequently, there are three groups of gainers (the consumers, the project and the Government) whose additional income must be enough to compensate the losers (exporters) and leave a remainder to compensate the loss implicit in the project costs, which are not shown in Table 3.1. As can be seen in this table, the balance in question is the willingness to pay for the consumption made possible by the increase in the supply of foreign exchange. This sum is the income remaining after the (potential) compensation of those affected by the increase in the supply of foreign exchange, available to compensate those who are net losers as a result of the project costs. Thus, valuing the additional foreign exchange according to willingness to pay for the consumption which it makes possible ensures that the potential compensation criterion is complied with for those affected by the additional supply of foreign exchange. Since the compensation is only potential, this valuation is all that is required by the application of the potential Pareto improvement criterion.

The same result can be achieved by assigning the same weight to all marginal income changes. In fact, this value judgment allows the columns in Table 3.1 to be added up horizontally. Thus, for example, in the first row, the gain by consumers is equal to the loss of the remaining exporters and the Government. As a result, the respective *net effect on total welfare* is nil. The net result of the horizontal sum of the columns is willingness to pay for the consumption made possible by the increase in the foreign exchange supply. We may therefore conclude that both from the point of view of the potential Pareto improvement criterion and from that of "efficiency analysis," the accounting price of foreign exchange is as follows:

$$APFE = \frac{\text{Willingness to pay for the consumption made possible by the additional foreign exchange } (S_1 - S_0)}{\text{Additional foreign exchange } (S_1 - S_0)}$$

2. The reader will recall that to add CVs, judgments are required concerning the "value" of changes in income for each consumer affected.
3. This is consistent with the approximation $EER_0 = EER_1$ which will be incorporated in the analysis later (see expressions [3.8] and [3.9]).

The fact that both approaches yield the same result is not surprising. In Chapter 1, we saw that both are based on the same distributional value judgment.

What has been explained so far enables us to write a simple formula for the accounting price of foreign exchange when the exchange rate adjusts the supply and demand of foreign exchange. In the simple example explained up to now, expression [3.3] shows that the sum of the compensating variations of the additional supply of foreign exchange will be the sum of the willingness to pay of each individual consumer for the additional consumption made possible.

$$WP(a_1 - a_0) = \tfrac{1}{2}\,(p_a^0 + p_a^1)\,(a_1 - a_0)$$
$$WP(b_1 - b_0) = \tfrac{1}{2}\,(p_b^0 + p_b^1)\,(b_1 - b_0)$$

[3.4]

Now defining

$$\Delta a = (a_1 - a_0)$$
$$\Delta b = (b_1 - b_0)$$

and substituting [3.1] in [3.4] we obtain

$$WP(\Delta a) = \Delta a\,\tfrac{1}{2}\,[CIF_a\,EER_0\,(1 + t_a) + CIF_a\,EER_1\,(1 + t_a)]$$
$$WP(\Delta b) = \Delta b\,\tfrac{1}{2}\,[CIF_b\,EER_0\,(1 + t_b) + CIF_b\,EER_1\,(1 + t_b)]$$

By rearranging the terms, the above expressions can be reduced to

$$WP(\Delta a) = \Delta a\,\tfrac{1}{2}\,(EER_0 + EER_1)\,(1 + t_a)\,CIF_a$$
$$WP(\Delta b) = \Delta b\,\tfrac{1}{2}\,(EER_0 + EER_1)\,(1 + t_b)\,CIF_b$$

[3.5]

and the accounting price of foreign exchange will be

$$\text{APFE} = \frac{WP(\Delta a) + WP(\Delta b)}{(S_1 - S_0)}$$

[3.6]

But as foreign exchange $S_1 - S_0$ is used entirely to import quantities Δa and Δb,

$$(S_1 - S_0) = CIF_a\,\Delta a + CIF_b\,\Delta b$$

[3.7]

Substituting [3.5] and [3.7] in [3.6] the accounting price of foreign exchange will be

$$APFE = \frac{\frac{1}{2}(EER_0 + EER_1)[CIF_a \Delta a (1 + t_a) + CIF_b \Delta b (1 + t_b)]}{CIF_a \Delta a + CIF_b \Delta b} \quad [3.8]$$

If now we consider that normally the increase in the supply of foreign exchange generated by a project has a minimum influence on the exchange rate, we can say that for all practical purposes,

$$\frac{1}{2}(EER_0 + EER_1) = EER$$

and expression [3.8] can be written as

$$APFE = \frac{EER [CIF_a \Delta a (1 + t_a) + CIF_b \Delta b (1 + t_b)]}{CIF_a \Delta a + CIF_b \Delta b} \quad [3.9]$$

However, the formula for the APFE is normally expressed as the relation between this accounting price and its market price (the EER). By calling this relation the *accounting price ratio of foreign exchange* (APRFE) we obtain

$$APRFE = \frac{APFE}{EER}$$

$$APRFE = \frac{CIF_a \Delta a (1 + t_a) + CIF_b \Delta b (1 + t_b)}{CIF_a \Delta a + CIF_b \Delta b} \quad [3.10]$$

Generalizing expression [3.10] for n imported consumer goods m_i we obtain

$$APRFE = \sum_{i=1}^{n} \varphi_i (1 + t_i) \quad [3.11]$$

in which

$$\varphi_i = \frac{CIF_i \Delta m_i}{\sum_{i=1}^{n} CIF_i \Delta m_i}$$

is the share of each good i in *additional* imports. It should be pointed out that the weights φ_i refer to the additional imports generated *exclusively* by the change in the exchange rate brought about by the increase in the supply of foreign exchange.[4] Consequently, they *cannot* be estimated by simply comparing the lists of imports between two periods since the Δm_i thus observed incorporate the effect of income changes.

The reader will recognize the expression [3.11] as the traditional formula for the APRFE as presented in UNIDO (1972) or Harberger (1973), except that in these two works $(1 + t_i)$ is replaced by a more general expression in order to allow for other forms of protection to be included such as an import quota, sold at a domestic price determined by the market and which will be expanded in accordance with the increase in the supply of foreign exchange. If, for example, imports were subject to a domestic "sales" tax of t_i^y, the formula for the foreign exchange accounting price ratio would be

$$APRFE = \sum_{i=1}^{n} \varphi_i (1 + t_i)(1 + t_i^y)$$ [3.12]

Elsewhere, the same expression [3.11] is shown in terms of the price elasticity of the demand functions of imported goods.

3.3 Income Transfers Generated by an Additional Supply of Exports

The simple example developed so far also enables us to present the income transfers generated by the additional supply of exports. The identification and quantification of these transfers, as will be seen later, is an important part of estimating the distribution of the income changes generated by a project. To do this, it is useful to begin with the direct effects of the increase in the supply of foreign exchange presented in Table 3.1. This will allow us to explain a series of assumptions implied in the subsequent analysis.

We have already mentioned that, for practical purposes, the effect of the change in the supply of foreign exchange on the EER is assumed to be small enough to be ignored. Thus,

$$EER_0 = EER_1 = EER$$

---

4. This is how Δa and Δb were defined in Figure 3.2. Strictly speaking, the weights will be:

$$\varphi_i = \frac{\partial m_i}{\partial EER} \frac{\partial EER}{\partial \text{foreign exchange}}$$

and the values corresponding to the first line of Table 3.1 will be nil. But if this is the case, from [3.1] and [3.2] it follows that

$$\tfrac{1}{2}\,(p_a^0 + p_a^1) = p_a$$

and consequently consumers' willingness to pay will be estimated simply as

$$p_a\,(a_1 - a_0) = CIF_a\,EER\,(1 + t_a)\,(a_1 - a_0)$$

From this it follows that the difference between consumers' willingness to pay and what is actually paid for the consumption that additional foreign exchange makes possible will be nil. To summarize, the only effect considered is the value of additional consumption, equal to the total income from the project plus the change in the Government's receipts from foreign trade taxes. Since the Government will not in practice alter its foreign trade tax policy as a result of a marginal increase in receipts, this will result in (most likely) an increase in expenditure, a reduction in the deficit, or (least likely) a reduction in other taxes, all of which will affect people's economic welfare.[5]

We can now give an example of the transfers caused by an increase in the supply of foreign exchange. Let us suppose that the project concerned generates exports (foreign exchange) whose value in the national currency is $100,[6] and that this foreign exchange is used to import $60 worth of additional units of a and $40 worth of additional units of b so that

$$CIF_a\,EER\,\Delta a = \$60$$

$$CIF_b\,EER\,\Delta b = \$40$$

Furthermore, assume that $t_a = 0.10$ and $t_b = 0.20$, from which

$$
\begin{aligned}
p_a\,\Delta a &= \$\ 60 + \$60 \times 0.1 \\
\underline{p_b\,\Delta b} &= \underline{\$\ 40 + \$40 \times 0.2} \\
\text{Total} &= \$100 + \$14
\end{aligned}
$$

in which the total shows the sum of the compensating variations of the $100 of foreign exchange. Consequently (see Table 3.2), what is income of $100 for the project is additional consumption of $114 for the economy as a whole and the difference is the $14 of additional taxes received by the Government. Logically, the accounting price ratio of foreign exchange is equal to 1.14.

The assumptions made in order to present this simple example will be the

---

5. These effects will not be discussed for the time being.
6. Henceforth the $ sign will always be used to refer to the national currency.

Table 3.2. Valuation at Efficiency Prices of Additional Exports, in Consumption Units

	Project	Government	Economic Valuation
Exports	100	14	114

same as those implied in the analyses given in subsequent chapters, where they will not be repeated. Later in this chapter, we introduce the import of intermediate goods, exports and the domestic production of imports, none of which alters what has been stated so far.

By the end of this chapter, the reader will realize that the difference between $100 and $100 × APRFE is explained, under the assumptions presented in this chapter, by the additional taxes for the import of consumer and intermediate goods, less the taxes lost through the reduction in exports plus the subsidies saved through this reduction. The corresponding numerical example is left for the reader.

3.4 The Accounting Price of Foreign Exchange When Intermediate Goods Are Imported

The simple example in Section 3.2 enabled us to present the derivation of the accounting price of foreign exchange in a direct and uncomplicated way, since we assumed that only consumer goods were imported. In this case, the sum of the CVs of the additional supply of foreign exchange can be calculated directly according to consumers' willingness to pay. When the import of intermediate goods (which are not produced domestically) is introduced, valuation is indirect through consumers' willingness to pay for the consumer goods that can be produced with these intermediate goods. According to the neo-classical formulation, under perfect competition, the demand function for an intermediate input (D_b in Figure 3.2(b)) will be a reasonable approximation of the value of the marginal product of that input, i.e. of the additional quantity that can be obtained from the good in whose production the input is used per additional unit of the input when the quantity of all the other inputs remains constant, the additional quantity of product being valued at its market price.[7] Thus, the market price of b will be

$$p_b^0 = \frac{\Delta c}{\Delta b} p_c^0$$

$$p_b^1 = \frac{\Delta c}{\Delta b} p_c^1$$

[3.13]

7. See Ferguson and Gould (1975) for an explanation of why it would only be an approximation.

in which c is the consumer good in the production of which input b comes in. Under these circumstances, substituting [3.13] in [3.4] yields

$$WP(\Delta b) = \tfrac{1}{2} \left(\frac{\Delta c}{\Delta b} p_c^0 + \frac{\Delta c}{\Delta b} p_c^1 \right) \Delta b$$

$$WP(\Delta b) = \tfrac{1}{2} (p_c^0 + p_c^1) \frac{\Delta c}{\Delta b} \Delta b$$

[3.14]

and we see that the willingness to pay for quantity Δb of the imported input would be equal to the willingness to pay for the additional consumption that it makes possible. Thus the formulas [3.11] or [3.12] for calculating the APRFE can be extended to the case of intermediate goods. By a similar process, again under conditions of perfect competition, this reasoning can be extended to "capital goods".

In the case of intermediate goods, it may not be enough to suppose that demand for the imported input is equal to the value of the marginal product, since the latter assumes that the quantities of all the other inputs used remain constant. If the quantities of the remaining inputs were also to change, willingness to pay for intermediate good b could be expressed as

$$WP(\Delta b) = \Delta c \tfrac{1}{2} (p_c^0 + p_c^1) - \sum_i \Delta q_{ic} \, p_i$$

[3.15]

that is, as willingness to pay for the change in the consumption of good c in the production of which it is used, less the value at market prices of the change in the quantities used of the *remaining* inputs ($\Sigma \, \Delta q_{ic} \, p_i$), i.e. excluding input b. If the (constant) market prices of the remaining inputs (p_i) can be accepted as reasonable approximations of the respective efficiency prices, willingness to pay for Δb will adequately reflect the sum of the CVs of Δb and the formula [3.11] or [3.12] for the APRFE will continue to be valid.

3.5 The Accounting Price of Foreign Exchange When Exports Are Taken into Account

In previous sections, it was assumed that the supply of foreign exchange (exports) was completely inelastic with respect to (small) variations in the exchange rate. However, this was only for the sake of simplification. In general, the supply of exports will be an increasing function of the exchange rate (Figure 3.3), reflecting the price elasticity of both domestic supply and demand of the goods exported.

Let us consider first the case in which only consumer goods are exported. The project under consideration will increase the supply of foreign exchange

Figure 3.3. The Effects of an Increase in the Supply of Foreign Exchange

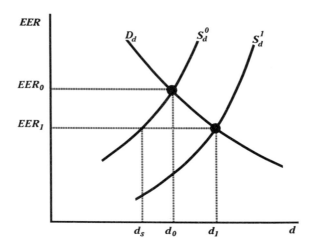

by $d_1 - d_s$, of which only $d_1 - d_0$ will be additional net availability, whereas $d_0 - d_s$ will replace the supply of other producers who will reduce their sales abroad because of the reduction in the exchange rate from EER_0 to EER_1. The additional net supply $d_1 - d_0$ will allow for additional imports of the same magnitude to be made and the sum of CVs per additional unit of foreign exchange can be calculated, for example, as

$$APFE_m = \sum_{i=1}^{n} \varphi_i (1 + t_i) EER \qquad [3.11]$$

bearing in mind that the weights φ_i have to be calculated with respect to the project's additional supply of foreign exchange. In algebraic form, the weights will be

$$\varphi_i = \frac{CIF_i \, \Delta m_i}{d_1 - d_s}$$

$$\sum_i \varphi_i = \frac{\sum_i CIF_i \, \Delta m_i}{d_1 - d_s}$$

$$\sum_i \varphi_i = \frac{d_1 - d_0}{d_1 - d_s}$$

44

that is, the CIF value of the additional imports of good i as a proportion of the additional foreign exchange produced by the project.

To arrive at the sum of the CVs of foreign exchange $d_0 - d_s$, it is necessary to turn to the markets of the only two export (and domestic consumption) goods e and h. Let us suppose that e is the good whose production increases, and that the firm will export all its additional production. Figure 3.4(a) and (b) show the long-term equilibrium positions in the markets of e and h. In Figure 3.4(a) it can be seen that additional production $e_1 - e_1^s$ will increase the *net* supply of the exports of e by

$$(e_1 - e_1^s) - (e_0^s - e_1^s) - (e_1^d - e_0^d)$$

since due to the effect on the exchange rate, it will replace other sources by $e_0^s - e_1^s$ and increase domestic consumption (reduce the exports of other producers) by $e_1^d - e_0^d$. If the domestic prices of the resources released by the reduction $e_0^s - e_1^s$ are acceptable approximations of their efficiency prices (in the consumption numeraire), the sum of the CVs in the market of e will be the willingness to pay for additional consumption

$$\tfrac{1}{2} (p_e^0 + p_e^1) (e_1^d - e_0^d) \qquad [3.17]$$

plus the value at efficiency prices of the resources released

$$\tfrac{1}{2} (p_e^0 + p_e^1) (e_0^s - e_1^s) \qquad [3.18]$$

In the market of h, Figure 3.4(b), the reduction in the equilibrium exchange rate will reduce the domestic price, increasing consumption by a total value of

$$\tfrac{1}{2} (p_h^0 + p_h^1) (h_1^d - h_0^d) \qquad [3.19]$$

and, on the assumption that the domestic market price of the good exported is equal to its long-run marginal cost at efficiency prices,[8] it will release resources by

$$\tfrac{1}{2} (p_h^0 + p_h^1) (h_0^s - h_1^s) \qquad [3.20]$$

Consequently, the foreign exchange produced by the project will be

$$FOB_e (e_1 - e_1^s)$$

---

8. If the assumption were not acceptable, the APRFE could be calculated by using input-output techniques through a process similar to that described in Chapter 13. See Londero (1994).

Figure 3.4. The Effects of the Reduction in the Exchange Rate on the Market for Exported Goods

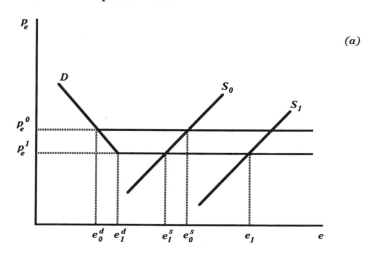

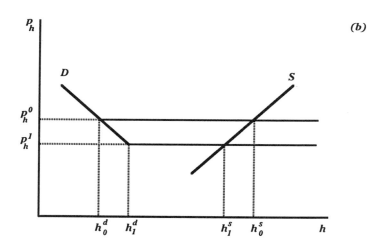

in which FOB_e is the f.o.b. price expressed in foreign exchange. This is partially compensated by the reduction in exports from other producers for a total of

$$FOB_e \, [(e_0^s - e_1^s) + (e_1^d - e_0^d)] + FOB_h \, [(h_0^s - h_1^s) + (h_1^d - h_0^d)]$$

46

and the difference between both quantities of foreign exchange is used to increase imports, i.e.

$$d_1 - d_0 = FOB_e \left[(e_1 - e_1^s) - (e_0^s - e_1^s) - (e_1^d - e_0^d) \right]$$
$$- FOB_h \left[(h_0^s - h_1^s) + (h_1^d - h_0^d) \right]$$

To summarize, from [3.17] and [3.18] we can see that the value of additional consumption in the market of e will be

$$\Delta C_e = \tfrac{1}{2} (p_e^0 + p_e^1) \left[(e_1^d - e_0^d) + (e_0^s - e_1^s) \right] \tag{3.21}$$

and, from [3.19] and [3.20], that in the market of h will be

$$\Delta C_h = \tfrac{1}{2} (p_h^0 + p_h^1) \left[(h_1^d - h_0^d) + (h_0^s - h_1^s) \right] \tag{3.22}$$

Following the same procedure as in the case of imports, and assuming again that the domestic transport and trade margins are nil, we can express the domestic prices of the two exported consumer goods as

$$p_e^0 = FOB_e \, EER_0 \, (1 - t_e)$$
$$p_e^1 = FOB_e \, EER_1 \, (1 - t_e) \tag{3.23}$$

$$p_h^0 = FOB_h \, EER_0 \, (1 - t_h)$$
$$p_h^1 = FOB_h \, EER_1 \, (1 - t_h) \tag{3.24}$$

in which FOB_i and t_i $(i = e, h)$ are the FOB prices in foreign exchange and the export tax rates, respectively.[9] Substituting [3.23] and [3.24] in [3.21] and [3.22] we get

$$\Delta C_e = \tfrac{1}{2} (EER_0 + EER_1) \, FOB_e \, (1 - t_e) \left[(e_1^d - e_0^d) + (e_0^s - e_1^s) \right] \tag{3.25}$$
$$\Delta C_h = \tfrac{1}{2} (EER_0 + EER_1) \, FOB_h \, (1 - t_h) \left[(h_1^d - h_0^d) + (h_0^s - h_1^s) \right]$$

Since for small changes in the supply of foreign exchange

$$\tfrac{1}{2} (EER_0 + EER_1) = EER$$

---

9. Export incentives, such as drawbacks or credits at interest rates lower than the discount rate, will be treated as "negative" taxes.

expressions [3.25] can be written as

$$\Delta C_e = EER\ FOB_e\ (1 - t_e)\ (\Delta e^d + \Delta e^s)$$
$$\Delta C_h = EER\ FOB_h\ (1 - t_h)\ (\Delta h^d + \Delta h^s)$$

[3.26]

As a result, the value of the additional consumption made possible by the increase in the supply of foreign exchange $d_1 - d_s$ would be equal to:

(a) that resulting from additional imports for an amount in foreign exchange equal to $d_1 - d_0$, whose value, according to the example in Section 3.2, will be

$$EER\ [CIF_a\ \Delta a\ (1 + t_a) + CIF_b\ \Delta b\ (1 + t_b)]$$

(b) that resulting from the increase in the domestic consumption of exported goods, the value of which, according to expressions [3.26], will be

$$EER\ [FOB_e\ \Delta e^d\ (1 - t_e) + FOB_h\ \Delta h^d\ (1 - t_h)]$$

(c) the value of the resources made available for the additional production of other goods, because of the reduction in the production of export goods

$$EER\ [FOB_e\ \Delta e^s\ (1 - t_e) + FOB_h\ \Delta h^s\ (1 - t_h)]$$

The increase in the supply of foreign exchange produced by the project being analyzed will consist of:

(a) the *net* addition to foreign exchange availability $(d_1 - d_0)$, which is used entirely for additional imports; and
(b) the reduction in exports from other producers due to the increase in the domestic quantity demanded (Δe^d and Δh^d) and the reduction in domestic production (Δe^s and Δh^s)

$$d_0 - d_s = FOB_e\ (\Delta e^d + \Delta e^s) + FOB_h\ (\Delta h^d + \Delta h^s)$$

Consequently, since the APFE has been defined as the sum of the CVs of the additional supply of foreign exchange per unit thereof, and in keeping with the assumptions already mentioned, this sum of CVs will be equal to total willingness to pay plus the value of the resources released, expression [3.6] can be redefined as

$$APFE = \frac{WP(\Delta a) + WP(\Delta b) + \Delta C_e + \Delta C_h}{d_1 - d_s}$$

and calculated in accordance with expressions [3.9] and [3.26]. Defining $CIF_i \, \Delta m_i$ as the increase in the value of the imports of good i per additional unit of foreign exchange $d_1 - d_s$ produced by the project and $FOB_j \, \Delta x_j$ as the reduction in the value of the exports of good j per unit of $d_1 - d_s$, the APFE will be

$$APFE = \frac{EER \left[\sum_{i=1}^{n} CIF_i \, \Delta m_i \, (1 + t_i) + \sum_{j=1}^{k} FOB_j \, \Delta x_j \, (1 - t_j) \right]}{\sum_{i=1}^{n} CIF_i \, \Delta m_i + \sum_{j=1}^{k} FOB_j \, \Delta x_j} \qquad [3.27]$$

Finally, since the accounting price ratio of foreign exchange has been defined as

$$APRFE = \frac{APFE}{EER}$$

defining

$$\varphi_i = \frac{CIF_i \, \Delta m_i}{\sum_{i=1}^{n} CIF_i \, \Delta m_i + \sum_{j=1}^{k} FOB_j \, \Delta x_j} \qquad [3.28]$$

$$\varphi_j = \frac{FOB_j \, \Delta x_j}{\sum_{i=1}^{n} CIF_i \, \Delta m_i + \sum_{j=1}^{k} FOB_j \, \Delta x_j} \qquad [3.29]$$

and substituting [3.28] and [3.29] in [3.27], the APRFE can be presented as

$$APRFE = \sum_{i=1}^{n} \varphi_i \, (1 + t_i) + \sum_{j=1}^{k} \varphi_j \, (1 - t_j) \qquad [3.30]$$

49

In other words, the APRFE is a weighted average of one plus *ad valorem* foreign trade taxes rates (or its equivalent for other types of restrictions or incentives) in which the weights represent the share of the change in the value of the imports or exports of each good, in the supply change generated. If imports and exports were also subject to domestic taxes t_i^y and t_j^y, respectively, the equivalent of [3.30] would be

$$APRFE = \sum_{i=1}^{n} \varphi_i \,(1 + t_i)(1 + t_i^y) + \sum_{j=1}^{k} \varphi_j \,(1 - t_j)(1 - t_j^y) \qquad [3.31]$$

If the change in exports includes intermediate or capital goods, expressions [3.30] and [3.31] will continue to be valid if:

(a) we can assume that domestic demand for such goods is a good approximation of the value of their marginal product (in consumption units) as shown in expression [3.14] for the case of imports; or
(b) the domestic prices of the inputs used in the production of consumer goods are regarded as good approximations of their efficiency prices (in the consumption numeraire), which would result in the same as shown in expression [3.15] for imported intermediate goods.

The calculation of the weights φ requires that the price elasticity of the supply of exported goods and of the domestic demand for imported goods be known, information which in practice is not available. As a result, the APRFE is frequently calculated on the assumption that the weights φ are equal to the average share of each product in total imports and exports. Thus, for example, in the case of imports, the weights are calculated as

$$\varphi_i = \frac{CIF_i \,\Delta m_i}{\displaystyle\sum_{i=1}^{n} CIF_i \,\Delta m_i + \sum_{j=1}^{k} FOB_j \,\Delta x_j} = \frac{CIF_i \,m_i}{\displaystyle\sum_{i=1}^{n} CIF_i \,m_i + \sum_{j=1}^{k} FOB_j \,x_j} \qquad [3.32]$$

Substituting [3.32] and its equivalent for exports in [3.27], and dividing by the EER we obtain

$$APRFE = \frac{M + T_m + X - T_x}{M + X} \qquad [3.33]$$

in which

$$M = \sum_{i=1}^{n} CIF_i \, m_i \, EER$$

$$T_m = \sum_{i=1}^{n} CIF_i \, m_i \, EER \, t_i$$

$$X = \sum_{j=1}^{k} FOB_j \, x_j \, EER$$

$$T_x = \sum_{j=1}^{k} FOB_j \, x_j \, EER \, t_j$$

The same expression has been presented in various texts as the formula for calculating the "standard conversion factor", which is used to convert values expressed in the consumption numeraire to the foreign exchange numeraire.[10]

3.6 The Accounting Price of Foreign Exchange When There Is Domestic Production of Marginally Imported Goods

Up until now, it was taken for granted that there was no domestic production of imported goods, avoiding the resulting complications of considering the effects on domestic production of marginally imported goods. This section analyzes those effects.

Suppose the imported good a is also produced domestically, as shown in Figure 3.5. If adjustment to an additional supply of foreign exchange takes place through a reduction in the EER, this will reduce the internal price of a by $p_a^0 - p_a^1$, reducing domestic production by $a_0^s - a_1^s$ and increasing imports by $(a_0^s - a_1^s) + (a_1 - a_0)$. Following a similar reasoning as in the case of exports, for small EER variations and taking the domestic price of a to be equal to its long-run marginal cost at efficiency prices,[11] the value at efficiency prices for

---

10. Squire and van der Tak (1975, Chapter IX), Bruce (1976), Gittinger (1982, Chapter 7), and Squire, et al. (1979, Appendix C). See Chapter 5 of this study.

11. As in the export case, if this assumption were unacceptable, the APRFE could be calculated using input-output techniques. See Londero (1994).

Figure 3.5. The Effect of an Exchange Rate Reduction on Markets for Domestically Produced, Marginally Imported Goods

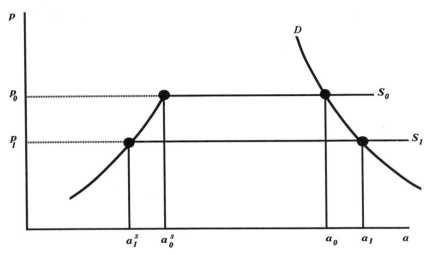

that part of the additional supply of foreign exchange which is devoted to import good a will also be

$$\Delta C_a = EER\ CIF_a\ (1 + t_a)\ [(a_0^s - a_1^s) + (a_1 - a_0)]$$

In other words, it is the willingness to pay for the additional consumption $a_1 - a_0$, plus the "value of the resources released" by the reduction in domestic production $a_0^s - a_1^s$. Given the assumption of equality between domestic price and long-run marginal cost at efficiency prices, there would be no (significant) distributional effects stemming from the reallocation of inputs to be registered, and the taxes on additional imported goods would explain the entire difference between the APFE and the EER coming from the domestic production of imported goods.

3.7 The Existence of Transport and Trade Margins

When defining the relation between the domestic and international prices of traded goods as

$$p_i = CIF_i\ EER\ (1 + t_i) \qquad\qquad [3.1]$$

$$p_j = FOB_j\ EER\ (1 - t_j) \qquad\qquad [3.23]$$

52

it was assumed that the domestic transport and trade margins were nil, which simplified presentation considerably. The appropriate corrections can now be made. If tra_i and com_i are the transport and trade margins per unit of imports i, the domestic price will be as follows:

$$p_i = CIF_i\, EER\, (1 + t_i) + tra_i + com_i \qquad\qquad [3.34]$$

If as a result of an increase in the supply of foreign exchange, which reduces the EER, imports of good i increase, the value of additional consumption will be $\Delta q_i\, p_i$ less the cost of providing transport and trade services valued at their efficiency prices, that is,

$$\Delta C_i = \Delta q_i\, (p_i - tra_i' - com_i')$$

in which p_i corresponds to the expression [3.34] and the superscripts ' indicate that the transport and trade margins are valued at efficiency prices. If we now replace p_i by its expression [3.34], we obtain

$$\Delta C_i = \Delta q_i\, [CIF_i\, EER\, (1 + t_i) + (tra_i - tra_i') + (com_i - com_i')]$$

In the case of exports, the reduction in the EER will result in an increase in domestic consumption Δq_j^d and a reduction in production Δq_j^s. The former will require more transport and trade services while the latter will release resources under the same heading. Consequently, the value of additional consumption will be

$$\Delta C_j = (\Delta q_j^d + \Delta q_j^s)[FOB_j\, EER\, (1 - t_j)]$$
$$+ (\Delta q_j^d - \Delta q_j^s)\, (tra_j - tra_j' + com_j - com_j')$$

in which, for the sake of simplification, it is assumed that the transport and trade margins for the domestic consumption of j are equal to those for exporting it.

If the value at market prices of these margins is, for practical purposes, equal to their value at efficiency prices, the effects $(tra - tra')$ and $(com - com')$ will be nil and the APRFE can be calculated according to equations [3.30] or [3.31], or to its operational version [3.33].

3.8 Summary

Calculation of the APRFE in accordance with expressions [3.30] or [3.31], or its operational version [3.33], presupposes that the following main conditions are met:

(a) the exchange rate is the instrument used to adjust the supply and demand of foreign exchange in the long run;

(b) the exchange rate corrected by the APRFE (or the one used to calculate the APFE) is the one that keeps the supply and demand of foreign exchange in long-run equilibrium;

(c) if other incentives or disincentives for imports or exports exist, they can be expressed through an equivalent tax or subsidy;

(d) the domestic demand functions for intermediate goods adequately reflect the value of the marginal product at efficiency prices or (more appropriately) the prices of the remaining intermediate goods adequately reflect their efficiency prices;

(e) the value at market prices of the transport and trade margins is equal to their value at efficiency prices.

Under these circumstances, an additional unit of foreign exchange expressed in the national currency at the (long-term equilibrium) exchange rate can be expressed in units of consumption by multiplying it by the APRFE calculated in accordance with what has been presented in this chapter.

CHAPTER 4

THE VALUATION
OF TRADED GOODS

4.1 Traded Goods

The system of foreign trade incentives and disincentives in most countries is
characterized by the diversity of the instruments used and by the variation in
the extent to which these instruments alter domestic prices in relation to
international prices. Some goods and services are traded internationally (are
imported or exported) at prices that are not subject to any other effect than the
level of the exchange rate. At the other extreme, others are not traded due to
the level of such incentives and disincentives. Moreover, in many countries
the existence of systems for promoting certain activities or firms results in
different domestic prices for different users of the same imported input.
However, in the example of imported inputs, the "efficiency" criterion dic-
tates that the cost of importing additional units is determined by the reduction
in the incomes of the persons affected (the sum of their CVs) by the use of the
resources required. This effect on incomes and its distribution among those
affected depends, as this chapter will show, both on the effective cost to the
importer and on the accounting price of foreign exchange.

   This chapter presents the most frequent cases in the valuation of traded
goods, with an emphasis on identifying the related distributional effects. For

this purpose, an APRFE will be used that corresponds to the expression [3.31] and which, as a consequence, depends on the validity of the assumptions already discussed in chapter III.

A good or service is said to be internationally traded at the margin (imported or exported), or simply traded, when the adjustment to an additional domestic demand or supply of that commodity is made entirely through a change in its exports or imports. It should be noted that describing a good as traded depends on what actually happens with the corresponding exports or imports, a feature that differentiates this classification from that in which groupings are made in accordance with what *would potentially happen if* export and import incentives and disincentives were altered or eliminated. In the latter case we speak of tradable (importable or exportable) goods and services.[1]

4.2 The Project Increases the Demand for Imported Goods

The immediate effect of a project that increases the demand for an imported good will be to displace towards the right the demand for the good concerned in the quantity required by the respective technical specifications. If this additional demand is insignificant with respect to world supply, the CIF price of the product can be considered constant and world supply infinitely elastic at that price. The price to the domestic purchaser will be

$$p_m = CIF_m \times EER \times (1 + t_m) + cp_m + tra_m + com_m$$

in which

$$t_m = \textit{ad valorem} \text{ tax rate}$$
$$cp_m = \text{costs of port handling, at market prices}$$
$$tra_m = \text{transport costs from the port to the user, at market prices}$$
$$com_m = \text{trading costs, at market prices}$$

Figure 4.1 shows the situation described when *cp, tra* and *com* can be assumed to be constant per unit of product for small changes in demand. In such a situation, the cost at efficiency prices (in the consumption numeraire) of providing the quantity $\Delta m = m_1 - m_0$ will include the cost of the foreign exchange required to import that quantity valued at the APFE

$$\Delta m \times CIF_m \times EER \times APRFE$$

---

1. The implications of the classification criterion adopted are discussed in V. Joshi (1972, Section IV), Dasgupta (1972, Sections 5.3 and 5.4), H. Joshi (1972) and Mishan (1982, Chapters 13 & 14).

Figure 4.1 The Project Increases the Demand for Imported Goods

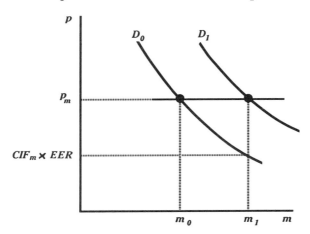

plus the cost at efficiency prices of the respective port handling (cp_m) transport (tra_m) and trading (com_m) services.

If the value at market prices of these services can be accepted as a reasonable approximation of their efficiency prices, an assumption already made in the previous chapter, obtaining the efficiency price of the imported input only requires the foreign exchange to be corrected. Let

$$
\begin{array}{rl}
CIF_m \; EER \; \Delta m = & 100 \\
t_m \; CIF_m \; EER \; \Delta m = & 10 \\
cp_m = & 2 \\
tra_m = & 1 \\
\underline{com_m = } & \underline{20} \\
\text{Total} = & 133
\end{array}
$$

be the cost to the purchaser, in this case to the project, of the additional imports, which we wish to value at efficiency prices, and let APRFE = 1.2 be the accounting price ratio of foreign exchange.

Table 4.1 shows the valuation of these imports at efficiency prices. The first column indicates the cost to the purchaser, or what the project pays to obtain these imports. The second records two effects on the Government's finances. The first one is the taxes on foreign trade no longer received due to the net balance resulting from the reduction in imports and increase in exports required to provide the foreign exchange needed for the project. As explained in Chapter 3, the latter is equal to the difference between the amount of the reduction in incomes needed to provide foreign exchange (-100×1.2) and

Table 4.1   Valuation at Efficiency Prices of the Cost to the Purchaser of Imports (Consumption Numeraire)

Breakdown	Project	Government	Total at Efficiency Prices
Foreign Exchange	−100	−20	−120
Taxes on Foreign Trade	−10	+10	−
Other Domestic Costs	−23	−	−23
Total	−133	−10	−143

its valuation at the EER (−100). The second effect is the import taxes it receives directly from the project. The last column shows the valuation at efficiency prices of the resources required to provide the imports concerned. It shows that the valuation at market prices (−133) underestimates the value at efficiency prices by the difference between willingness to pay for the reduction in consumption needed to release the foreign exchange (−100 × APRFE = −120) and what is actually paid for the imports that they make possible (−100 − 10). At the same time, this last column shows that the loss in income of those involved (the project and the Government) is 143. In other words, the resources used to provide the imports concerned require a reduction in incomes of 143, consisting of 133 from the (owners of the) project and 10 from the (users of the services of the) Government.

4.3 The Project Increases the Demand for Exported Goods

Let us consider the case of a good e which is exported and whose international price is not affected by small variations in the country's supply to the international market. The producer receives a price equal to the export price less the corresponding taxes and less port, transport and trading costs,

$$p_e^p = FOB_e \, EER \, (1 - t_e) - cp_e - tra_e^x - com_e^x \qquad [4.1]$$

in which the superscript x indicates that these are transport and trade margins for export. Since the domestic producer does not distinguish between purchasers, he sells the product to anybody who pays price p_e^p for it. Thus, the price to the domestic purchaser will be equal to the producer's price plus domestic transport and trade costs

$$p_e^u = p_e^p + tra_e + com_e$$

58

Replacing the producer's price by its expression [4.1] we obtain

$$p_e^u = FOB_e \, EER \, (1 - t_e) - cp_e + (tra_e - tra_e^x) + (com_e - com_e^x)$$

If the incremental transport and trading expenses are nil, the purchaser's price will simply be

$$p_e^u = FOB_e \, EER \, (1 - t_e) - cp_e$$

Figure 4.2 shows the case in question. In the situation without the project (D_0), quantity e_0 of domestic production e_t is for domestic consumption and the remainder $(e_t - e_0)$ for export. As the producer's price is determined by the international price, the increase $D_0 - D_1$ in domestic demand generated by the project will not affect the domestic price. As a consequence, there will not be increases in production or reductions in domestic demand and the additional quantity demanded will be provided through a reduction in exports equal to

$$\Delta e = e_1 - e_0$$

whose value at the prices paid by the project will be

$$\Delta e \, p_e^u = \Delta e \, FOB_e \, EER \, (1 - t_e) - \Delta e \, cp_e$$

Figure 4.2 The Project Increases the Demand for Exported Goods

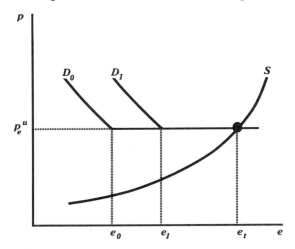

Table 4.2   Valuation at Efficiency Prices of the User's Cost of the Reduction in Exports (Consumption Numeraire)

	Project	Government	Total at Efficiency Prices
Foreign Exchange	−100	−20	−120
Taxes on Foreign Trade	10	−10	−
Other Costs	2	−	2
Total	−88	−30	−118

Let, for example,

$$\begin{array}{rcl} \Delta e \, cp_e &=& -2 \\ \Delta e \, FOB_e \, EER &=& 100 \\ -t_e \, \Delta e \, FOB_e \, EER &=& -10 \\ \hline \Delta e \, p_e^u &=& 88 \end{array}$$

be the value of the exported goods used by the project, whose valuation at efficiency prices is shown in Table 4.2. The APRFE is equal to 1.2 and the value at market prices of port services is assumed to be equal to their value at efficiency prices. The first column is merely the breakdown of what the input costs the project, as explained when the expression for the price to the domestic purchaser was deduced. The second shows the effects on the Government, which sees its tax revenue reduced for two reasons: (a) the net balance resulting from the lower imports and greater exports needed to adjust the foreign exchange market after exports have been reduced by 100; and (b) the export taxes it no longer receives when exports have been reduced by 100. In short, the cost at efficiency prices of the exported input is equal to the cost to the purchaser plus the reduction in Government revenue.

4.4 The Projects Substitutes for Imports

Let us begin by considering the case of a project that substitutes for imports in the context of *existing* incentives and disincentives to foreign trade; for example, the existing import tariff will not be altered as a consequence of the project. In addition, the reduction in international demand for the imported product (at the margin) does not affect the corresponding CIF price. This situation is reflected in Figure 4.3 in which m_d is domestic production and $m_0 - m_d$ imports, both in the "without project situation". The purchaser's

Figure 4.3 The Project Substitutes for Imports at the Prevailing Tariff

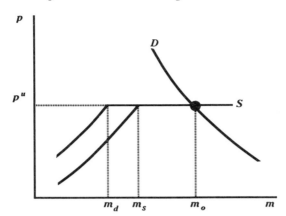

price of the product is determined by the international price plus domestic port handling, transport and trade expenses

$$p^u = CIF_m \, EER \, (1 + t_m) + cp_m + tra_m + com_m \qquad\qquad [4.2]$$

and will remain unaltered in response to the additional supply of the project $(m_s - m_d)$. As price p^u is given, the project will sell at a price equal to p^u less the domestic transport and trade costs between the project and the purchaser. Thus the price to the producer (project) will be

$$p^p = p^u - tra - com$$

in which *tra* and *com* are the transport and trade margins of domestic production. Replacing p^u by its expression [4.2] we obtain

$$p^p = CIF_m \, EER \, (1 + t_m) + cp_m + (tra_m - tra) + (com_m - com)$$

Assuming, to simplify presentation, that the net transport and trade balances are nil, the producer's price of the substituted import will simply be

$$p^p = CIF_m \, EER \, (1 + t_m) + cp_m$$

61

Consequently, sales from the project will equal the quantity $(m_s - m_d)$ at price p^p. For example, let

$$
\begin{array}{rcl}
cp_m\,(m_s - m_d) &=& 3 \\
CIF_m\,EER\,(m_s - m_d) &=& 100 \\
t_m\,CIF_m\,EER\,(m_s - m_d) &=& 30 \\
\hline
p^p\,(m_s - m_d) &=& 133
\end{array}
$$

be the breakdown of the value of sales in savings on port costs, savings in foreign exchange and the reduction in import tax revenue. The valuation of these sales at efficiency prices is given in Table 4.3 on the assumption that the market value of port costs adequately reflects the corresponding value at efficiency prices. The value at efficiency prices of the imports substituted is equal to that of the foreign exchange saved plus that of the resources corresponding to the port costs saved. The difference between this total and the price to the producer is explained by the net effect on the collection of taxes by the Government, consisting of: (a) the reduction of 30 through the imports substituted; and (b) the increase of 20 due to the effect of the reduction in the demand for foreign exchange on receipts from taxes on foreign trade.

Consider now the case in which the Government wished to make privately profitable the substitution of an imported *consumer* good that is not produced domestically. With this objective in mind, the Government increases the prevailing tariff t_0 in Δt, an increase which would not be effected if the project(s) were not carried out. This situation is illustrated in Figure 4.4, in which p_0 is the price to the user of the imported product when the import tariff is t_0 and p^* is that price when the tariff is $t_1 = t_0 + \Delta t$. Given that, at the new tariff, the price to the purchaser of imports (p^*) is greater than that of domestic production supply (p_1), imports m_0 will be reduced to zero by the substitution of quantity m_1 and the reduction in domestic consumption by $m_0 - m_1$ due to the price increase $p_1 - p_0$.

Table 4.3   Valuation at Efficiency Prices of the Imports Substituted (Consumption Numeraire)

	Project	Government	Total at Efficiency Prices
Foreign Exchange	100	20	120
Taxes on Foreign Trade	30	−30	—
Other Costs	3	—	3
Total	133	−10	123

Figure 4.4 The Project Substitutes for Imports by Increasing the Tariff

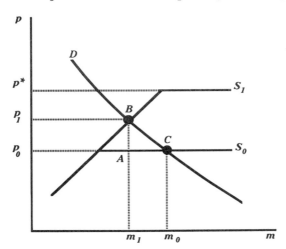

Assuming that m is a consumer good, the price increase results in a welfare loss for the consumers, measured by the respective compensating variations whose sum is shown in Figure 4.4 by the area p_0BCp_1.

The numerical example of Table 4.4, constructed on the basis of the data

$$
\begin{aligned}
m_0 &= 1000 \\
m_1 &= 950 \\
p_0 &= 9 \\
p_1 &= 10
\end{aligned}
$$

will allow for a clearer presentation of the income changes caused by the project. The effect on the consumers, measured by the sum of their CVs of the price increase, can be shown as the increase in the cost of consuming m_1 plus their willingness to pay for $m_0 - m_1$ less what they actually do pay for such consumption:

Willingness to pay for $(m_0 - m_1)$ =	$-\frac{1}{2}(p_0 + p_1)(m_0 - m_1)$ =	-475
Paid for $(m_0 - m_1)$ =	$p_0(m_0 - m_1)$ =	450
Increase in the market value of m_1 =	$-m_1(p_0 - p_1)$ =	-950
Total =		-975

The project receives income through the sale of m_1, which is equal to the domestic value of the imports substituted ($m_1 p_0$) plus the increase in this

Table 4.4 Valuation at Efficiency Prices of Imports Substituted (Consumption Numeraire)

	Project	Consumers	Importers	Government	Total at Efficiency Prices
Compensating Variation					
Willingness to Pay for $(m_0 - m_1)$	—	−475	—	—	−475
Paid for $(m_0 - m_1)$	—	450	−450	—	—
Increase in the Market Value of m_1	950	−950	—	—	—
Import Substitution	8550	—	−8550	—	—
Savings by the Importer and Other Costs					
Foreign Exchange	—	—	6000	1200	7200
Taxes	—	—	1350	−1350	—
Port Costs	—	—	150	—	150
Transport	−100	—	100	—	—
Trade	−1400	—	1400	—	—
Total	8000	−975	—	−150	6875

value $m_1 (p_1 - p_0)$. Since these values are expressed at the prices paid by the purchaser of the imports substituted, the corresponding transport and trading costs have to be charged to the project. The importers no longer receive income from the sale of m_0 and, at the same time, stop paying for the corresponding costs, including "normal" profits. The Government no longer receives import taxes corresponding to m_0 while it receives the net taxes on foreign trade resulting from the reduction in the demand for foreign exchange. Assuming that the port costs valued at the prices paid for the service are equal to its value at efficiency prices and that the (saved) transport and trading costs of imports are equal to those (incurred) of domestic production, presentation of the effects of import substitution has been completed. The Total row in Table 4.4 shows that the project receives $8,000 worth of income, the consumers lose the compensating variation of the price increase of $975, the importers are unaffected and the Government loses $150 of revenue. Total gains and losses of those involved, equal to the value at efficiency prices of the reduction in imports ($7,200 + $150) less willingness to pay for the reduction in consumption ($475), gives the valuation at efficiency prices of the production of the project.

It should be noted that in the example in Table 4.4, the CVs of the consumers are added together, which implies the interpersonal value judgment of efficiency analysis. If we wish to break the total down into consumers grouped together according to their monetary income level, we must remember that the total of the CVs of consumers i can be expressed as

$$\sum_i CV^i = \Delta p \sum_i m_0^i + \tfrac{1}{2} \Delta p \sum_i \frac{\Delta m^i}{\Delta p} \Delta p$$

Since the first term depends on quantities consumed in the without project situation, it can be broken down by income brackets using the data from a household expenditure survey. The second term, on the other hand, depends on the *change* in consumption per unit of change in price and, in general, this information is not available and very difficult to estimate. However, since the second term will be very small in relation to the first, the distribution of the total CVs will be dominated by that of the change in expenditure in quantity m_0 and, from a practical point of view, the distribution of expenditure by income brackets in the without project situation can be used as an approximation.

If on the other hand we were dealing with an intermediate good, the price change would be translated into a change in purchasers' costs which they would try to pass on in successive steps of intersectoral transactions to the consumers, who would receive the total or partial effect. Discussion of this case, the characteristics of which are common to price variations in general, is postponed until Chapter 7.

4.5 The Project Increases Exports

Consider the case of a project that increases exports under existing export incentives and disincentives when this increase in exports does not affect the international price of the product.

Since the price to the domestic producer is determined by the export price, the project will not affect domestic consumers (Figure 4.5) and will result in an increase in the value of exports by $FOB_e \, EER \, (e_1 - e_0)$. However, this is not the value received by the domestic producer because of the existence of port, transport and trading costs. In addition, exports are subject to a tax t_e per unit of sales on the foreign market. In this way, the price to the producer will be

$$p^p = FOB_e \, EER \, (1 - t_e) - cp - tra - com$$

Consequently, the producer's sales revenue can be presented, for example, as

$$
\begin{array}{rcr}
FOB_e \, EER \, (e_1 - e_0) & = & 100 \\
-t_e \, FOB_e \, EER \, (e_1 - e_0) & = & -5 \\
-cp \, (e_1 - e_0) & = & -2 \\
-tra \, (e_1 - e_0) & = & -1 \\
-com \, (e_1 - e_0) & = & -12 \\
\hline
\text{Value of sales} & = & 80
\end{array}
$$

Figure 4.5 The Project Increases Exports

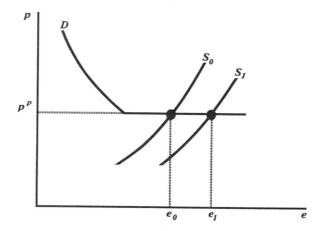

Table 4.5   Valuation at Efficiency Prices of Additional Exports (Consumption Numeraire)

	Project	Government	Total at Efficiency Prices
Foreign Exchange	100	20	120
Taxes on Exports	−5	5	—
Port Costs	−2	—	−2
Transport	−1	—	−1
Trading	−12	—	−12
Total Sales	80	25	105

whose valuation at efficiency prices is given in Table 4.5. The case presented assumes that payments for port, transport and trading services are equal to their respective values at efficiency prices. The table shows additional Government revenue from tax t_e plus the additional revenue it receives from the (net) taxes on foreign trade due to the increase in the supply of foreign exchange.

CHAPTER 5

FOREIGN EXCHANGE AS A NUMERAIRE

5.1 From the Consumption to the Foreign Exchange Numeraire

The publication of an OECD manual for appraising industrial projects, as well as two widely-read subsequent books on the topic,[1] led many economists to believe that it was preferable to use foreign exchange expressed in the national currency at the equilibrium exchange rate as a numeraire. Presented in this way, this is merely a change in the unit of account in which the costs and benefits of a project are expressed, and to that extent, the change in the numeraire does not present any difficulties. In order to express a certain quantity of foreign exchange at efficiency prices in the consumption numeraire, it has to be multiplied by the APRFE. Conversely, any other cost or benefit already valued at efficiency prices in the consumption numeraire can be expressed in the "foreign exchange numeraire" by dividing it by the APRFE, while the costs and benefits in foreign exchange will already be expressed in the numeraire. Presented in this way, the choice of numeraire would seem to be merely a question of practical convenience.

---

1. See Little and Mirrlees (1969 and 1974) and Squire and van der Tak (1975).

68

Let us suppose that a Government project substitutes imports for

$$CIF_s \, EER \, \Delta m_s \, (1 + t_s) = 200$$

using imported inputs for

$$CIF_i \, EER \, \Delta m_i \, (1 + t_i) = -30$$

Suppose also that

$$t_s = 1.0$$
$$t_i = 0.5$$

In such a case, and following the presentation in Chapters 3 and 4, the corresponding valuation when $APRFE = 1.2$ will be

$$(CIF_s \, EER \, \Delta m_s - CIF_i \, EER \, \Delta m_i) \times APRFE = (100 - 20) \times 1.2$$

which is shown in Table 5.1. The imports substituted generate a saving in foreign exchange (100) and a reduction in receipts from taxes (100), while the price paid for the imported inputs is broken down into 20 of foreign exchange and 10 of additional taxes for the Government. Consequently, the project increases the supply of foreign exchange by $100 - 20 = 80$, the use of which produces additional revenue for the Government of $(100 - 20) \times 0.20$, in which 0.20 is the foreign exchange premium $(APRFE - 1)$.

If we wish to express this valuation in the foreign exchange numeraire *regardless of its distribution*, it amounts to asking what increase (reduction) in

Table 5.1 Valuation of the Net Use of Foreign Exchange (Consumption Numeraire)

	Project	Government	Total at Efficiency Prices
Value of Production			
Foreign Exchange	100	20	120
Taxes	100	−100	—
Value of Imported Inputs			
Foreign Exchange	−20	−4	−24
Taxes	−10	10	—
Total	170	−74	96

Table 5.2   Valuation of the Net Use of Foreign Exchange (Foreign Exchange Numeraire)

	Project	Government	Total at Efficiency Prices
Net Use of Foreign Exchange	141.7	−61.7	80

the supply (demand) of foreign exchange ΔS would have resulted in an increase in total consumption of 96, that is

$$96 = \Delta S \times APRFE$$

of which

$$\Delta S = \frac{96}{1.2} = 80$$

The changes in the revenue of the Government and the project can be expressed in the new numeraire using the same *algebraic operation* (see Table 5.2).

Note that the above does *not* purport to answer the question of how much foreign exchange will have to be transferred to (the owners of) the project nor how much will have to be taken away from the Government to produce an equivalent result, since the project does *not* give rise to such changes for itself or the Government; it only gives rise to changes in their real *income*. Nor does the change in the numeraire try to measure the changes in the use of foreign exchange that would result from spending such income changes. Cost-benefit analysis does not, in general, take into account such indirect effects.[2] It tries only to estimate the income changes of those affected before adding them up in accordance with a distributional value judgment. The change in numeraire, as its name indicates, involves only a *change in the unit of measurement*, in the same way as a distance can be measured in centimeters or in inches. Thus, the use of any particular numeraire cannot bring about any difference in the final result. In fact, if B_t is the net benefit from a project in period t, d the rate of discount and r the project's internal rate of return, it is clear that:

$$\sum_{t=1}^{n} \frac{B_t}{(1+d)^t} > 0 => \frac{1}{APRFE} \sum_{t=1}^{n} \frac{B_t}{(1+d)^t} > 0$$

$$\sum_{t=1}^{n} \frac{B_t}{(1+r)^t} = 0 => \frac{1}{APRFE} \sum_{t=1}^{n} \frac{B_t}{(1+r)^t} = 0$$

---

2. To do so would require taking into account the benefits deriving from such expenditure as well.

5.2 Valuation in the "Uncommitted Public Income" Numeraire

Let us suppose now that for some reason, income in the hands of the Government is considered more valuable than in the hands of the private sector, and that "uncommitted public income" is chosen as the numeraire. In such a case, a review of Table 5.1 will reveal that if the additional revenue generated can be freely used by the Government, the valuation is already in the numeraire since private income has not been directly affected. If now we want this public revenue to be expressed in foreign exchange at the equilibrium exchange rate, the Little and Mirrlees (1974) numeraire, no possibility exists other than the valuation shown in Table 5.2.

The numerical example used in the tables mentioned corresponds to the first two rows in Table I presented by Little and Mirrlees (1974, page 149), but with different results. A detailed comparison of both will reveal that the example of these authors omits the changes in Government revenue resulting from the adjustment of the foreign exchange market to the additional supply created by the project. This omission explains that what is paid for net import substitution (200 − 30), less the import taxes included in the respective prices (−100 + 10), is equal to the net foreign exchange revenue valued at the EER, which constitutes an accounting identity and not a measure of the net effect on Government income (the numeraire).

It should be pointed out that the omission mentioned above does not affect the result of the analysis when it seeks only to determine whether the project satisfies the *potential* compensation criterion. However, it does affect the results if the objective is to obtain the information required to make compensation effective, to make distributional value judgments different from the one assigning equal weights to all marginal income changes, or to discard the assumption of equality between the rate of discount and the marginal rate of return on investment.

CHAPTER 6

ACCOUNTING PRICES FOR LABOR

6.1 The Supply of Labor

In neoclassical microeconomics, the supply of labor and the demand for consumer goods are treated in a similar way. It is assumed that the time dedicated to work in exchange for a certain sum of money has other uses for the individual and that the welfare derived from the additional purchasing power acquired competes with the welfare derived from these alternative uses. Furthermore, it is assumed that the additional income required to persuade an individual to perform an additional hour's paid work of a certain type rises in relation to the number of hours worked. Thus, his supply function of working hours for a particular job i takes the shape shown by function S^i in Figure 6.1. At wage w_0 the individual works L_0^i hours per day, and a higher wage w_1 is needed to persuade him to do an additional hour's paid work i. At the same time, it can be shown that the area w_0ABw_1 is approximately equal to the compensating variation corresponding to the wage increase $w_1 - w_0$, that is the sum of money that his income would need to be reduced by so that, after the increase $w_1 - w_0$, he would be at the same level of welfare as before the increase.[1]

---

1. See Mishan (1981), where some of the problems associated with the interpretation of the area enclosed by the supply curve and the wage increase are discussed.

Figure 6.1 The Labor Supply

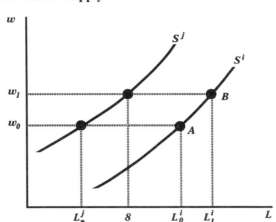

Bear in mind that S^i in Figure 6.1 refers to the supply of hours of paid work *of a certain type*, since if we were dealing with occupation j, an individual might be willing to work a smaller number of hours for the same hourly wage. In addition, this representation is suitable for jobs in which the worker may work the number of daily hours that he wishes at the prevailing wage. However, if the existing jobs j consist of a day with a fixed number of daily hours, for example 8, the minimum daily wage that a worker will be willing to accept for one of these jobs will be that for which the excess CV of those hours whose valuation is less or equal than the wage equals the compensation needed to persuade him to work the remaining hours. Thus, in Figure 6.1, w_0 is this minimum wage in job j and the excess CV of L_*^j hours is equal to the income needed to compensate him for working $8 - L_*^j$ hours. Consequently, each time that the worker obtains a job of type j at a wage w_1 he will increase his welfare by the equivalent of $8(w_1 - w_0)$, equal to the difference between the daily wage received $8w_1$ and the minimum daily wage he is willing to accept.

The market supply function will be the horizontal aggregate of the individual supply functions and an increase in the demand for labor $L_1 - L_s$ (Figure 6.2) will result in an increase in the equilibrium wage. If the jobs are ones in which the number of hours can be adjusted freely, $w_1 - w_0$ can be interpreted as the wage increase required to bring about additional hours $L_1 - L_0$; in the second case, Δw will be the increase in the daily wage required to obtain the additional days needed. The area w_0ABw_1 will be an approximation of the

Figure 6.2 An Increase in the Demand for Labor

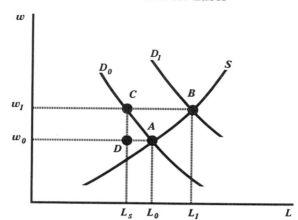

sum of the CVs of the wage increase $w_1 - w_0$ for workers L_1, which can be expressed as

$$w_0 ABw_1 = (w_1 - w_0) L_s + \tfrac{1}{2} (w_1 - w_0) (L_0 - L_s)$$

$$+ \tfrac{1}{2} (w_1 - w_0) (L_1 - L_s) \qquad [6.1]$$

Alternatively, the CV of the wage increase for employment level L_1 can be expressed as the sum of two components. The first is the increase in the income of workers L_0 already employed at wage w_0, the CV of which is by definition this additional income. The second component is the difference between what is received by the workers $L_1 - L_0$ less the minimum compensation that they are willing to receive, that is, the difference between their additional income and the CV of the job. The latter will be equal to the area $L_0 ABL_1$ which, by analogy with the concept of willingness to pay, will be called *willingness to receive*. Thus, the CV of the wage increase $w_1 - w_0$ for job L_1 can be broken down in the following way:

$$\begin{aligned}
\text{Increase in income for } L_s &= (w_1 - w_0) L_s \\
\text{Increase in income for } (L_0 - L_s) &= (w_1 - w_0) (L_0 - L_s) \\
\text{Income for } (L_1 - L_0) &= w_1 (L_1 - L_0) \\
\underline{\text{Willingness to receive by } (L_1 - L_0)} &= \underline{-\tfrac{1}{2} (w_1 + w_0) (L_1 - L_0)} \\
CV^L &= (w_1 - w_0) L_0 + \tfrac{1}{2} (w_1 - w_0) (L_1 - L_0)
\end{aligned}$$

74

Figure 6.3 Effects of a Wage Increase

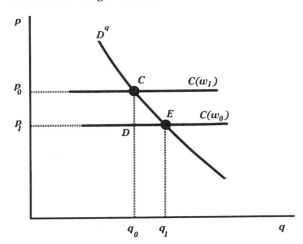

6.2 The Efficiency Price of Labor

From the "efficiency" analysis perspective, it is of interest to know the sum of the CVs of the effects attributable to the increase in the demand for labor generated by a project. The efficiency price of labor for this additional demand will be the quotient between this sum of CVs and the additional demand in question. In most cases, however, the efficiency price of labor can be calculated as the sum of the CVs attributable to a unitary excess demand. As the previous analysis showed, if a project increases the demand for labor by $L_1 - L_s$ (Figure 6.2) when there is no "involuntary unemployment", the workers will come from a reduction in employment in other jobs ($L_0 - L_s$) and from an increase in workers who join the market due to the wage increase ($L_1 - L_0$). As indicated in the previous section, the cost at efficiency prices of the latter will be given by their *willingness to receive*. However, jobs $L_0 - L_s$ in the project will be filled at the cost of employment in other sectors, which will see their costs rise because of the wage increase. The effects of such a situation are shown in Figure 6.3 in which, for the sake of simplicity, it is assumed that in the without project situation, labor L_0 is used only to produce the quantity q_0 of consumer good q. If in addition it is assumed that Δw is sufficiently small not to bring about substitution between labor and the other inputs (the average long-run technical coefficients are equal to the marginal coefficients)[2], and

---

2. This assumption does not seem very restrictive if we consider that the long-run effect of the price increase produced by Δw will most probably be limited to postponing the entry sequence of a given set of plants.

that the prices of the remaining inputs are equal to their efficiency prices and are not affected, the difference between long-run average costs $C(w_1)$ and $C(w_0)$ will be

$$C(w_1) - C(w_0) = p_1 - p_0 = (w_1 - w_0) L_s/q_1 = (w_1 - w_0) \Delta L/\Delta q \quad [6.2]$$

The increase in the market value of quantity q_1 of the consumer good will be

$$p_1 CDp_0 = (p_1 - p_0) q_1 \quad [6.3]$$

Substituting [6.2] in [6.3] we see that

$$p_1 CDp_0 = (w_1 - w_0) \frac{L_s}{q_1} q_1 \quad [6.4]$$

$$p_1 CDp_0 = (w_1 - w_0) L_s$$

The complement of the CV of the consumers of q will be

$$CDE = \tfrac{1}{2} (p_1 - p_0) (q_0 - q_1) \quad [6.5]$$

Substituting [6.2] in [6.5] we see that

$$CDE = \tfrac{1}{2} (w_1 - w_0) \frac{(L_0 - L_s)}{(q_0 - q_1)} (q_0 - q_1) \quad [6.6]$$

$$CDE = \tfrac{1}{2} (w_1 - w_0) (L_0 - L_s)$$

The sum of the consumers' CVs can then be obtained as the sum of [6.4] and [6.6], that is

$$CV^{cons} = (w_1 - w_0) L_s + \tfrac{1}{2} (w_1 - w_0) (L_0 - L_s) \quad [6.7]$$

If we now compare [6.1] with [6.7] we can see that the difference between the sum of the CVs of workers L_1 and that of the consumers will be

$$CV^L - CV^{cons} = \tfrac{1}{2} (w_1 - w_0) (L_1 - L_s)$$

equal to the area ACB in Figure 6.2. In other words, an important part of the gain to workers L_1 is offset by the loss to the consumers.

It is now possible to summarize the effects of the additional demand for labor and to identify the sectors affected (see Table 6.1). The workers employed in the without project situation $L_s + (L_0 - L_s)$ gain the equivalent of wage increase $w_1 - w_0$ for this volume of employment. The additional workers $L_1 - L_0$ gain the difference between their wage income and their willingness to receive or the minimum income they are willing to accept. The total effect on the workers is equal to the sum of their CVs. As shown in [6.4], the additional income of employment L_s corresponds, under the simplifying assumptions adopted, to the loss to the consumers through greater expenditure on quantity q_1 of the consumer good. The consumers also lose the difference between their valuation of $q_0 - q_1$ and what they actually pay. The project pays the hired workers wage w_1 and the firms producing the consumer good no longer receive revenue from sales $q_0 - q_1$ and at the same time stop paying for the resources required to produce that quantity. If the market prices of these resources are acceptable approximations of their efficiency prices, the value of these resources at market prices is taken as a gain.

The reader can imagine that data in Table 6.1 could have been disaggregated at the level of *each* worker, consumer and owner of the project and of the other firms, in which case the columns could have been added up vertically without resorting to interpersonal comparisons. However, it should be noted that any horizontal sum requires a value judgment regarding the contribution to "total welfare" of the changes in individuals' income. From the point of view of the potential compensation criterion, the comparison of the vertical totals indicates that the gain of workers CV^L is insufficient to compensate the consumers (CV^{cons}) and the employers (the project). Consequently, the "total" loss that can be attributed to hiring $L_1 - L_s$ workers is recorded in the *Total* column and shows the minimum income that their employment ought to generate to make compensation possible.

Application of the value judgment that assigns equal weights to all marginal income changes allows for columns in Table 6.1 to be added up, and the total in the last column to be interpreted according to efficiency analysis. This total consists of the cost of the additional employment for the workers, their willingness to receive (WR), equal to

$$WR(L_1 - L_0) = -\tfrac{1}{2}(w_1 + w_0)(L_1 - L_0)$$

plus the consumers' willingness to pay (WP) for the quantities $q_0 - q_1$ of consumer goods that they will stop consuming

$$WP(q_0 - q_1) = -\tfrac{1}{2}(w_1 - w_0)(L_0 - L_s) - p_0(q_0 - q_1)$$

77

Table 6.1. Economic Valuation of the Additional Demand for Labor (Consumption Numeraire)

	Workers	Consumers	Project	Other Firms	Total
CV^L					
Increase in Income for L_s	$(w_1-w_0)L_s$	$-(w_1-w_0)L_s$	—	—	—
Income of (L_0-L_s) with the Project	$w_1(L_0-L_s)$	—	$-w_1(L_0-L_s)$	—	—
Income of (L_0-L_s) without the Project	$-w_0(L_0-L_s)$	—	—	—	$-w_0(L_0-L_s)$
Income of (L_1-L_0) with the Project	$w_1(L_1-L_0)$	—	$-w_1(L_1-L_0)$	—	—
Willingness to Receive for (L_1-L_0)	$-\frac{1}{2}(w_1+w_0)(L_1-L_0)$	—	—	—	$-\frac{1}{2}(w_1+w_0)(L_1-L_0)$
Consumers					
Willingness to Pay for (q_0-q_1)	—	$\frac{1}{2}(w_1-w_0)(L_0-L_s)$ $-p_0(q_0-q_1)$	—	—	$-\frac{1}{2}(w_1-w_0)(L_0-L_s)$ $-p_0(q_0-q_1)$
Paid for (q_0-q_1)	—	$p_0(q_0-q_1)$	—	$-p_0(q_0-q_1)$	—
Resources Released				$p_0(q_0-q_1)$	$p_0(q_0-q_1)$
Total	$CV^L - CV^{cons} = \frac{1}{2}(w_1-w_0)(L_1-L_s)$	—	$-w_1(L_1-L_s)$	—	$-\frac{1}{2}(w_0+w_1)(L_1-L_s)$

less the value of the resources released (*VRR*) by this reduction in consumption and which remain available for use in the rest of the system, which consequently excludes quantity $L_0 - L_s$ used by the project,

$$VRR = p_0 (q_0 - q_1) - w_0 (L_0 - L_s)$$

Thus, looked at from the "value of resources" angle, the cost at efficiency prices (*CEP*) of jobs $L_1 - L_s$ will be[3]

$$CEP(L_1 - L_s) = - WR(L_1 - L_0) - WP(q_0 - q_1) + VRR$$

It is worth recalling here that the previous example, although illustrative of the *logic* of the valuation of labor, is based on the assumption that the wage increase does not lead to any substitution of inputs in the production of consumer goods. If such a substitution existed or if the average long-run technical coefficients were different from the marginal coefficients, the change in the unit costs of production of q would not be equal to the wage change multiplied by the labor requirements per unit of product. Conversely, income from other "primary factors" would be affected and the identification and quantification of these effects per group would not be practicable.[4] However, whenever the labor demand of the project $L_1 - L_s$ is small in relation to the respective employment, the change in wages will be insignificant and, as a consequence, the change in the price of the goods using this labor will be negligible. In this case, the cost of labor $L_1 - L_s$ at efficiency prices (*CEP*) will simply be

$$
\begin{aligned}
-WR(L_1 - L_0) &= -w (L_1 - L_0) \\
-WP(q_0 - q_1) &= -p (q_0 - q_1) \\
\underline{VRR} &= \underline{p (q_0 - q_1) - w (L_0 - L_s)} \\
CEP(L_1 - L_s) &= -w (L_1 - L_s)
\end{aligned}
\qquad [6.8]
$$

Table 6.2 presents its breakdown in terms of the effects on various sectors.

Finally, this line of reasoning enables us to arrive at the criterion normally used in practice. If all the labor employed by the project $(L_1 - L_s)$ is taken from alternative occupations, the cost at efficiency prices of the additional employment will be

$$
\begin{aligned}
CEP(L_1 - L_s) &= -WP(\Delta q) + VRR(\Delta q) \\
CEP(L_1 - L_s) &= -w (L_1 - L_s)
\end{aligned}
\qquad [6.9]
$$

---

3. The expression $-WP(q_0 - q_1) + VRR$ substitutes for the value of the marginal product of labor withdrawn from the production of consumer goods.

4. See Mishan (1982, Chapter 10 and 1981, Part V)

Table 6.2. Economic Valuation of the Additional Demand for Labor When Changes in Wages Are Negligible (Consumption Numeraire)

	Workers	Consumers	Project	Other Firms	Total
CV^L					
Increase in Income for L_s	—	—	—	—	—
Income of L_0-L_s with the Project	$w(L_0-L_s)$	—	$-w(L_0-L_s)$	—	—
Income of L_0-L_s without the Project	$-w(L_0-L_s)$	—	—	—	$-w(L_0-L_s)$
Income of L_1-L_0 with the Project	$w(L_1-L_0)$	—	$-w(L_1-L_0)$	—	—
Willingness to Receive of L_1-L_0	$-w(L_1-L_0)$	—	—	—	$-w(L_1-L_0)$
Consumers					
Willingness to Pay for q_0-q_1	—	$-p(q_0-q_1)$	—	—	$-p(q_0-q_1)$
Paid for q_0-q_1	—	$p(q_0-q_1)$	—	$-p(q_0-q_1)$	—
Resources Released	—	—	—	$p(q_0-q_1)$	$p(q_0-q_1)$
Total	—	—	$-w(L_1-L_s)$	—	$-w(L_1-L_s)$

the consumers' valuation of the loss in consumption Δq less the value of the resources released, excluding the labor used by the project. On the other hand, if all the jobs created by the project were to be done by workers joining the market because of higher wages, and provided employment in the remaining sectors were not affected, the efficiency value of the additional employment would be

$$CEP(L_1 - L_s) = -WR(L_1 - L_s)$$

$$CEP(L_1 - L_s) = -w\,(L_1 - L_s)$$

[6.10]

the willingness to receive for these jobs.[5]

It should be noted that when the wage is the variable that adjusts the labor market, and the distributional value judgments of efficiency analysis are made, the economic cost of labor is always $w\,\Delta L$. However, when labor is withdrawn from alternative jobs (expression [6.9]), use of the valuation $w\,\Delta L$ requires the following additional assumptions: (a) the market price of the good in the production of which it would be used in the without project situation is accepted as its accounting price; and (b) the market prices of the remaining resources released (VRR) are also accepted as their accounting prices. Assumption (a) does not present any problems if the good in question, q in the example given, is a non-traded consumer good. However, if q were a traded good it would be necessary to correct its market price in the manner indicated in Chapter 4. This case will be dealt with in Section 6.4. If on the other hand, q were a non-traded intermediate good, use of the valuation $w\Delta L$ would require assumptions (a) and (b) to be valid along the entire inter-industrial chain up to the non-traded consumer goods or the traded goods.

6.3 The Accounting Price of Skilled Labor

The traditional approach holds that skilled labor is fully employed and that its supply is completely inelastic in relation to small changes in wages. As a consequence, additional hiring is done at the cost of reducing employment in alternative occupations. In such a situation, the corresponding cost at efficiency prices is the loss in consumption due to the withdrawal of labor from

---

5. Lal (1973) has questioned the inclusion of WR in the calculation of the accounting price of unskilled labor. See also Hamilton's (1976 and 1977) critique of Lal's position.

such jobs and, consequently, its efficiency price (APL_s) can be calculated on the basis of [6.9] as follows:

$$APL_s = \frac{WP(\Delta q) - VRR(\Delta q)}{\Delta L}$$

If the market prices of all the resources released are considered acceptable approximations of their efficiency prices, it follows from expression [6.8] that the wage paid will be the appropriate efficiency price and there will be no distributional effects significant enough to be recorded.

If the skilled labor were to be hired abroad, it would be appropriate to treat it as an imported good. In fact, since the Government is only interested in the welfare of "nationals" when it performs cost-benefit analyses, the effects of hiring on the income of skilled labor abroad or on the production of goods for which it would be employed in the without project situation does not count in the analysis. Conversely, what does matter are the costs that this hiring imposes on "nationals." Since the wages for imported labor are normally paid in foreign exchange, of which only a part is remitted, the cost of employment is given by the value of the foreign exchange remitted (FER) plus the value at efficiency prices of domestic expenditure on goods and services (DE). If the market prices of the latter are considered as acceptable approximations of their efficiency prices, the corresponding efficiency wage will be

$$APL_{imp} = FER \times APRFE + DE$$

Let, for example, $W_{cal} = \$100$ be the equivalent in the national currency of the monthly salary of a foreign professional recruited for the project. This salary is paid in foreign exchange, and it is estimated that $50 is spent in the country, $40 is remitted to the country of origin and $10 is income taxes paid to the Government. This situation is shown in Table 6.3, in which the part of wages remitted in foreign exchange has been corrected by the APRFE, and the loss in Government revenue due to lower expenditure of foreign exchange

Table 6.3. Valuation of the Employment of "Imported" Labor

	Project	Government	Value at Efficiency Prices
Salary			
• Foreign Currency Remitted	−40	−8	−48
• Domestic Expenditure	−50	—	−50
• Tax	−10	+10	—
Total	−100	+2	−98

82

Table 6.4. Valuation of Employing a Worker Who Would Have Emigrated Without the Project

	Project	Worker	Government	Total
With the Project				
Wage	$-W_{dom}$	W_{dom}	—	—
Willingness to Receive	—	$-WR_{dom}$	—	$-WR_{dom}$
Without the Project				
Wage	—	$-(1-k)W_{ext}-kW_{ext}$	$-kW_{ext}(APRFE-1)$	$-(1-k)W_{ext}-kW_{ext}APRFE$
Willingness to Receive	—	WR_{ext}	—	WR_{ext}
Total	$-W_{dom}$	$W_{dom}-WR_m$	$-kW_{ext}(APRFE-1)$	$-WR_m-kW_{ext}(APRFE-1)$

on uses subject to the payment of import tax has been recorded. Since without the project, this professional would not have been employed in the country that hires him, the income tax is attributable to the project and as such is shown as a transfer from the project to the Government.

Finally, consider the case in which the demand for skilled workers generated by the project is covered by people who, in the absence of the project, would have emigrated due to the lack of jobs. In such a case, there would be no reduction at all in domestic production, although the situation with the project could imply a reduction in output in the country of destination of the potential migrant. However, current value judgments in cost-benefit analysis only take account of the effects on the economic welfare of the "nationals". These effects are summarized in Table 6.4.

In the situation with the project, the worker would receive a wage W_{dom} which will have to be greater than or equal to his willingness to receive WR_{dom} when the alternative of emigration does not exist. The latter requires WR_{dom} to be completed with the possible gain $W_{ext} - WR_{ext}$ resulting from the difference between his wage abroad and the respective willingness to receive. Since the worker remits a proportion k of his wage to his family when he emigrates, the Government loses the corresponding foreign exchange premium. The compensating variation of accepting the job in the project, and consequently of not migrating, will then be

$$WR_m = WR_{dom} + (W_{ext} - WR_{ext})$$

which will be the minimum sum he is prepared to accept. His net gain will be $W_{dom} - WR_m$. The sum of the totals of each column indicate the minimum income to be created by his employment in the project which is required to make the compensation possible. This minimum income will be equal to

$$WR_m + k W_{ext} (APRFE - 1)$$

the compensating variation WR_m plus the loss in Government revenue due to the foreign exchange that would not come in. Assigning the same weights to all marginal income changes allows for the columns to be added up horizontally and the welfare loss (measured by total CVs) corresponding to the job in the project to be obtained in accordance with this value judgment. This will be equal to his willingness to receive for not migrating, plus the premium on the foreign exchange, which he would have remitted if he had emigrated.

6.4 The Accounting Price of Unskilled Labor

The simplified analysis in Section 6.2 made it possible to show that the accounting price of labor depends on the way in which the market adjusts in response to project demand. Some alternative examples of adjustment are presented in this section to show their consequences on the efficiency price of unskilled labor. These examples may be used as the basis for applying the basic reasoning to other particular cases.

Suppose first that the project being analyzed is located in the metropolitan area of the capital city, where a high level of underemployment exists. Fulltime unskilled jobs are concentrated in the formal sector, in which wages are relatively high, determined principally through negotiations between workers and employers, and which are considerably above the respective supply price (willingness to receive). Thus, the supply of unskilled labor faced by employers in the sector is infinitely elastic at the prevailing wage. The other sector, the informal one, includes ". . . most of the self-employed, domestic staff and those employed in excessively small undertakings, which are not formally organized and engage in marginal activities". In this sector, wages ". . . tend to be situated at a relatively adequate level in relation to the other options offered by the labor market, becoming the adjustment variable that determines the number of suppliers in a given informal activity".[6]

Suppose now that the jobs created by the project will be filled by workers from the informal sector, in which the abundance of self-employed workers whose working hours can easily be adjusted results in an almost infinitely elastic supply at the prevailing wage so that minimum variations in wages are enough to make the adjustment. This situation is illustrated in Figure 6.4. The increase in the demand for labor in the formal sector $(L_1^f - L_0^f)$ results in a reduction in the supply in the informal sector which, though it practically does not alter wages in that market, reduces the under-employment of the remaining workers. In such a case, the workers now employed in the formal sector increase their income by $(w^f - w^i)(L_1 - L_0)$ while those in the informal

---

6. PREALC (1977, Chapter V, pp 258–59).

Figure 6.4 Adjustment of the Unskilled Urban Labor Market

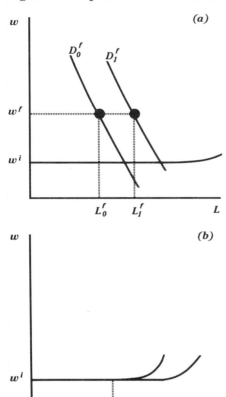

sector increase their weekly hours of work at a wage w^i equal to their willingness to receive. Consequently, part of the labor cost to the project is a transfer to the new workers now employed in the formal sector.

Table 6.5 contains a schematic presentation of the preceding explanation. The first column records the cost to the project. The second shows the increase in the incomes of the new workers employed in the formal sector. The third column shows that the remaining workers in the informal sector increase their employment level at a wage equal to their willingness to receive, and so are not affected by the new situation. Finally, the distributional value judgment that assigns equal weights to all marginal income changes enables us to arrive at the fourth column, which contains the net income changes according

Table 6.5. Valuation at Efficiency Prices of Additional Jobs Created in the Formal Sector When Labor Comes from the Informal Sector (Consumption Numeraire)

	Project	Workers $L_1^f - L_0^f$	Remainder of the Informal Sector	Value at Efficiency Prices
Formal Sector				
• Wages	$-w^f(L_1^f - L_0^f)$	$w^f(L_1^f - L_0^f)$	—	—
• Willingness to Receive		$-w^i(L_1^f - L_0^f)$	—	$-w^i(L_1^f - L_0^f)$
Informal Sector				
• Wages	—	—	$w^i(L_1^f - L_0^f)$	$w^i(L_1^f - L_0^f)$
• Willingness to Receive			$-w^i(L_1^f - L_0^f)$	$-w^i(L_1^f - L_0^f)$
Total	$-w^f(L_1^f - L_0^f)$	$\Delta w(L_1^f - L_0^f)$	—	$-w^i(L_1^f - L_0^f)$

to source. The totals in each column can be interpreted as the basis for checking that the potential compensation criterion is complied with. In this case, the increase in workers' income ΔL^f is not sufficient to compensate the cost (loss) to the project, and the necessary complement will have to come from the production resulting from their employment in the project. From the point of view of efficiency analysis, the *net* loss $w^i \Delta L^f$ will have to be lower than the value of production (at efficiency prices) resulting from such employment.

Let us now take a case in which an additional job created in the formal urban sector is filled by an informal sector worker, which in turn gives rise to the migration of *one* rural worker who replaces the former in the informal sector. In such a case, the workers who remain in the informal sector would not be affected and the entire impact would be transferred to the rural sector. Suppose also that the source of rural labor is family small-holdings in which the effect on family production of the withdrawal of one member can be compensated through the increase in working hours of those remaining.[7] Table 6.6 outlines this situation. The wage paid for the project is w^f and the worker previously occupied in the informal sector gains, as in the previous case, wage difference $w^f - w^i$. The migrant rural worker enters the informal sector earning w^i, at the same time as he stops receiving his share of rural family income y^r. The rural family gains y^r, stops receiving the income from wages w^x which the migrant earned away from the farm during the harvest of export crops, loses the value of the marginal product of the migrant worker on the farm v_m^r but compensates for it (totally or partially) with the additional

---

7. The method of presentation used in the following paragraphs is based on Sen (1966 and 1972).

86

Table 6.6. Economic Valuation of an Additional Job in the Formal Sector When Labor Comes from the Rural Economy (Consumption Numeraire)

	Project	Informal Sector Worker	Migrant Worker	Rural Family	Farming Company	Government	Total
Change in Income	$-w^f$	$(w^f - w^i)$	$(w^i - y^r)$	$(y^r - w^x - v^f_m + v^f_r)$	$(w^x - v^x)$	$-q_x p^{fob}(t_x + APRFE - 1)$	$-\Delta v^f - v^x - q_x p^{fob}(t_x + APRFE - 1)$
Additional Work	—	$-d^f + d^i$	$-d^i + d^r + d^x$	$-d^r$	—	—	$-d^f + d^x$

production v_r^r resulting from the increase in working hours of the remaining members. The farming company stops paying wage w^x at the same time as it stops receiving the market value of the marginal product v^x, since during the harvesting period the labor supply is completely inelastic.[8] However, v^x is the value of the marginal product valued at the farm gate, that is

$$v^x = p^x q^x \qquad\qquad [6.11]$$

in which q^x is the marginal product and p^x the farm gate price. The latter will be equal to

$$p^x = p^{fob} (1 - t_x - dc) \qquad\qquad [6.12]$$

the f.o.b. price less the taxes on exports equivalent to an *ad valorem* rate t_x less domestic transport, processing and trading costs expressed as a proportion (dc) of the f.o.b. price. Consequently, the marginal product that is lost by hiring the worker, valued at farm gate market prices, can be broken down in the following way:[9]

$$
\begin{array}{rcl}
\text{Foreign exchange} &=& q^x p^{fob} \\
\text{Taxes on exports} &=& -q^x p^{fob} t_x \\
\underline{\text{Domestic costs}} &=& \underline{-q^x p^{fob} dc} \\
\text{Farm gate value } (v^x) &=& q^x p^{fob} (1 - t_x - dc)
\end{array}
\qquad [6.13]
$$

Note that the valuation at market prices includes foreign exchange valued at the exchange rate, less taxes and less the domestic costs required to export the agricultural product. However, the taxes that are no longer paid are revenue that the Government no longer receives, to which must be added the revenue it would have received from the use of the foreign exchange that it loses. The total effect on the Government will consequently be

$$q^x p^{fob} t_x + q^x p^{fob}(APRFE - 1) = q^x p^{fob} (t_x + APRFE - 1) \qquad [6.14]$$

which is that shown in the *Government* column in Table 6.6.

If, for the sake of simplicity, the market value of domestic costs ($q^x p^{fob} dc$) is assumed equal to their value at efficiency prices, the income that transporters, processors and traders stop receiving will be equal to what they stop

---

8. See, for example, Londero (1981).

9. Gittinger (1982, Chapter 3) shows the breakdown of the farm gate price of a traded good in more detail.

paying for the resources used. Consequently, there will be no changes in their income to be recorded under this heading.

The second row in Table 6.6 shows the CVs of the additional work of those affected. The rural family will have to compensate for the work done by the migrant worker by intensifying or extending the working day, d^r being the respective CV. The migrant worker will stop working on the family holding and, assuming that his CV for such work is equal to that of the family, will gain d^r, the respective CV. He will also gain the CV of not working in export agriculture d^x. At the same time he will occupy the vacancy created in the informal sector whose CV is assumed to be equal to that of the worker in the informal sector d^i. The latter gains d^i at the same time that he loses the CV of his working time in the formal sector d^f. The efficiency price of unskilled labor (APL_u) can now be obtained in the same way:

$$APL_u = \Delta v^r + v^x + q^x p^{fob} (t_x + APRFE - 1) + d^f - d^x \qquad [6.15]$$

This indicates the minimum income that will have to be generated by the project job to make compensation possible or, looking at the *Total* column, the loss in "total welfare", corresponding to the efficiency analysis value judgments, resulting from reduced production and increased work. The previous expression for APL_u can be simplified if the rural family compensates fully for the marginal product of the migrant ($\Delta v^r = 0$). In such a case, [6.15] is reduced to

$$APL_u = v^x + q^x p^{fob} (t_x + APRFE - 1) + d^f - d^x \qquad [6.16]$$

A different set of assumptions on compensating variations d allows us to obtain the most frequently used expression for APL_u. If the CVs of each hour of work are equal in the rural, export, informal and formal sectors, $d^f - d^x$ can be estimated as the number of hours of work in the formal sector, less the hours worked in export agriculture, all times the minimum hourly wage that a farm worker is willing to accept (his "reservation wage"). Thus, [6.16] will indicate that the APL_u will be equal to the value of the marginal product during the period of full employment in the farming sector (v^x in the example) valued at efficiency prices plus the "reservation farm wage" during the period in which there is underemployment or unemployment in the rural sector.

Expression [6.16] can also be presented only in terms of v^x obtaining from [6.13]

$$q^x p^{fob} = \frac{v^x}{(1 - t_x - dc)}$$

and substituting it in [6.16]. Thus we arrive at

$$APL_u = v^x \left[1 + \frac{t_x + APRFE - 1}{(1 - t_x - dc)} \right] + d^f - d^x \qquad [6.17]$$

The calculation of expression [6.17] does however require that the farm gate market value of the marginal product in export agriculture v^x be estimated. This could be avoided if during the period of peak demand, wages equalled the market value of the marginal product ($v^x = w^x$). Thus, expressions [6.17] can be calculated on the basis of

$$APL_u = w^x \left[1 + \frac{t_x + APRFE - 1}{(1 - t_x - dc)} \right] + d^f - d^x \qquad [6.18]$$

It can easily be shown that expression [6.18] is the traditional valuation of labor at efficiency prices. This will be equal to the value at efficiency prices of the marginal product (in this example, the value of foreign exchange less the domestic costs saved) during the period of full employment in the farm sector plus the compensating variation $d^f - d^x$ measured through the "reservation wage" during the period in which there is unemployment or underemployment in the rural sector:

$$APL_u = q^x p^{fob} APRFE - q^x p^{fob} dc + d^f - d^x$$

Using [6.12], $p^{fob} dc$ can be replaced by

$$p^{fob} dc = p^{fob} (1 - t_x) - p^x$$

to obtain

$$APL_u = q^x p^{fob} APRFE - q^x [p^{fob} (1 - t_x) - p^x] + d^f - d^x$$

after working out the products and regrouping, we arrive at expression [6.16]

$$APL_u = q^x p^x + q^x p^{fob} (APRFE - 1 + t_x) + d^f - d^x$$

which is the one used as the basis for deducing [6.18].

Some authors have pointed out that an increase in employment in the formal urban sector may lead to the migration of more than one rural worker.[10] Such

---

10. See Harris and Todaro (1970), Harberger (1971a) and Mazumdar (1976).

migrants would become part of the urban labor supply, which is infinitely elastic at the prevailing wage in both sectors (formal and informal). As a consequence, the number of unemployed or underemployed will increase if the fixed number of informal jobs is distributed among a larger number of workers. In this situation, expression [6.18] for the APL_u will have to be modified since it was deduced on the assumption that only one rural worker would migrate for each additional job created in the formal urban sector. For this purpose, it would be useful to revise, and make the corresponding adjustment to, each column in Table 6.6 for the situation in which more than one worker migrates. The first two columns will remain unaltered since the project would continue to employ a worker from the informal sector. To simplify presentation, assume now that h rural migrants would share the working hours released in the informal sector. Thus, the total of the effects on the migrant workers would be

$$w^i - \sum_{j=1}^{h} y_j^r - d^i + \sum_{j=1}^{h} d_j^r + d_j^x$$

whereas those on the rural family (families) would be

$$\sum_{j=1}^{h} y_j^r - w_j^x - v_j^r - d_j^r$$

As for the farm companies, they would be affected by the departure of h workers

$$\sum_{j=1}^{h} (w_j^x - v_j^x)$$

and the Government would see its revenue reduced by

$$\sum_{j=1}^{h} q_j^x p^{fob} (t_x + APRFE - 1)$$

Finally, using the same assumptions as for [6.18] the accounting price of unskilled labor would be

$$APL_u = \sum_{j=1}^{h} w_j^x \left[1 + \frac{t_x + APRFE - 1}{(1 - t_x - dc)} \right] + d^f - \sum_{j=1}^{h} d_j^x$$

that is, the value of the marginal product of h migrant workers, plus the CV of the single additional job created, less the sum of the CVs of not working in export agriculture.

6.5 The Treatment of Contributions to a Compulsory Social Security System

The existence of a compulsory social security system introduces a difference between the cost to the employer of hiring a unit of labor and the monetary income received by the worker. The cost to the employer will be equal to the wage received by the worker plus the contributions of the latter and the employer to the social security system. In this section the main aspects to be taken into account for the allocation of these contributions in distributional analysis will be presented.

The wage appearing in the *Project* column of the tables that present the effects of the additional job created corresponds to the cost to the employer of hiring labor, since this is the sum of money that the project has to pay for hiring. If this sum is represented by w, the sum of money received by the worker will be $w(1 - t_{ss})$ in which t_{ss} is the proportion of the cost to the employer that is transferred to the social security system as the sum of contributions from the employer and the worker. The latter receives a benefit from his participation in the system, which he values at B_{ss}, the CV of participating in the system. Consequently, we have the following set of effects

Project	$-w$
Worker	$w(1 - t_{ss}) + B_{ss}$
Social Security System	$w t_{ss} - C_{ss}$

in which C_{ss} is the cost of providing the service. Although C_{ss} can be estimated, at least as the average cost per member, B_{ss} will not normally be known and some drastic simplification will be required. Assume, for example, that $w t_{ss}$ is the payment for a worker who joins a medical insurance scheme to participate in the system and that this is the only service of such a type to which the worker has access. If it can be assumed that $w t_{ss} = B_{ss}$, then the total wage w will be income for the worker. Assume, on the other hand, that the worker is employed in an area that is very far from social security medical care centers, and he consequently will not make use of these services, even though both employer and worker will have to pay the corresponding contributions. However, the project will provide the medical services which the worker values at B_{sp}. In such a case, the effects to be recorded will be

Project	$-w - C_{sp}$
Worker	$w(1 - t_{ss}) + B_{sp}$
Social Security System	$w\,t_{ss}$

in which the cost of the service provided by the project (C_{sp}) will be included with the other costs. Again, if $B_{sp} = w\,t_{ss}$ is a reasonable assumption, all of wage w will be income for the worker. As for the social security system, it will receive revenue without incurring any costs.

Let us now consider a case where the workers hired already participate in a pension scheme and would continue to do so in the situation without the project, as might be the case with skilled labor. Hiring these workers for the project would not affect their situation (if their wages did not change) since they would continue to pay ($w\,t_{ss}$) and receive (B_{ss}) from the system as they would in the without project situation. Their original employer would not be affected either if the cost to this employer is assumed to be equal to the value of the marginal product, and the social security system continued to receive the same revenue and incur the same costs. In the case of workers who belong to the system and are expected to continue to belong to it until their retirement, as might be the case with unskilled jobs created in the formal sector, the only approximation possible may be to assume that $B_{ss} = w\,t_{ss}$. However, in the case of *temporary* hiring of rural labor which is not expected to succeed in obtaining benefits from the system, the effects will be as follows:

Project	$-w$
Worker	$w(1 - t_{ss})$
Social Security System	$w\,t_{ss}$

The worker's income will be less than his wage and the social security system will receive a transfer $w\,t_{ss}$.

Given the difficulty (not to say the impossibility) of estimating the benefits B_{ss}, the solution that is always adopted will include an element of arbitrariness on the part of the analyst. However, common sense should enable him to come up with an acceptable approximation.

6.6 An Example

Consider the case of an industrial project in the formal sector of the economy, which will be located in the metropolitan area of the capital city and will hire unskilled labor for a present value of 31,887. This sum corresponds to the cost for the project of hiring labor, and therefore includes not only the worker's monetary income, but also contributions to the social security system ($w^f\,t_{ss}$)

estimated at 2,232. We know that the labor force comes (at the margin) from the farming sector, in which workers are fully employed for a period of three months for the harvest of an export crop. During this period, the supply of labor is totally inelastic to small changes in wages and the latter effectively determine the allocation of available labor among big farms. During the remainder of the year, the farm workers are under-employed. The demand for labor from small-holdings (the providers of labor during the period of peak demand) plus the requirements of the big farms are considerably less than what is available. This is clearly shown by the fact that during the latter period "landless farm workers" have great difficulty finding jobs, even temporary ones, and thus finance their consumption to a certain extent from income earned during the period of peak demand. For these reasons, for the purposes of estimating the APL_u, the year has been divided into these two periods.

The income from wages earned during the period of peak demand (w^x), which rises to 20% of the annual cost to the employer or the project $(w^x = 0.2 \, w^f)$, is considered a reasonable approximation of the farm gate value of the marginal product $(w^x = v^x)$. Consequently, in accordance with [6.13]

$$q^x \, p^{fob} \, (1 - t_x - dc) = 0.2 \, w^f$$
$$q^x \, p^{fob} \, (1 - t_x - dc) = 6377$$

It is also known that an export tax of 4% $(t_x = 0.04)$ is levied on agricultural produce and that the domestic processing, transport and trading costs are 15% $(dc = 0.15)$ of the f.o.b. price. Consequently, the farm gate value of the marginal product can be broken down into

Foreign exchange $(q^x \, p^{fob})$	=	−7873
Export taxes $(0.04 \, q^x \, p^{fob})$	=	315
Savings in domestic costs $(0.15 \, q^x \, p^{fob})$	=	1181
Farm wages (w^x)	=	−6377

Contributions to the social security system are not included in this breakdown since in practice they are not paid.

During the rest of the year, the labor force is underemployed and the output of the rural economy and the farms is assumed to be unaffected $(-v_m^r + v_r^r = 0)$. Consequently, the valuation during this period corresponds to the CV of the job, less the CV of not working in export agriculture, all valued at the reser-

Table 6.7. Effects of Hiring Unskilled Labor

	Project	Unskilled Workers	ISS	Government	Total
Foreign Exchange $(-q^x p^{fob})$	−7873	−	−	−787	−8660
Taxes $(t_x q^x p^{fob})$	315	−	−	−315	−
Cost Savings $(dc\, q^x p^{fob})$	1181	−	−	−	1181
Reservation Wage $(d^f - d^x)$	−9566	−	−	−	−9566
Social Security $(w^f t_{ss})$	−2232	−	2232	−	−
ISS Benefits (B_{ss})	−	2800	−2232	−568	−
Other Transfers (Δw)	−13712	13712	−	−	−
Total (w^f)	−31887	16512	−	−1670	−17045

vation wage in the farm sector. The result is equivalent to 30% of the wage paid by the project $(d^f - d^x = 0.3w^f)$, that is

$$d^f - d^x = 0.30 \times 31887$$
$$d^f - d^x = 9566$$

Thus, the cost to the employer (the project) of the labor to be hired for the project will be

$$w^f = w^x + d^f - d^x + w^f t_{ss} + \Delta w$$
$$31887 = 6377 + 9566 + 2232 + 13712$$

in which Δw is the increase in the *monetary* income of the workers hired for the project less the CV total of the jobs.

With this information and the breakdown already presented for w^x, almost all of the first column of Table 6.7 has been constructed. The remaining entry, *ISS Benefits*, corresponds to the benefits that the workers will receive from the Institute of Social Security (ISS) estimated as equal to the average costs per member of the Institution $(B_{ss} = C_{ss})$. Since the cost of providing these services is greater than the contributions received to finance them $(w^f t_{ss} < C_{ss})$, the Government is shown as financing the difference (-568). The column *Unskilled Workers* summarizes the effects which in Table 6.6 are divided into the categories *Informal Sector Workers*, *Migrant Workers* and *Rural Family*. The members of this group receive benefits from the ISS (2800) and the transfer (13712) consisting of the difference between the increase in their net monetary income and the CVs of their work. The ISS receives contributions $w^f t_{ss}$, which it returns as 2800 of services $(B_{ss} = C_{ss})$, of which it finances only 2232 (the contributions), while the remaining 568 is financed by the Government.[11] The latter also loses the foreign exchange premium ($APRFE - 1 = 0.1$) and the export taxes (-315) because of the reduction $q^x p^{fob}$ in exports. Finally, the column totals are the total gains and losses of those affected and the horizontal sum of these totals indicates the minimum additional income that hiring the workers must generate to make compensation *possible*.

---

11. Note the implied assumption that the cost of the services at market prices is equal to their value at efficiency prices.

CHAPTER 7

FIRST APPROXIMATION OF
THE VALUATION OF
NON-TRADED GOODS AND SERVICES

7.1 Non-Traded Goods at the Margin

A good or service is said to be non-traded at the margin, or simply non-traded, when adjustment to an increase in domestic demand for a commodity takes place through an increase in domestic production, its withdrawal from alternative domestic uses or a combination of both effects. Similarly, adjustment in response to additional domestic supply takes place through an increase in the quantity consumed domestically, a reduction in the output of other producers or a combination of both effects. Describing a good as non-traded depends, consequently, on what *actually happens* in response to changes in demand or supply. As in the case of traded goods, this classification must be distinguished from that based on what would *potentially happen* *if* the existing incentives or disincentives to foreign trade were altered or eliminated, in which case we speak of non-tradeable goods.

The objectives of this chapter are: (a) to present, at least in introductory form, the problems involved in the valuation of non-traded goods; (b) to explain the assumptions implied in accepting the market price as being equal

Figure 7.1 The Project Generates Excess Demand for a Non-Traded Good or Service

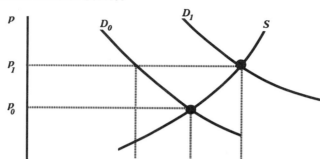

to the efficiency price; and (c) to pave the way for presenting the use of input-output techniques in Part II. Since our interest lies in the distributional aspects, special attention will be given to price changes brought about by the project and to the possibility of estimating the distribution of the corresponding CVs.

7.2 The Project Demands Non-Traded Inputs

Starting from an equilibrium situation, the additional demand generated by a project at the prevailing market price can be represented graphically (see Figure 7.1). Additional demand generated by the project is $q_1 - q_s$, and the respective adjustment is to produce $q_1 - q_0$ additional units and to reduce their alternative uses by $q_0 - q_s$, both brought about by the increase $p_1 - p_0$ in the price. Using Figure 7.1, it is now possible to work out an initial approximation of the changes in income caused by the additional demand for q created by the project, shown in Table 7.1.

The project pays $p_1(q_1 - q_s)$ for its purchases and the remaining purchasers incur additional costs $(p_1 - p_0)q_s$. The producers of q receive these sums as additional income and incur additional costs $C[q_1] - C[q_0]$, in which $C[q_i]$ is the long-run total cost of producing quantity q_i and the square bracket indicates "function of". Finally the purchasers who no longer buy quantity $q_0 - q_s$ stop spending $p_0(q_0 - q_s)$ but lose $\Sigma CV(q_0 - q_s)$. This first approximation enables us to discuss each change in income and the possibility of distributing it according to beneficiaries: in particular, the purchasers of $q_0 - q_s$ in the situation without the project, the producers of q and the users of q_s.

Table 7.1. Income Changes Due to Excess Demand Generated by the Project. The Competitive Model

	Project	Purchasers of q_s	Producers of q	Purchasers of $q_0 - q_s$	Total at Efficiency Prices
Purchases by the Project	$-p_1(q_1 - q_s)$		$p_1(q_1 - q_s)$		
Increase in the Value of Purchases by Other Users		$-(p_1 - p_0)q_s$	$(p_1 - P_0)q_s$		
Costs Attributable to Additional Production $(q_1 - q_0)$			$-C[q_1] + C[q_0]$		$-C[q_1] + C[q_0]$
Reduction in Purchases by Other Users			$-p_0(q_0 - q_s)$	$p_0(q_0 - q_s)$	
Value of Purchases $(q_0 - q_s)$ for Other Users				$\Sigma CV(q_0 - q_s)$	$\Sigma CV(q_0 - q_s)$

Source: Figure 7.1.

Figure 7.2 The Competitive Model

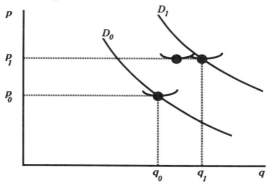

Let us begin discussion with the area $(p_1 - p_0)q_s$, since this is the one that can entail important distributional effects, although they are very difficult, if not impossible, to identify. For that purpose, two situations will be considered which differ in the type of competition and, consequently, in the type of adjustment involved.[1] In the first place, consider the case in which the real situation can be approximated by a totally competitive model without restrictions on access to technology, without economies of scale and in which no abnormal private profits exist, the latter being defined as those resulting from the difference between the rate of return on investment at market prices and the minimum profitability required for businessmen to invest. This situation is reflected in Figure 7.2 in which the individual long-run average cost functions (including "normal" profits) are equal for all producers and depend on the volume of production. In other words, for each volume of total production q_i there exists an average cost $c[q_i]$ equal for all. But since $p_i = c[q_i]$ for all, the additional income $(p_i - p_0)q_i$ is simply what is needed to pay the total additional costs $C[q_i] - C[q_0]$ incurred by each producer (if the industry could expand at constant costs, $p_i - p_0$ would be nil). This additional income (costs) for the producer of q can represent income changes ranging from *additional* abnormal profits per product unit in the inter industrial chain supplying the inputs, to changes in relative factor prices that increase the price of product q relative to that of others. This type of distributional effect is difficult to even approximate and in practice is ignored.

Let us now consider the case shown in Figure 7.3, in which there are economies of scale, restrictions on all the producers having access to the same technology and entry barriers. The "big" producers, with average long-run

---

1. Consulting Mishan (1968, 1981a, Part V and 1982, Chapter 10) will help to shed light on a problem not often dealt with in the literature on applied welfare economics.

Figure 7.3 An Oligopolistic Model

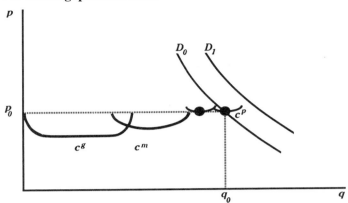

costs including "normal" profits $c^b[q]$, and the "medium-sized" ones ($c^m[q]$) allow the existence of "small" firms, and it is to their costs ($c^s[q]$) that the market price corresponds.[2] The effects of the demand increase created by the project are also difficult, if indeed possible, to estimate. If additional output came from the "small" firms, there would not be abnormal profits for them, although the problem of relative price changes could arise for the competitive case already discussed. Conversely, if the additional output came from the expansion of medium-sized or large firms it is very likely that they would enjoy abnormal profits since the price determination "model" implies that the small firms are not eliminated completely.[3]

The difficulties in approximating the distributional effects of the changes $p_i - p_0$ (if they existed) are obvious and, in practice are usually ignored. This raises the question of how important the effects omitted are. In the case of producers with different costs (Figure 7.3), the greater the difference between the price and the average cost of the firms that expand output in response to excess demand, the greater the magnitude of the effect. Conversely, in more competitive markets (Figure 7.2) the effects are likely to be less important. In this regard, it can be shown that for small changes $q_1 - q_s$,

$$p_1 - p_0 \approx \frac{\alpha p_0}{\epsilon - \eta}$$

2. See Sylos Labini (1966).
3. See Sylos-Labini (1966) and the works by Mishan mentioned at the beginning of this section.

Table 7.2. Practical Approximation of Income Changes Due to Excess Demand Generated by the Project. The Competitive Model

	Project	Producers of q	Total at Efficiency Prices
Purchases of $(q_1 - q_s)$	$-p(q_1 - q_s)$	$p(q_1 - q_s)$	
Costs of Producing $(q_1 - q_s)$		$-c(q_1 - q_s)$	$-c(q_1 - q_s)$
Total	$-p(q_1 - q_s)$	$(p - c)(q_1 - q_s)$	$-c(q_1 - q_s)$

Source: Figure 7.1.

in which α is demand increase $q_1 - q_s$ as a proportion of q_0, ϵ is price elasticity of supply and η price elasticity of demand.[4] Consequently,

$$(p_1 - p_0)\, q_0 \approx \frac{(q_1 - q_s)\, p_0}{\epsilon - \eta}$$

will be smaller, the greater the supply and demand elasticities are in absolute terms. Given that, in general, supply elasticity will be sufficiently high, ignoring the distributional effects implicit in this area is not expected to have major repercussions on the final result. If we ignore the area $(p_1 - p_0)\, q_0$, we can redefine the effect on the producers of q, limiting it to the difference between their marginal income and their marginal costs (at prices prevailing in the situation *without* the project)

$$p\,(q_1 - q_s) - c\,(q_1 - q_s)$$

in which c is now the constant long-run marginal cost. The analysis is thus conducted *as if* all the demand increase were met by additional output and thus disregarding the (minor) effects on the purchasers of $q_0 - q_s$. Consequently, the effects which in practice could be considered are project expenditure, its counterpart as additional income for producers, and the marginal costs (at the prices prevailing in the without project situation), shown in Table 7.2. Recall that equality between price, marginal cost at market prices and marginal cost at efficiency prices was already assumed in Section 3.4. This assumption, maintained throughout Part I, results in the valuation of non-traded inputs at their market price. Part II includes a brief discussion on the use of input-output techniques to approximate the valuation of marginal costs at efficiency prices, and to identify the main transfers involved in the difference between the price and marginal costs at market and efficiency prices.

---

4. See Fontaine (1981).

7.3 The Project Produces Consumer Goods

The examples of market functioning briefly presented in the previous section will be useful for discussion here on additional supply of consumer goods. We will consider the cases in which price reductions can be either expected or not and in which, consequently, it will or will not be necessary to estimate changes in consumers' surpluses. Let us consider first the competitive case in which all enterprises use the same technique and none obtains abnormal private profits. In such a case, it is unlikely that a project using the same technique would come up for analysis, unless for *short-run* reasons the firms are making such profits temporarily and the investment being considered is what causes the adjustment. Under these circumstances, the elimination of abnormal private profits through a price reduction is not a transfer that can be *attributed* to the project for a longer period than is necessary for another enterprise to expand capacity in the *without* project situation. These short-run effects are not often estimated and, more important from a practical point of view, it is even less probable for the public sector to assess projects with these characteristics.

A second case in a competitive market would be a situation where the introduction of a new technique would reduce costs (at the prevailing relative prices), in which case the price would continue to be dominated for a (possibly lengthy) time by marginal producers, and the effect of the project would be to replace some of them. This will continue as long as there are no restrictions on access to the particular technique and the price will not fall until (at least in theory) the last producer using the old technique has been eliminated. In this instance again, it is unclear whether the resource savings stemming from the introduction of the new technique must be *attributed* to a particular project when the market behavior model itself implies that introduction of the new technique will take place inevitably for one firm or the other.

An interesting exception to the foregoing would be projects such as credit projects for small farmers to introduce "improved" methods of cultivation. In these cases, the objective is to achieve or speed up a reduction in unit costs or an increase in production, which would not take place without the project (credit). But even in this case, there would only be an effect on the price of outputs insofar as what can be attributed to credit is the eradication of the "old" technique or the speeding up of the process. Otherwise the price would continue to be determined by the costs of the producers with the old technique and the effect of the project would simply be the saving in resources resulting from producing the same quantity at lower costs.

Price reductions following the complete replacement of a technique by another should not be attributed separately to credit but to a technical development and dissemination program of which credit is only a part. Figure 7.4

Figure 7.4 Producers Use the "Traditional", "Modern" and "Most Efficient" Techniques

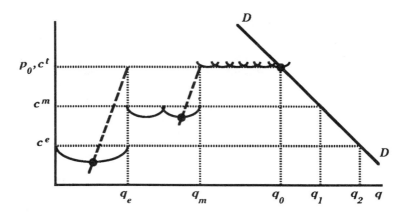

Figure 7.5 A "Modern" Producer Turns to the "Most Efficient" Technique

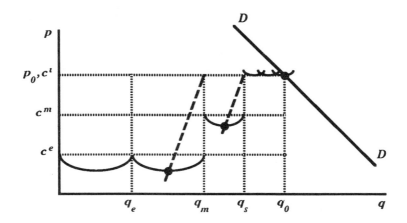

provides an example that shows the long-run average cost curves of individual producers who use the "traditional" technique ($q_0 - q_m$), those who use the "modern" technique ($q_m - q_e$) and the most "efficient" one (q_e), on the assumption that all the plots are the same size and that there are no differential rents within each group. Only if the program goes as far as including the producers of $q_0 - q_m$ needed to reach q_1 with the new technique, will there be a reduction in prices (the CVs of which will not only be attributable to credit) as well as a release of resources because higher production per surface unit could displace some of the producers who use the "traditional" technique. If the project does not affect marginal producers, it will not affect prices, nor, consequently, will it affect the differential rents of the remaining producers. On the other hand, it will create differential rents for the beneficiaries of the project. If the project affects all marginal producers, and consequently the price, it will reduce the differential rents of other producers by an extent that will depend on the technique introduced. Furthermore, it can give rise to differential rents for the direct beneficiaries of the project (producers who change their technique) only if costs in the situation *with* the project convert *other* producers into marginal producers. In the example this would occur if the project benefited the producers of $q_0 - q_m$ by bringing them to the "most efficient" technique without eliminating all those who use the "modern" technique.

A second example consists of irrigation projects, which are a particular instance of technical change. There again, there will only be reductions in prices and a release of resources if irrigation is introduced in marginal holdings. Otherwise, there will only be a release of resources and differential rents. This case will be considered in more detail in Chapter 12.

We can then conclude that in general, in situations that can be represented by the competitive model, there will be no price reductions that can be attributed to the project, unless it reduces the unit costs of marginal producers, and this reduction in costs would not have taken place without the project being analyzed.

Now we can look at two examples of the introduction of a new technique on the basis of Figure 7.4, which shows the situation *without* the project. To simplify presentation, assume that production per surface unit of a "modern" producer is half that of an "efficient" one. Let us first consider, for example, the case of an irrigation project, which affects only one of the producers of $q_m - q_e$, that is one who uses the "modern" technique, and that as a result of the project this producer will move to the category of the most "efficient". This situation *with* the project is represented in Figure 7.5, which shows that the effect of the project is to displace some of the marginal producers without eliminating them altogether. Consequently, the price will continue to be p_0,

Table 7.3. The Project Introduces the "Most Efficient" Technique to a "Modern" Producer

	"Modern" Producer	"Traditional" Producers	Total
Changes in Sales	$p_0(q_s - q_m)$	$-p_0(q_s - q_m)$	—
Changes in Costs	$-c^e(q_m - q_e) + c^m(q_s - q_m)$	$c^t(q_s - q_m)$	$-c^e(q_m - q_e) + (c^m + c^t)(q_s - q_m)$
Total	$(p_0 + c^m)(q_s - q_m) - c^e(q_m - q_e)$	$(c^t - p_0)(q_s - q_m)$	$-c^e(q_m - q_e) + (c^m + c^t)(q_s - q_m)$

Source: Figure 7.5.

and there will be no direct effects either on the consumers of q, the remaining "modern" producers or the most "efficient" ones.

One of the main effects of the project, as indicated in Table 7.3, consists in increasing the differential rents of the "modern" producer benefiting from the project. The second effect will be to displace the marginal producers to other activities without however, it is assumed, affecting their earnings since they did not in any event receive any differential rents. If the unit costs at market prices c^t, c^m and c^e were equal to costs at efficiency prices, there would be no more effects to be recorded. Conversely, if the market prices of the inputs were different from their efficiency prices, it would also be necessary to take into account the transfers that constitute the difference between market and efficiency prices. A clear example of this is the price of water, since the tariff charge is often less than the costs of providing it. In this case, we have to compute the investment, operating and maintenance costs of the irrigation system, annualized and at efficiency prices, to compare them with the tariff. This correction is always estimated in these projects, since to start with, the costs of providing the water are computed, and the tariff is considered a mere transfer between farmers and the irrigation authority (see Chapter 12).

Note that the sum in the *Total* column, or net benefits at efficiency prices, is the difference between the costs saved by displacing the traditional producers and by discarding the "modern" technique, less the costs incurred in using the efficient technique. This result is logical since, as the price is not affected, there will be no additional sales and all benefits at efficiency prices will be cost savings. The reader will also notice that in practice the market prices of costs c^m and c^e are corrected, but the correction of the effects that might be caused by the displacement of marginal producers is omitted, i.e. it is assumed implicitly that the market price in the without project situation is equal to the average cost at market prices of the displaced producers ($p_0 = c^t$), that this is equal to the corresponding cost at efficiency prices, and that there are no income changes for the displaced producers. If $p_0 = c^t$, the sum of the total column can be expressed as

$$p_0(q_s - q_m) - [c^e(q_m - q_e) - c^m(q_s - q_m)]$$

106

Figure 7.6 The "Traditional" Producers Turn to the "Modern" Technique

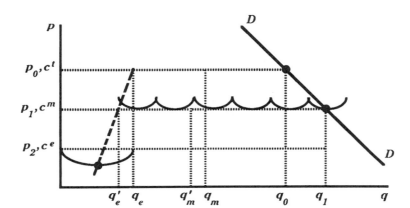

that is, the additional sales of the producers affected by the project less their additional costs, which is the traditional way of presenting the results of projects of this type.

Let us now consider a case in which the project will introduce irrigation for producers who use the "traditional" technique with unit costs c^t, bring them to the modern technique with unit costs c_1^m and, consequently, reduce the price from p_0 to p_1. The without project situation is shown in Figure 7.4 and that with the project in Figure 7.6. Since a price change is brought about, consumers and all producers are affected by the project. This gives rise to various effects, which are worth considering step by step according to the group affected. To simplify the presentation of the effects on the different people, given in Table 7.4, consumers are treated as a single whole and the *Consumers* column shows the sum of their CVs. The reader will bear in mind that if the objective is to present the distribution of income changes, it will be necessary to distinguish between groups of consumers, as will be done later in Chapter 10.

Beginning with the consumers of q, each one benefits by the CV of the price reduction. The total of consumers' CVs has been broken down into savings from the purchase of q_0, willingness to pay for additional purchases $q_1 - q_0$, and what is actually paid for them. What the consumers stop spending on q_0 is income that the producers no longer receive in proportion to their participation in sales q_0. What they pay for additional purchases $q_1 - q_0$ is additional income for producers who increase their output, i.e. the "traditional" producers who adopt the "modern" technique, and is shown in that column as part of the *Project sales*. The "efficient" producers will reduce their sales to $q_e - q'_e$ as a result of the price fall and lower production will reduce their total costs by

$$(c_0^e - c_1^e)(q_e - q'_e)$$

in which c_i^e is the average cost of the corresponding sales at price p_i. The effects on the producers who already used the "modern" technique in the *without* project situation are similar, since they reduce production by $q_m - q'_m$ and stop incurring the corresponding costs. The "traditional" producers, that is those who adopt the "modern" technique as a consequence of the project, are considered in two stages: first as if they were eliminated by the project, in which case they also no longer receive $p_1(q_0 - q_m)$ and no longer incur costs $c'(q_0 - q_m)$; and then as if they reappeared using the "modern" technique, so that they receive income from their sales. These include what the "traditional" producers produced previously $(q_0 - q_m)$, plus reductions $(q_e - q'_e)$ and $(q_m - q'_m)$ in the output of other producers caused by the price reduction and plus additional purchases by consumers $(q_1 - q_0)$. At the same time, they incur corresponding costs c_1^m per unit produced.

It should now be noted that Table 7.4, although it carefully records all the effects on consumers and producers, is very complex to use in practice. The reader can imagine what it would be like if we discarded the assumption of a single product q, only three techniques and a single farm size. In practice, however, it is assumed that the effects of the price reduction on the quantities produced by the "efficient" and "modern" producers in the without project situation are insignificant, that is,

$$q_e - q'_e = q_m - q'_m = 0$$

As a result, the entire increase in output by producers who adopt the "modern" technique is additional sales for the market as a whole, so that Table 7.4 can be considerably simplified.

The new results are shown in Table 7.5. The vertical sum of the columns indicates the income changes of the various persons affected by the project. In the case of consumers, they gain the total of the CVs of the price change measured by the change in consumers' surplus. The "efficient" and "modern" producers in the without project situation see their income differentials reduced to zero because the project has converted the users of this technique into marginal producers. Finally, the effects on the "traditional" producers

Table 7.4. Income Changes Brought About by the Project. Turning "Traditional" into "Modern" Producers

	Consumers	"Efficient" Producers	"Modern" Producers in the Without Project Situation	"Traditional" Producers	Total
Savings from the Purchase of q_0	$(p_0 - p_1)q_0$	$-(p_0 - p_1)q_e$	$-(p_0 - p_1)(q_m - q_e)$	$-(p_0 - p_1)(q_0 - q_m)$	—
Willingness to Pay for $q_1 - q_0$	$\frac{1}{2}(p_0 - p_1)(q_1 - q_0) + p_1(q_1 - q_0)$	—	—	—	$\frac{1}{2}(p_0 - p_1)(q_1 - q_0) + p_1(q_1 - q_0)$
Paid for $q_1 - q_0$	$-p_1(q_1 - q_0)$	—	—	—	$-p_1(q_1 - q_0)$
Reduction in Sales	—	$-p_1(q_e - q_e')$	$-p_1(q_m - q_m')$	$-p_1(q_0 - q_m)$	$-p_1\{(q_e - q_e') + (q_m - q_m') + (q_0 - q_m)\}$
Reduction in Costs	—	$(c_0^e - c_1^e)(q_e - q_e')$	$(c_0^m - c_1^m)(q_m - q_m')$	$c'(q_0 - q_m)$	$(c_0^e - c_1^e)(q_e - q_e') + (c_0^m - c_1^m)(q_m - q_m') + c'(q_0 - q_m)$
Project Sales	—	—	—	$p_1\{(q_e - q_e') + (q_m - q_m') + (q_1 - q_0)\}$	$p_1\{(q_e - q_e') + (q_m - q_m') + (q_1 - q_0)\}$
Project Costs	—	—	—	$-c_1^m\{(q_e - q_e') + (q_m - q_m') + (q_1 - q_0)\}$	$-c_1^m\{(q_e - q_e') + (q_m - q_m') + (q_1 - q_0)\}$

Source: Figures 7.4 and 7.6.

109

can best be presented in two stages. The first consists in their discarding the "traditional" technique

$$-p_0 (q_0 - q_m) + c^t (q_0 - q_m)$$

and the second in their adopting the "modern" technique

$$p_1 (q_1 - q_m) - c_1^m (q_1 - q_m)$$

The example given is also simplified in the sense that it assumes that *all* the "traditional" producers adopt the new technique and that the market absorbs all that is produced as a result at a price no lower than their average costs. If this were not the case, and some of the "traditional" producers were transferred from q to another crop z, the respective column would also have to include the relevant additional income and costs:

$$p^z \Delta q^z - c^z \Delta q^z$$

Adding up the *Total* column in this table we obtain

$$\text{Willingness to pay} \qquad + \text{ Cost savings } - \text{ Project costs}$$
$$\tfrac{1}{2}(p_0 - p_1)(q_1 - q_0) + p_1(q_1 - q_0) + c^t(q_0 - q_m) - c_1^m(q_1 - q_m)$$

If input market prices are equal to their efficiency prices, the above expression will represent the net benefits of the project at efficiency prices. Otherwise it will be necessary to correct the valuation of these inputs. In this regard, the valuation of foreign exchange and labor has already been discussed, and as pointed out in Part I, the assumption of equality between market price and efficiency price of non-traded goods is maintained. Finally, the reader will note that the sum in the *Total* column reproduces the operational rule of efficiency analysis, viz: willingness to pay for additional consumption, plus the costs saved by displacement of a technique, less the costs incurred by adopting that of the project.

7.4 The Project Produces Intermediate Goods

When the effect of the project is only to replace other producers without affecting the price, the situation is similar to that already presented for consumer goods. Conversely, if it affects prices, it is necessary to reconsider the

Table 7.5. Practical Approximation of the Income Changes Brought About by the Project. Turning "Traditional" into "Modern" Producers

	Consumers	"Efficient" Producers	"Modern" Producers in the Without Project Situation	"Traditional" Producers	Total
Savings from the Purchase of q_0	$(p_0 - p_1)q_0$	$-(p_0 - p_1)q_e$	$-(p_0 - p_1)(q_m - q_e)$	$-(p_0 - p_1)(q_0 - q_m)$	—
Willingness to Pay for $q_1 - q_0$	$\frac{1}{2}(p_0 - p_1)(q_1 - q_0) + p_1(q_1 - q_0)$	—	—	—	$\frac{1}{2}(p_0 - p_1)(q_1 - q_0) + p_1(q_1 - q_0)$
Paid for $q_1 - q_0$	$-p_1(q_1 - q_0)$	—	—	—	$-p_1(q_1 - q_0)$
Reduction in Sales	—	—	—	$-p_1(q_0 - q_m)$	$-p_1(q_0 - q_m)$
Reduction in Costs	—	—	—	$c^t(q_0 - q_m)$	$c^t(q_0 - q_m)$
Project Sales	—	—	—	$p_1\{(q_0 - q_m) + (q_1 - q_0)\}$	$p_1\{(q_0 - q_m) + (q_1 - q_0)\}$
Project Costs	—	—	—	$-c_1^m\{(q_0 - q_m) + (q_1 - q_0)\}$	$-c_1^m\{(q_0 - q_m) + (q_1 - q_0)\}$

Source: Figures 7.4 and 7.6.

first column of Tables 7.4 or 7.5. In the case of consumer goods, the final user of the goods whose price has been affected has been reached and it is possible to estimate changes in consumers' surpluses. On the other hand, where intermediate goods are involved, the price reduction will be a reduction in costs for other producers. These in turn will be forced to transfer part or all of these savings to the following stage in the intersectoral chain through prices, and so on until the producers of consumer goods are reached and, through them, the consumers. This raises various problems for estimating the distributional effects. In the first place, the cost saving will "travel" forward along the interindustrial chain and at each stage or transaction, market conditions will determine the percentage of this saving that "continues the journey" forward through prices and the percentage retained as additional profits. This makes it difficult, if not impossible, to estimate which percentage of the initial saving reaches consumers taken as a whole. In the second place, this initial cost saving may affect producers of various goods and services, each of whom will in turn sell to other producers of other goods, and so on. This makes it difficult to estimate the effects on consumers benefitting from the cost saving, since what is received will depend not only on the transfer process but also on the particular composition of the consumer basket.

From a practical point of view, these problems are difficult to solve. With regard to the distribution of the total saving between the percentage that reaches consumers and the percentage retained as additional profits, it will be difficult for the analyst to go beyond determining a *range* of transfer, taking into account the type of input involved. As for the effect of the transfer on different consumer groups, the use of input-output techniques may allow for an approximation of the incidence of the saving transferred to be made, although it will be possible to use it only if the following three conditions are met: if the input-output table is sufficiently disaggregated, if the good in question can be reasonably identified with some sector of the matrix or can be incorporated into it, and if the consumption column can be broken down according to the desired groups of consumers.

Let us assume that the project being analyzed will reduce the price of a good that is both a final consumer good and an intermediate good. As a result, people consume it not only directly but also indirectly through the consumer goods that use it directly or indirectly as an input. As the structure of total consumption, direct and indirect, of the good in question per type of consumer will not be equal to that of direct consumption, it would be useful to know the composition of this total consumption by group of consumers. With the assistance of some simplifying assumptions, and using an input-output matrix, it is possible to approximate the direct and indirect requirements of the consumption baskets of each group. Let

$$X = (I - A)^{-1} D$$
$$X = T D$$

[7.1]

be the traditional equation of input-output analysis that relates the vector for sectoral gross production values X with the final demand matrix D through the matrix of total direct and indirect requirements $T = (I - A)^{-1}$, in which I is the identity matrix and A the matrix for intersectoral transactions in non-traded goods.[5] To simplify presentation, assume that X has only three columns corresponding to "products" (1), (2) and (3) and that the final demand matrix D can be broken down into the following vectors: consumption of people with low incomes (C^b), consumption by the rest of the families (C^r), Government consumption (C^g) and the remainder of final demand (D^r). Thus, system [7.1] can be written as

$$\begin{bmatrix} X_1 \\ X_2 \\ X_3 \end{bmatrix} = \begin{bmatrix} T_{11} & T_{12} & T_{13} \\ T_{21} & T_{22} & T_{23} \\ T_{31} & T_{32} & T_{33} \end{bmatrix} \begin{bmatrix} C_1^b & C_1^r & C_1^g & D_1^r \\ C_2^b & C_2^r & C_2^g & D_2^r \\ C_3^b & C_3^r & C_3^g & D_3^r \end{bmatrix}$$

[7.2]

The total requirements, direct and indirect, for product (3) corresponding to the consumption basket of the low-income group will be

$$X_3(C^b) = T_{31} C_1^b + T_{32} C_2^b + T_{33} C_3^b$$

which can be interpreted in the following way. In order to provide one peso's worth of product (1) it is necessary to produce T_{31} pesos of (3), so that $T_{31} C_1^b$ indicates the production value of (3) "contained" in C_1^b peso's worth of consumption of product (1). Thus, $X_3(C^b)$ will be the value of product (3) directly and indirectly contained in the consumption basket of the low-income group, made up of their direct consumption C_3^b and by indirect consumption

$$X_3(C^b) - C_3^b = T_{31} C_1^b + T_{32} C_2^b + (T_{33} - 1) C_3^b$$

---

5. See Chenery and Clark (1963) or Bulmer-Thomas (1982).

through the quantity of product (3) required to produce basket C_j^b. We could calculate in the same way, the total consumption, direct and indirect, of product (3) by the rest of the families and the Government, thus obtaining the total consumption of each group:

$$X_3(C^b)$$
$$X_3(C^r)$$
$$X_3(C^g)$$

Then the reduction in value of direct sales to final consumers could be distributed in proportion to direct consumption, while the reduction in the value of the intermediate sales which it is assumed reaches the final consumers could be distributed according to the share of indirect consumption of each group in the indirect consumption of all the consumer groups. Thus, for example, suppose that the composition of direct consumption of product (3) is

$$
\begin{aligned}
C_3^b &= 0.20 \\
C_3^r &= 0.70 \\
\underline{C_3^g} &= \underline{0.10} \\
\text{Total} &= 1.00
\end{aligned}
$$

that of indirect consumption is

$$
\begin{aligned}
X_3(C^b) - C_3^b &= 0.15 \\
X_3(C^r) - C_3^r &= 0.74 \\
\underline{X_3(C^g) - C_3^g} &= \underline{0.11} \\
\text{Total} &= 1.00
\end{aligned}
$$

and the reduction in the value of sales to final consumers is $500, and that to intermediate users is $2000. If we assume that only 60% of the effect of the sales price reduction for intermediate consumption reaches the final consumers, each group of consumers will benefit by

$$
\begin{aligned}
\text{Group } b &= 0.20 \times \$500 + 0.60 \times 0.15 \times \$2000 = \$ \ 280 \\
\text{Group } r &= 0.70 \times \$500 + 0.60 \times 0.74 \times \$2000 = \$1238 \\
\underline{\text{Group } g} &= \underline{0.10 \times \$500 + 0.60 \times 0.11 \times \$2000} = \underline{\$ \ 182} \\
\text{Total} &= \qquad \$500 + 0.60 \times \$2000 \qquad = \$1700
\end{aligned}
$$

and the remaining $0.40 \times \$2000 = \$800$ would be retained by producers along the inter-industrial chain.

The procedure described has not escaped drastic simplification. In addition to the well known limitations of the input-output model, it ignores effects on imports and exports, and distributes the savings from sales which are not for consumption (which includes sales to sectors producing investment goods) in accordance with the total content of consumption baskets. Although the simple model presented could be extended to include an approximation of this type of effect, it would do so at the price of greater complexity and more demanding requirements for data not often available, while it is unlikely that it would add much precision to the final result.

CHAPTER 8

THE DISCOUNT RATE

Preceding chapters have dealt with the identification of direct distributional effects at a given moment in time. An investment project, however, is also a proposal to allocate or reallocate income over time. The same resources required to invest in a project today in order to receive a future flow of consumption, can also be used to produce more consumer goods today. Thus a method is required to compare additional present consumption against additional future consumption. This is the topic of this chapter.

It should be recalled that the discount rate is a parameter of vital importance, as well as one of the most controversial, in project appraisal. The details of this controversy are beyond the scope of this chapter, which will merely indicate the salient aspects of the controversy and provide references to the main works on the subject.

8.1 Intertemporal Allocation from the Individual Point of View

As pointed out in Chapter 1, most proposals for applying cost-benefit analysis are based on the principle that those affected are the ones who define the nature of the effects, quantified by means of the respective CV. For the sake of consistency therefore, weights for intertemporal comparison in principle ought to be derived on the basis of these criteria. This is in fact the approach followed by efficiency analysis advocates and for that reason, this section presents the rationalization prevailing in the neo-classical theory of consumer behavior regarding decisions on intertemporal consumption allocation. This will make it possible to discuss the concept of the discount rate from an individual point of view as well as its relationship with the interest rate of a perfect capital market, the profitability rate of marginal investments, and application of the compensation criterion.

A simple illustration of two periods will be used for this purpose. Let us begin by considering an individual who receives income Y_0 in this period and who knows *for certain* that he will receive income Y_1 in the following period. If a "perfect" capital market exists, without "distortions" such as an income tax, in which a real interest rate i prevails, Mr. R has before him two extreme hypothetical options. The first consists in devoting all his income Y_0 to present consumption and in addition borrowing an amount $Y_1/(1+i)$, also for consumption in this period, a debt which at interest rate i he will be able to pay in the following period (consuming zero in that period) from his income Y_1. Thus, maximum present consumption possible will be

$$\max C_0 = Y_0 + \frac{Y_1}{1 + i}$$

The alternative extreme option is not to consume anything in this period and to invest his income Y_0 at rate i in order to consume

$$\max C_1 = Y_0 (1 + i) + Y_1$$

in the following period. In more general terms, his consumption in the following period will be equal to his saving in the previous period plus the interest between both periods, plus his income from the following period, i.e.

$$C_1 = (Y_0 - C_0) (1 + i) + Y_1 \qquad [8.1]$$

This expression corresponds to a straight line with a slope $-(1 + i)$ and represents the maximum combinations between present and future consumption available to the individual at rate i (Figure 8.1). The combination to be chosen will depend on his preferences between present and future consumption. These preferences are represented on the graph by indifference curves U_0 and U_1, which show the different combinations of present and future consumption that result in the same level of welfare for the individual. It should

Figure 8.1 Possible Combinations of Present and Future Consumption

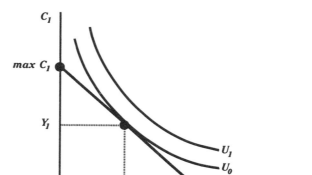

be noted that in order for him to know the utility level of a certain combination of expenditure on present and future consumption, he also needs to know the prices in effect in both periods. An indifference curve shows what quantity of additional future consumption ΔC_1 is required to compensate him for a reduction $-\Delta C_0$ in present consumption, without altering his level of welfare. Let,

$$-\frac{\Delta C_1}{\Delta C_0} = -(1 + d)$$

be this relation, which is equal to the slope of the indifference curve at the point concerned. Thus, starting from a given level of present consumption, the individual will be willing to reduce this consumption by quantity ΔC_0 if he can obtain $\Delta C_0 (1 + d)$ in the following period, in which d is the so-called time preference rate. Consequently,

$$\Delta C_1 = (1 + d) \Delta C_0$$

The maximum indifference curve between present and future consumption that the individual can reach is that which is tangential to his constraint [8.1], and the point of tangency determines his intertemporal allocation of income. At this point, the slope of the straight line is found to be equal to the slope of the indifference curve, i.e.

$$-(1 + i) = -(1 + d)$$
$$i = d$$

118

This equilibrium position is reached by granting and taking loans. If the individual's time preference rate is less than the rate of interest, he will save since the increase in his future consumption $(Y_0 - C_0)(1 + i)$ will be greater than the minimum he is willing to accept $(Y_0 - C_0)(1 + d)$ for a reduction in his present consumption. Conversely, if $d > i$ he will borrow, since his valuation today of the loss in future consumption $(C_0 - Y_0)(1 + i)/(1 + d)$ is less than the increase in present consumption $(C_0 - Y_0)$. It should be noted that the adjustment requires the possibility of lending and borrowing at rate i.

8.2 The Interest Rate as the Discount Rate

For given levels of present and future income, the higher the rate of interest, the more the individual will save $(Y_0 - C_0)$, i.e. his supply of savings rises with the interest rate. The horizontal aggregation of these individual saving functions gives rise to the market savings supply function (Figure 8.2). At the same time, those drawing funds in this period can invest these savings in projects available to them, which can be classified in descending order according to their certain profitability q, without considering interest paid as costs. Since it is assumed that no investments are made that fail to show a profit after interest payments, all investments made will verify that $q > i$. Consequently, for the equilibrium investment level, the marginally undertaken (or rejected) investment will verify that

$$q_m = i = d$$

Figure 8.2 The Savings Market

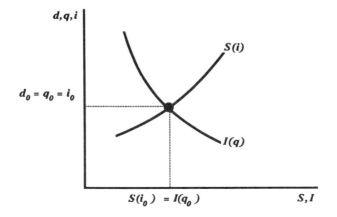

119

Table 8.1 Flows of Costs and Benefits of Two Hypothetical Projects

Project	Year 0 Government	Year 1 Mr. P	Year 2 Mr. R
P^1	-100	110	—
P^2	-100	—	130

In this way, a perfect capital market, without "distortions" such as income taxes, would ensure equality between individual discount rates, the interest rate and the profitability of marginally undertaken (or displaced) investments.

Now, if all the individuals affected by a project participate in this market, equality between the interest rate and the individuals' discount rate ensures that use of the equilibrium interest rate as a discount rate will comply with the potential Pareto improvement criterion. Let us consider the comparison between Government projects P^1 and P^2 in Table 8.1 when the equilibrium interest rate is 10% per year. Both require initial expenditure of 100 to obtain:

(a) in the case of P^1, benefits of 110 to Mr. P the following year; and
(b) in the case of P^2, benefits of 130 to Mr. R at the end of two years.

Since the option of transferring the 100 to Mr. P or to Mr. R exists, carrying out project P^1 is "equivalent" to effecting these transfers. It is indifferent to P whether he receives 100 this year or 110 next year. If this sum were transferred to R, he could compensate P for the loss involved in not carrying out P^1. However, when considering project P^2, Mr. R will prefer 130 at the end of two years, compared with 100 today, since he is prepared to reduce his consumption today by 100 if he can obtain at least $100(1+0.1)^2 = 121$ at the end of two years. Furthermore, 130 would enable him to compensate Mr. P in the third year for the 110 he lost in the second by not carrying out P^1. This would require $110(1+0.1) = 121$, and leave a remainder of $130 - 121 = 9$.

The above *appears* to indicate that sticking strictly to the principles of who determines the nature of effects and how they are measured would lead us to consider the rate of interest in a "perfect" market, without "distortions," as the appropriate discount rate. However, innumerable criticisms have been made of this formulation of the problem.

8.3 Criticism of the Use of the Interest Rate as the Discount Rate

The first type of criticism focusses on the existence of the conditions required for the market to reveal rate d. Not only are future prices and incomes not even known as random variables, they are also subject to uncertainty. More-

Figure 8.3 Positions of Intertemporal Equilibrium of Mr. P

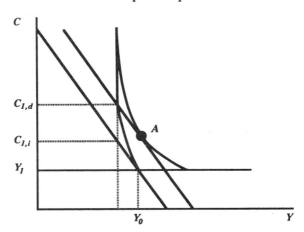

over, the market interest rates are expressed in nominal terms so that any intertemporal consumption plan requires the future inflation rate to be known.[1] In addition, the existence of income tax introduces special complications. In this case, person j will equal his individual discount rate d^j with the rate of interest after taxes $i(1 - t^j)$ in which t^j is the marginal income tax rate corresponding to that person. Consequently, unless t^j is the only rate for *all* persons, a single interest rate will correspond to various individual discount rates and there will be a different "average" discount rate for each project, which will depend on the interpersonal and intertemporal distribution of costs and benefits.[2] Finally, application of the compensation criterion to the intertemporal allocation described in Section 8.2 requires *both individuals to participate in the "savings market."* Let us consider for example the case shown in Figure 8.3, in which the future income of P is less than or equal to the minimum acceptable consumption in this period, while his present income is somewhat higher than the respective minimum consumption. In such a situation, P does not want to borrow since this would mean an unacceptable reduction in his future consumption. At the same time, the prevailing rate of interest i is less than his time-preference rate d so that

$$(Y_0 - C_0)(1 + i) < (Y_0 - C_0)(1 + d)$$

the increase in future consumption possible at rate i ($C_{1,i} - Y_1$ in Figure 8.3) is less than the minimum required to persuade him to save ($C_{1,d} - Y_1$). In this

---

1. See Section 9.3 below.

2. Cf. Mishan (1982, Chapter 35). The author wishes to thank Professor Mishan for an exchange of correspondence on this point.

case, the compensation criteria cannot be implemented by using a single rate i since this rate is different from the time-preference rate of Mr. P. A change in the distribution of present or future income in favor of P could take him to a point such as A at which he would participate in the savings market. However, a generalized redistribution would affect the savings market and would give rise to a different interest rate than that which would have prevailed without redistribution. As a consequence, even if a perfect market existed, the resulting rate of interest might not be the appropriate one for implementing the compensation criterion if one or more individuals did not participate in the market. It should also be noted that the interest rate is not independent of (present or future) income distribution between individuals.

The second type of criticism is based on the impossibility, in the field of intertemporal decisions, of complying with the principle that it is those who are affected who determine the nature of effects, since these extend beyond the life of the present generation. Mishan (1981a, 1981c, and 1982) has put this in terms of the impossibility of applying the criterion of the potential Pareto improvement when gainers and losers do not co-exist in time. Let us suppose that project P^r, which costs the Government 100, will show benefits the following year of $100(1 + q^r)$ received entirely by Mr. R, and that $q^r > d$. Alternative project P^f, which also costs 100, will provide benefits $100(1 + q^f)^{100}$ received entirely by Mr. F in year 100, in which $q^f = d$.[3] Obviously,

$$\frac{100(1 + q^r)}{1 + d} > \frac{100(1 + q^f)^{100}}{(1 + d)^{100}}$$

and application of the present value criterion would result in P^r being selected. However, as Mr. R would not be alive in year 100, it would not be *possible* to effect compensation unless a mechanism existed for transfers between generations that could *potentially* take compensation $100(1 + d)$ in year 1, and reinvest it at rate d for 99 years in order to compensate Mr. F. Given that this mechanism depends not only on the possibility of transfers between members of the same generation, but in *addition* on the possibility of transfers between generations, Mishan has called it *"potential* potential Pareto improvements" and expressed objections to the use of the present value criterion without explicit consideration of the intergenerational problem.[4]

Other economists have questioned acceptance of the interest rate of a perfect market on the basis of denying the ability or even possibility of individuals of the present generation to make intertemporal comparisons that affect

---

3. The assumption should be noted that d today is equal to d in 100 years.
4. In this regard, see also Pearce and Nash (1981).

members of future generations. Even in the (unrealistic) case of perfect certainty about future prices and incomes, there would be no certainty about the date of death, and this uncertainty of the present generation, which would be expressed through higher discount rates, is not a defensible argument for discounting the benefits of future generations.

The criticism would be equally strong if the claim were made to use a "pure" time-preference rate. In the words of Sen (1961):

> A distant object "looks" smaller, and we tend to value, it is claimed, a unit of consumption in the future less than we value the same now... If the difference is only due to distance in time, then the position is symmetrical. A future object looks less important now, and similarly, a present object will look less important in the future. While it is true that the decision has to be taken now, there is no necessary reason why today's discount of tomorrow should be used, and not tomorrow's discount of today.

These concisely put criticisms are by no means exhaustive. However, they do illustrate the difficulties in accepting even the interest rate of a reasonably competitive market as the discount rate.[5]

8.4 The Social Discount Rate

If a "pure" time preference rate is unacceptable and the uncertainty of the present generation is not accepted as a criterion for discounting the benefits of future generations, why should future benefits be discounted at all? What one gets as an answer is based on rejecting, totally or partially, the intertemporal preferences revealed by the present generation and sticking to the "principle of the diminishing marginal utility of consumption." Since the future generation will be richer than the present one (per capita consumption rises), an additional unit of future consumption is less valuable than an additional unit of present consumption.[6] This enables us to deduce and interpret a formula for the discount rate based on the "principle of diminishing marginal utility of consumption" and on a value judgment made explicit by postulating a "total economic welfare" function. Various proposals exist, of course, regarding this function, of which only one will be presented here.[7]

---

5. The reader interested in more details of the controversy can consult, in addition to the works mentioned, Dobb (1960) and Marglin (1963). Layard (1972) and Pearce and Nash (1981) provide summaries of the discussions. Sen (1982) provides a more advanced treatment of the discount rate including the subjects of the following sections.

6. The reader will note that the same argument can be applied to members of the present generation. In this case, a unit of additional income for a poor person *today* will be more valuable than the same unit for a rich person. This topic will be considered in Chapter 15.

7. Ray (1984) discusses this in detail. Also see Sen (1982).

Let us suppose that the level of "total economic welfare" is a function of per capita consumption and let

$$B_0, B_1, B_2, \ldots, B_k$$

be the flow of costs and benefits from an investment project. As the population (N_t) and its growth are independent of the project, B_t/N_t will be the change in per capita consumption brought about by the project in year t. If w_t is the contribution to "total welfare" of an additional unit of per capita consumption in year t, the project's contribution to "total welfare" will be

$$\Delta W = w_0 \frac{B_0}{N_0} + w_1 \frac{B_1}{N_1} + \ldots + w_k \frac{B_k}{N_k}$$

and the project will be accepted if ΔW is greater than zero. However, the analyst does not need to know the weights w_t or express costs and benefits in per capita terms. If ΔW is positive, then

$$\Delta W_0 = \frac{\Delta W N_0}{w_0}$$

$$\Delta W_0 = B_0 + \frac{w_1}{w_0} \frac{N_0}{N_1} B_1 + \ldots + \frac{w_n}{w_0} \frac{N_0}{N_k} B_k$$

will be also, from which we can deduce that ΔW_0 is equal to the present value of flow B_t and a simple expression for the discount rate corresponding to the "total welfare" function W.

If in order to simplify, we assume that the population grows at a constant rate n, the weight assigned to benefits obtained in year $t + 1$ compared with the one they are assigned the previous year will be

$$\frac{w_t}{w_{t-1}(1 + n)} = \frac{1}{1 + d_t} \tag{8.2}$$

so that we can write

$$\Delta W_0 = B_0 + \frac{w_1}{w_0(1 + n)} B_1 + \frac{w_2}{w_0(1 + n)^2} B_2 \tag{8.3}$$

$$+ \ldots + \frac{w_k}{w_0(1 + n)^k} B_k$$

Assuming now, as is customary in cost-benefit analysis, that weights w_t also diminish at a constant rate, we can write the following:

$$\frac{w_1}{w_0 (1 + n)} = \frac{1}{1 + d}$$

$$\frac{w_2}{w_0(1 + n)^2} = \frac{w_2}{w_1(1 + n)} \frac{w_1}{w_0(1 + n)} = \frac{1}{(1 + d)^2}$$

$$\vdots$$

$$\frac{w_t}{w_0(1 + n)^t} = \frac{w_t}{w_{t-1}(1 + n)} \frac{w_{t-1}}{w_{t-2}(1 + n)} \cdots \frac{w_1}{w_0(1 + n)} = \frac{1}{(1 + d)^t}$$

in which d is the discount rate. Consequently, [8.3] can be written as

$$\Delta W_0 = B_0 + \frac{B_1}{1 + d} + \frac{B_2}{(1 + d)^2} + \cdots + \frac{B_k}{(1 + d)^k}$$

which is the traditional formula for present value.

We now need to ask ourselves about the relation between the discount rate obtained this way (d), the "marginal utility of per capita consumption" (w) and the rate of growth of the population (n), which will enable us to obtain a simple formula for d. On the basis of [8.2] we can write

$$1 + d = \frac{w_t(1 + n)}{w_{t+1}}$$

and bearing in mind that $w_t = w_{t+1} - \Delta w$, the preceding expression becomes

$$1 + d = \left(1 - \frac{\Delta w}{w}\right)(1 + n)$$

Multiplying and dividing by the expected per capita consumption growth rate $(\Delta c/c)$ we obtain

$$1 + d = \left(1 - \frac{c}{w} \frac{\Delta w}{\Delta c} \frac{\Delta c}{c}\right)(1 + n)$$

Note now that, given that Δw is a function of the change in per capita consumption,

$$e = \frac{c}{w} \frac{\Delta w}{\Delta c}$$

is the elasticity of the "marginal utility of per capita consumption." Consequently, expression [8.2] can finally be written as

$$1 + d = (1 - e\,\dot{c})\,(1 + n) \qquad\qquad [8.4]$$

in which $\dot{c} = \Delta c / c$ is the expected per capita consumption growth rate.

If the expected per capita consumption and population growth rates can be considered as given, the problem is reduced to parameter e, for which some authors have proposed estimation procedures on the basis of data on prices and quantities consumed.[8] The advantage claimed for this approach is that it is consistent, at least in part, with the principle of accepting individual preferences. In other words, of all the reasons that the members of the present generation may have for discounting future consumption, the one accepted is that of "diminishing marginal utility of consumption" and it is assumed that the rate at which it diminishes does not change between the generations affected.[9] Conversely, for other authors, parameter e ought simply to be considered as a value judgment by the "political authority."[10]

Whatever the position adopted regarding parameter e, the question of considering the per capita consumption growth rate as a datum must still be discussed. If in accordance with the operational rule of efficiency analysis, investment has to expand until the profitability of marginal investment is equal to the discount rate, the future per capita consumption growth rate will be a function of the discount rate through investment. To avoid this problem, Marglin (1963) has proposed that we begin by determining the (possible) growth rate desired, in order to derive from that the investment required to reach it. Given that for whoever makes decisions, this investment rate is optimal by definition, the rate of return of marginal projects is the discount rate, since otherwise we would reduce present consumption even more to the benefit of investment (future consumption). From this we deduce that when, in efficiency analysis, the rate of return of marginal projects is used as the discount rate, the investment rate is assumed to be optimal in a normative

---

8. Helmers (1979, Section 9.2) gives a summary of the procedures used and the results obtained.

9. The reader interested in more detail can consult Dasgupta and Pearce (1972, Chapter 6).

10. Weisbrod (1968), UNIDO (1972) and Scott, et al. (1976).

sense, i.e. it is not different because the political authority considers it optimal.

8.5 Summary

If the intertemporal preferences revealed by the present generation are accepted as the criterion for intertemporal aggregation, it is then necessary to ask ourselves if the financial market complies with all the requirements necessary for the prevailing rate of interest or a derivative thereof to be considered as the *common* discount rate for *all* individuals. If the answer were in the affirmative, the practical problem of the discount would be solved. Conversely, if the conclusion were that the preferences revealed by individuals indicated the existence of different individual discount rates, the problem of intertemporal comparisons would become considerably more complicated since, from a theoretical point of view, the discount rate of each individual would have to be used. The extent of the practical problem will depend on the spread of the different individual rates. Only after solving this part of the problem should we go on to discussing the relationship between the rate of return of marginal investment and the discount rate(s).

If, on the other hand, the revealed intertemporal preferences are rejected as a criterion for intertemporal comparisons, it will be necessary to explain the principles of the alternative criterion to be used (including not discounting) and ensure that it is consistent with the interpersonal aggregation criterion.[11] This should all be done before comparing the resulting discount rate with the rate of return of marginal investment.

In the remaining chapters of Part I and in Part II of this study, we shall be working on the assumptions of the operational version of efficiency analysis, i.e. we assume that the discount rate is equal to the profitability at efficiency prices of marginal investment. The consequences of relaxing this assumption will be discussed in Part III.

---

11. See Chapter 15.

CHAPTER 9

COST-BENEFIT ANALYSIS OF AN INDUSTRIAL PROJECT

9.1 Introduction

The preceding chapters have presented the principles of cost-benefit analysis, tracing the path that goes from the compensating variation as a criterion for measuring changes in individuals' "economic welfare", to the formulas for estimating accounting prices for foreign exchange and labor. These formulas correspond to a specific set of assumptions, some of which oversimplify, but which will be maintained in this chapter. In particular, each time non-traded goods appeared on the scene in preceding chapters, their market prices were assumed to be good approximations of their efficiency prices. This assumption, which will be maintained in this chapter, simplifies presentation considerably and allows us to make an initial approach to applied cost-benefit analysis when the distributional effects are identified. This simplified presentation is useful from an instructional point of view insofar as it provides the reader, usually more familiar with efficiency analysis than with identification of distributional effects, an introduction to the problem of estimating these effects by applying principles presented in the preceding chapters to a simple example.

Let us consider the case of an industrial project submitted to the National Development Bank (NDB) to obtain a long-term credit. A state bank, the NDB is an integral part of the industrial promotion system and thus grants these credits at preferential terms compared with commercial banks with regard to repayment periods and interest rates. The project analysis presented in this chapter is carried out exclusively as a cost-benefit analysis, one of the criteria that the NDB takes into account for granting loans.

9.2 Valuation of Real Flows

Table 9.1 shows the present value of the project's cash flow from the perspective of the sponsoring firm. In this table, the project inputs have already been classified into the most appropriate categories for economic analysis. Thus, for example, a distinction has been made between imported and non-traded inputs and between skilled and unskilled labor. The project will be analyzed according to the major categories of this classification, and in the order in which they appear in the table.

Following the valuation criteria explained in Chapter 4, the factory gate value of the sales of the project's outputs has been broken down into its main components. Output A is an intermediate good currently imported directly by its users, which in the future will purchase directly from the project, i.e., the commercial sector is not affected. However, the project will be located close to the user firms, which will permit transport cost savings because of the difference between such costs for port-purchaser and project-purchaser journeys. Since project-purchaser transport is carried out by the latter, these costs are not included in Table 9.1, in which output A is valued at factory gate prices. The corresponding price is set so that it equals the customs gate price of the imported good, with the saving in transport costs thus being transferred to purchasers as an incentive to maximize utilization of domestic production capacity. We assume that the saving will be kept by the purchaser firms in the form of bigger profits. Ultimately, the factory gate price can be expressed as the total of the foreign exchange saved, the import taxes no longer paid and the savings on port costs. Thus, the Government stops receiving taxes corresponding to the imports substituted (20,000). The foreign exchange now needs to be valued at efficiency prices by using the APRFE, which has been estimated according to expression [3.33] as

$$APRFE = \frac{M + T_m + X - T_x}{M + X} = 1.1$$

Table 9.1 Present Value of the Flow of Funds from the Industrial Project (In $)

Source	Amount
Sales	630,000
• Output A	525,000
• Output B	124,000
• Sales Tax	−19,000
Current Costs	−450,600
• Imported Inputs	−202,100
• Non-traded Inputs	−173,900
• Skilled Labor	−37,800
• Unskilled Labor	−31,500
• Payments for Technology and Trademarks	−5,300
Fixed Capital Investments	−145,000
• Construction	−30,000
• Imported Machinery and Equipment	−110,000
• Non-traded Equipment	−2,200
• Non-traded Inputs	−250
• Imported Inputs	−350
• Technical Assistance	−200
• Skilled Labor	−1,500
• Unskilled Labor	−500
Circulating Capital Investments	−11,600
• Imported Inputs	−5,100
• Non-traded Inputs	−2,200
• Semi-finished Goods	−300
• Finished Goods	−4,000
Finance	44,500
• Long-Term Credits	86,000
• Repayments	−48,000
• Short-Term Credits	72,000
• Repayments	−65,500
Sub Total	67,300
Direct Taxes	−6,730
Total	60,570

Consequently, use of the foreign exchange released will increase tax revenue by

$$500,000 \times (APRFE - 1) = 50,000$$

The production of A yields B as a by-product, which is not used by domestic industry and is exported subject to a tax of 5%. It is exported by an intermediary firm whose trade margin c is 10% of the sales value, so that the factory gate price p^f will be

$$p^f = p^{fob} (1 - t_x) (1 - c)$$
$$p^f = p^{fob} (1 - 0.05) (1 - 0.10)$$

With these data, the factory gate value of exports can be broken down into foreign exchange, taxes and trade margins as shown in Table 9.2. Finally the sales tax paid by the project is additional revenue for the Government, which is added to the net balance resulting from the changes in revenue caused by the import substitution and the exports. Thus, the valuation at efficiency prices will be equal to the changes in the income of those affected: the project, the purchaser firms and the Government.

Current costs can be considered together with investments in stocks. The present value of the annual increases in stocks of inputs can be added to the present value of the respective annual consumption since the goods are the same. Stocks of semi-finished and finished foods are valued at the production cost, so that the corresponding value can be broken down into inputs and labor according to the structure of these costs. In this case, payments for technology and trademarks, which are paid on sales, must be omitted and logically so must administrative and marketing costs. The result of this procedure is

Table 9.2   Valuation of Sales at Efficiency Prices (In $)

Source	Project	Purchasers of A	Government	Total at Efficiency Prices
Imports Substituted (A)	525,000	—	30,000	555,000
• Foreign Exchange	500,000	—	50,000	550,000
• Taxes	20,000	—	−20,000	—
• Port Costs	5,000	—	—	5,000
Savings in Transport Costs	—	4,200	—	4,200
• Port-User Transport	—	6,500	—	6,500
• Project-User Transport	—	−2,300	—	−2,300
Exports (B)	124,000	—	21,754	145,754
• Foreign Exchange	145,029	—	14,503	159,532
• Taxes	−7,251	—	7,251	—
• Trade	−13,778	—	—	−13,778
Sales Taxes	−19,000	—	19,000	—
Total	630,000	4,200	70,754	704,954

shown in Table 9.3 together with the quantification of the effects resulting from the economic valuation. The vast majority of inputs would be imported tax-free as part of the industrial incentives granted to the project. These inputs are valued delivered to the project, so that the relevant transport costs have been separated. The remaining imported inputs will be purchased locally, which is why the corresponding taxes and transport and trade margins have been separated. Foreign exchange has been valued at efficiency prices, using an APRFE = 1.1, and the values at market prices of transport and trade services have been accepted as equal to their values at efficiency prices. The latter criterion was also used for non-traded inputs and skilled labor. Unskilled labor will be ultimately withdrawn from the agricultural sector and has been valued according to the presentation in Chapter 6, Section 6.6. Finally, the payments for technology and trademarks are made to a foreign firm in foreign exchange. This foreign exchange is expressed in domestic currency, which is why the corresponding amount has been corrected using the APRFE.

Fixed capital investments include construction, domestic and imported machinery and equipment (including spare parts), technical assistance for instal-

Table 9.3 Valuation at Efficiency Prices of Current Costs and Stocks (In $)

Source	Project	Government	Unskilled Workers	Total at Efficiency Prices
Imported Inputs	−209,264	−17,744	—	−227,008
• Foreign Exchange	−199,448	−19,945	—	−219,393
• Taxes	−2,201	2,201	—	—
• Transport	−3,200	—	—	−3,200
• Trade	−4,415	—	—	−4,415
Non-traded Inputs	−177,691	—	—	−177,691
Skilled Labor	−38,058	—	—	−38,058
Unskilled Labor[a]	−31,887	−1,670	16,512	−17,045
• Foreign Exchange	−7,873	−787	—	−8,660
• Taxes	315	−315	—	—
• Other Domestic Costs	1,181	—	—	1,181
• Reservation Wages	−9,566	—	—	−9,566
• Social Security	−2,232	−568	2,800	—
• Transfers to Workers	−13,712	—	13,712	—
Payments for Technology and Trademarks	−5,300	−530	—	−5,830
Total	−462,200	−19,944	16,512	−465,632

a. From Table 6.7.

Table 9.4   Valuation at Efficiency Prices of Construction Costs (In $)

Source	Project	Unskilled Workers	Government	Total at Efficiency Prices
Imported Inputs	−6,780	—	−520	−7,300
• Foreign Exchange	−6,500	—	−650	−7,150
• Taxes	−130	—	130	—
• Transport	−150	—	—	−150
Non-Traded Inputs[a]	−14,060	—	—	−14,060
Skilled Labor	−6,220	—	—	−6,220
Unskilled Labor	−2,940	1,470	−150	−1,620
Total	−30,000	1,470	−670	−29,200

a. Includes the capital cost that could not be disaggregated.

lation and assembly, and assembly and start-up costs. The latter two items have been broken down into their main components to better value them at efficiency prices, which was the same valuation approach used for current costs. In the case of construction, a different procedure has been followed. It consists of breaking down such costs according to the main types of inputs (see Table 9.4) and valuing each of these separately. The imported inputs and unskilled labor required for construction have been valued by following the same criteria as those already explained. Since it was not possible to disaggregate capital costs ("depreciation plus profits") these were grouped together with non-traded inputs, and their market value, like that of skilled labor, was accepted as equal to their value at efficiency prices. This assumes that the market prices of the equipment used are equal to their efficiency prices and that the activity receives "normal" profits (its rate of return is equal to the discount rate). This procedure, although imperfect, should give a better valuation than simply accepting the market value of construction as being equal to its value at efficiency prices.[1]

The results of valuing construction costs in such a way are shown in Table 9.4 and the *Total* column has been transferred to Table 9.5 to include it with the other investment costs. Machinery and equipment will be imported tax-free, which is why these costs, except for 5,000 of port-project transport costs, are foreign exchange. The remaining items have been valued in accordance with the principles already presented and only "technical assistance" deserves a special mention. This item includes the salaries of the professional

1. The reader will notice that a similar approximation can be adopted for the main non-traded inputs shown in Table 9.1. This will be dealt with more completely in Chapter 11 when the use of input-output techniques for estimating accounting prices is discussed.

Table 9.5   Valuation at Efficiency Prices of Investment Costs (In $)

Source	Project	Unskilled Workers	Government	Total at Efficiency Prices
Construction	−30,000	1,470	−670	−29,200
Imported Machinery & Equipment	−105,000	—	−10,500	−115,500
Transport	−5,000	—	—	−5,000
Non-Traded Equipment	−2,200	—	—	−2,200
Non-Traded Inputs	−250	—	—	−250
Imported Inputs	−350	—	−11	−361
Technical Assistance	−200	—	−10	−210
Skilled Labor	−1,500	—	—	−1,500
Unskilled Labor	−500	250	−26	−276
Total	−145,000	1,720	−11,217	−154,497

and technical staff of the firm supplying the licence. It is estimated that only 50% of these salaries will be spent within the country and that the remainder will be transferred abroad.

9.3 Treatment of Financial Flows

The economic analysis of projects is normally effected on the basis of a flow of funds expressed at constant prices. However, flows of funds expressed at "constant prices" are often found in which the receipt and repayment of loans have not been deflated by the expected rate of inflation. As this section will show, this inconsistency does not affect the "efficiency" analysis, but does have important consequences for the identification and quantification of distributional effects.

Let us consider the case of a $100 loan received at the beginning of year zero, and repaid in five equal annual payments from the beginning of year one at a nominal interest rate of 10%. This financial transaction will appear in a flow of funds at *current* prices as shown in the first four rows of Table 9.6. However, given the existence of a non-zero inflation rate, the reductions in future income required to repay the loan each year cannot be compared with one another, or with the amount of the loan received, until all these values are expressed in the same unit, i.e. in prices of the same year. Given that in cost-benefit analysis, year zero is traditionally used as the base period, it will be necessary to deflate the repayment flow by using the inflation rate in years one to five, which we assume is known, constant and equal to 10%. Thus, to construct the last two columns of Table 9.6, each annual repayment amount R_t

Table 9.6   Flows of Funds from a Loan

Source	Present Value	Year					
		0	1	2	3	4	5
Flows at Current Prices							
• Loan	—	100	—	—	—	—	—
• Amortization	—	—	−20	−20	−20	−20	−20
• Interest	—	—	−10	−8	−6	−4	−2
Total	—	100	−30	−28	−26	−24	−22
Flows at Constant Prices							
• Loan	100	100	—	—	—	—	—
• Repayment	78	—	−27.3	−23.1	−19.5	−16.4	−13.7

must be divided by $(1 + 0.1)^t$; for example, the outflow of funds in year three, R_3, can be expressed at constant prices as

$$R_3^* = \frac{-26}{(1+0.1)^3}$$

$$R_3^* = -19.5$$

Given that in this example the nominal interest rate is equal to the future inflation rate, the *real* interest rate is equal to zero. In fact, by using Table 9.6 the reader may check that

$$\sum_{t=1}^{5} \frac{R_t}{(1+0.1)^t} = 100$$

that is, the amount of the loan received is equal to total repayment values expressed at constant prices. Now, once they have been expressed in real terms, future income flows will have to be discounted at year zero using discount rate d, which will also be assumed equal to 10%. Consequently the present value of the repayment flow at constant prices R_t^* will be equal to

$$PV(R_t^*) = \sum_{t=1}^{5} \frac{R_t^*}{(1+d)^t} = \sum_{t=1}^{5} \frac{R_t^*}{(1+p)^t (1+d)^t}$$

$$PV(R_t^*) = 78$$

in which p is the inflation rate. In other words, the recipient of a loan in the circumstances indicated will repay only 78% of what he has received or, in other words, will receive a transfer equal to 22% of the loan.

In more general terms, if the project receives various loans for an annual total at current prices P_t in each year t, the present value of the inflow for a constant inflation rate p will be

$$PV(P_t^*) = \sum_{t=1}^{k} \frac{P_t}{(1+p)^t (1+d)^t}$$

If R_t is the annual debt servicing at current prices of the loans, the present value of repayments at year zero prices will be

$$PV(R_t^*) = \sum_{t=1}^{n} \frac{R_t}{(1+p)^t (1+d)^t}$$

and the present value of transfers $T_t^* = P_t^* - R_t^*$ will be

$$PV(T_t^*) = PV(P_t^*) - PV(R_t^*)$$

Quantifying the present value of the transfers received through long-term finance (not indexed) means knowing future inflation rate p, which obviously would not be possible. In some countries, in which the type of economic policy expected in the future does not differ substantially from that followed in the past, the analyst will be able to make an approximate projection of a constant rate p. In others, the margin of error will be considerably bigger and there will be no way of avoiding them.[2]

Deciding who grants transfer $PV(T_t^*)$ will be postponed until Sections 9.4 and 9.5, but for the moment let us only consider the direct effect, meaning that it is the lending bank that grants the transfer.

We can now go back to Table 9.1, which contains the present value of the flows generated by the project, and consider the values that appear under the heading *Finance*. In accordance with the notation used,

$$PV(P_t^*) = 86,000$$

---

2. There are countries whose rate of inflation is determined by that of some developed countries, so that the economic policy of the country concerned is not the only determining factor. In the United States, "when Richard Nixon came to power in January 1969 he was greeted by 5% inflation, a figure which in the eighties would cause rejoicing in the higher spheres, but which at that time alarmed a public used to practically stable prices and worried by the trend away from the stability of the previous three or four years" (Lekachman, 1982, Page 37). In Argentina in 1971 ($p_{71} = 0.35$), nobody in his right mind would have forecast the rate of inflation in 1984 ($p_{84} \simeq 6$).

Table 9.7 Present Value of Credits and Their Repayments (In $)

Source	Project	NDB	Commercial Banks	Total
Long-Term Credits	86,000	−86,000	−	−
Repayments	−48,000	48,000	−	−
Short-Term Credits	72,000	−	−72,000	−
Repayments	−65,500	−	65,500	−
Total	44,500	−38,000	−6,500	−

is the present value of the long-term loans received and

$$PV(R_t^*) = 48,000$$

the present value of the corresponding repayment flow. The loan would be granted by the National Development Bank (NDB), which in Table 9.7, is shown granting a loan to the project of 86,000 and receiving repayments of 48,000.

According to the financial statements contained in the project document, during the first few years, the project will have to rely on short-term loans to finance the formation of working capital. These financial statements show that, as time goes by, the short-term loans will be replaced by internally generated funds. However, short-term credit is offered (and supposedly will continue to be offered during the life of the project) at real interest rates appreciably below the profit rates firms can achieve from the use of such funds. As a result, the demand for such loans greatly exceeds availability and credit is rationed by the banking system. Considering that due to its characteristics, the project is not expected to experience difficulties in obtaining short-term credit, the initial loan will not be replaced by internally generated funds. Instead, the original line of credit will be maintained and renewed periodically. It will then be useful to explain the procedure for calculating the present value of short-term loans received and the present value of their repayments, shown in Table 9.7.

Let us suppose that at the beginning of period k the project receives a loan P_k to be repaid within 180 days whose value at year zero prices is $P_k^* = P_k/(1+\bar{p})^k$.[3] At the end of the period, the project will have to repay the loan for a total at year zero prices of $P_k^*(1+\bar{i})/(1+\bar{p})$. At the same time, it will obtain another loan for an amount at year zero prices equal to what is

---

3. The hyphen above the variables $\bar{p}$ and further on $\bar{i}$ and $\bar{d}$ indicates that the variable is defined for the duration of the loan. For example, if the period is three months, $\bar{d}$ will indicate the quarterly discount rate equivalent to annual rate d.

necessary to replace the previous loan, plus the project's additional working capital requirements ΔP_k^*. Thus, in period $k+1$

$$P_{k+1}^* = P_k^* + \Delta P_k^*$$

At the end of this period, the project will pay $P_{k+1}^*\,(1+\bar{i})/(1+\bar{p})$ and will take out a loan P_{k+2}^*, and so on until the period $k+n+1$ begins when it will repay $P_{k+n+1}^*\,(1+\bar{i})/(1+\bar{p})$. The flows resulting from these operations are given in schematic form in Table 9.8. The present value of the loans received, less the present value of their repayments, both at year zero constant prices, will be equal to

$$PV(T_t^*) = \sum_{t=k}^{k+n} \frac{P_t^*}{(1+\bar{d})^t} - \sum_{t=k}^{k+n} \frac{P_t^*(1+\bar{i})}{(1+\bar{p})\,(1+\bar{d})^{t+1}}$$

By rearranging the terms, the above expression can be rewritten as

$$PV(T_t^*) = \sum_{t=k}^{k+n} \frac{P_t^*}{(1+\bar{d})^t}\left[1 - \frac{1+\bar{i}}{(1+\bar{p})\,(1+\bar{d})}\right] \qquad [9.1]$$

where the expression between square brackets indicates the proportion of the present value of the loans that the project receives (grants) as a transfer due to a real interest rate that is less (greater) than the discount rate. Note that if this interest rate is equal to the discount rate, the transfer is nil.

Formula [9.1] is valid when the term limit for all the loans is the same which, although not necessarily true in practice, is a reasonable approximation if we keep in mind that we will be working with annual estimates of the use of short-term loans.

Furthermore, recall that the financing being considered is for working *capital* and not for current *assets*, even though the value of current assets better approximates the additional needs for short-term financing for the economy as a whole attributable to the project. For example, if the firm makes

Table 9.8 Receipt and Repayment of Short-Term Loans

Source	Year					
	k	$k+1$	$k+2$	...	$k+n$	$k+n+1$
Loans	P_k^*	P_{k+1}^*	P_{k+2}^*	...	P_{k+n}^*	—
Repayments	—	$\dfrac{P_k^*(1+\bar{i})}{1+\bar{p}}$	$\dfrac{P_{k+1}^*(1+\bar{i})}{1+\bar{p}}$	...	$\dfrac{P_{k+n-1}^*(1+\bar{i})}{1+\bar{p}}$	$\dfrac{P_{k+n}^*(1+\bar{i})}{1+\bar{p}}$

purchases of $100 per month due in 30 days and sells goods for $250 payable in 30 days, the monthly demand for 30-day finance created is $350. However, the need for working *capital* for the project is $350−$100=$250 since the remaining $100 is financed by the supplier.[4]

9.4 Summary of the Distribution of Income Changes Generated by the Project

Having analyzed the distribution of income changes generated by the project (sections 9.2 and 9.3), we can now group together such effects according to their source and the groups affected. This grouping is shown in Table 9.9, in which each row corresponds to the *Total* row of one of the preceding tables. The total in the first column coincides, of course, with the corresponding one in Table 9.1, since both show the present value of the income changes for the project sponsors. The totals in the remaining columns show the gains or losses of the others affected. The purchasers of input *A* increase their profits by not transferring through prices the saving in transport costs. The unskilled workers gain the difference between the wages paid in their new jobs and their income from alternative jobs. The Government has a positive net tax balance, while the banks are shown granting the transfer contained in short and long-term credits. The total of the effects on the groups in question is the value of net benefits at efficiency prices. However, to complete the distributional effect, it is necessary to reconsider the allocation of transfers implied in bank loans.

The NDB is shown transferring $38,000 caused by a real interest rate below the discount rate. This explains why the Government has to periodically make capital transfers to the NDB in order to maintain the volume of promotional credit growing *pari passu* with industrial investment. Consequently, it is the Government, which in reality pays the transfer received by the project, and which would not be required to compensate the NDB for the transfer had the loan not been granted. As the reader will remember from Chapter 1, the fact that in the *without project* situation another industrial project would have received the transfer, is connected with the distribution of *net* income changes attributable to the project. This will be discussed in the following section.

In the case of short-term loans granted by the commercial banks, the depositors can be considered, for the time being, the ones who grant the transfer since they receive on their deposits an interest rate that is lower than the

---

4. Strictly speaking, the $100 overestimates the requirements for short-term financing for the economy as a whole by the component (direct and indirect) of profits plus depreciation, and underestimates it by the increases in stocks of raw materials, semi-finished and finished goods required to expand production.

Table 9.9 Distribution of the Income Changes Brought about by the Project—First Approximation (In $)

Source	Project	Purchasers of A	Unskilled Workers	Government	NDB	Commercial Banks	Total at Efficiency Prices
Sales	630,000	4,200	—	70,754	—	—	704,954
Current Costs and Stocks	−462,200	—	16,512	−19,944	—	—	−465,632
Investment Costs	−145,000	—	1,720	−11,217	—	—	−154,497
Financing							
• Long-term	38,000	—	—	—	−38,000	—	—
• Short-term	6,500	—	—	—	—	−6,500	—
Direct Taxes	−6,730	—	—	6,730	—	—	—
Total	60,570	4,200	18,232	46,323	−38,000	−6,500	84,825

Source: Tables 9.2, 9.3, 9.5 and 9.7.

discount rate.[5] In short, the Government and depositors would grant the transfers contained in long and short-term financing respectively. If we include such changes, we obtain Table 9.10, which shows the estimate of the distribution of project costs and benefits.

9.5 Distribution of Net Income Changes Attributable to the Project

As we saw in Chapter 1, in order to estimate the distribution of *net* income changes from the project, i.e. those that are *attributable* to the project, it is necessary to know the distribution of income changes from the alternative course of action, or without project situation. In this case, it is clear that, given that an NDB loan is granted on preferential terms and is rationed, in the absence of the project, the NDB would use these funds to finance other project(s) displaced by the one being analyzed. The first row in Table 9.11 shows the distribution of the income changes of the project being analyzed, in which the effects on the Government have been separated into two parts: the transfer contained in the NDB loan and the remaining transfers. The second row shows the distribution of the income changes of the alternative project, on the simplifying assumption that it would require the same long-term credit as the project being analyzed. Thus, in the without project situation, the alternative project would receive the transfer of $38,000 plus a transfer of $7,500 from the "depositors," since the alternative project requires more short-term finance. Since it is a project that would produce exported goods, it does not affect domestic consumers and only the Government and unskilled workers are the remaining groups affected.

The distribution of the net income changes from the project being analyzed will be the difference between the distribution of its income changes and the distribution of those from the alternative course of action. Each one of the groups affected gains (or loses) the difference between what it receives from the project and what it would have received from the alternative course of action, which in this case is another project. It should be noted, however, that the balance in the *Depositors* column shows that they would gain 1,000 with the project, which is not true, since the project's lower demand for short-term credit compared with its alternative will not affect depositors' incomes, but will enable other lenders to gain the 1,000. Finally, the total net benefits at efficiency prices are the sum of the net incomes of all the groups affected.

---

5. The analysis assumes equality between lending and borrowing rates and consequently omits quantification of financial intermediation costs.

Table 9.10 Final Distribution of the Income Changes Brought about by the Project (In $)

Source	Project	Purchasers of A	Unskilled Workers	Government	Depositors	Total at Efficiency Prices
Sales	630,000	4,200	–	70,754	–	704,954
Current Costs and Stocks	–462,200	–	16,512	–19,944	–	–465,632
Investment Costs	–145,000	–	1,720	–11,217	–	–154,497
Financing						
• Long-term	38,000	.	–	–38,000	–	–
• Short-term	6,500	–	–	–	–6,500	–
Direct Taxes	–6,730	–	–	6,730	–	–
Total	60,570	4,200	18,232	8,323	–6,500	84,825

Source: Table 9.9

Table 9.11 Distribution of Income Changes from the Project Analyzed and from the Alternative Project (In $)

Project	Firms	Purchasers of A	Unskilled Workers	Government Loan	Other	Depositors	Total at Efficiency Prices
(1) Analyzed	60,570	4,200	18,232	−38,000	46,323	−6,500	84,825
(2) Alternative	13,865	—	6,320	−38,000	25,320	−7,500	5
Balance (1)–(2)	46,705	4,200	11,912	—	21,003	1,000	84,820

Source: Table 9.10.

Table 9.12   Present Value of Flows Attributable to Financing (In $)

	Project	Foreigners	Government	Total
Loan Received	86,000	−86,000	8,600	8,600
Repayments	−48,000	48,000	−4,800	−4,800
Total	38,000	−38,000	3,800	3,800

9.6 Effects of Changes in Financing

The objective of this section is to discuss the consequences of changes in financing on profitability at efficiency prices and on distributional effects. Consider first a change in the financing of fixed investment resulting in a reduction of (the present value of) long-term financing, which is compensated by an increase in internal funds. The effect of this change will be to reduce the present value of net income for the project's owners since the real interest rate is below the discount rate. This reduction in income will be compensated by an increase in the income of those who receive loans not granted to the project. This will affect the distribution of income changes from the project without any impact on its profitability at efficiency prices.

Secondly, the case may be considered in which the foreign suppliers of machinery provide all the long-term credit. In order not to introduce numerical complications, it will be assumed that credit conditions are the same. Table 9.12 shows the present value of the corresponding flows, considering that the suppliers' credit is "tied" to the project.[6]

The project receives a present value of $86,000 to finance the purchase of imported machinery and equipment. The loan is provided by the "foreigner," who receives the present value of the respective repayment flow. Since the machinery was valued at its c.i.f. price times the APRFE when investment costs were being considered, the credit received must be regarded as foreign exchange income and, consequently, also corrected by the APRFE. Thus, what is actually paid for the machinery is its c.i.f. value (105,000), less the loan received (86,000), plus repayment of it (48,000), all multiplied by the APRFE, i.e.

$$(-105,000 + 86,000 - 48,000)APRFE = -67,000 \times APRFE$$

Now, as cost-benefit analysis takes into account the CVs of the effects on "nationals," the loss to the "foreigners" must not be shown as a project

---

6. Financing would not be received if the project were not carried out, i.e. income and repayment of the loan are flows of foreign exchange *attributable* to the project.

"cost." In other words, one of the *benefits* of the project would be, in this case, obtaining a 38,000 transfer in foreign exchange from the foreigner, whose value at efficiency prices is[7]

$$38,000 \times APRFE = 38,000 \times 1.1 = 38,000 + 3,800$$

Consequently, the effect of the financing will be recorded in the cost-benefit analysis accounts as shown in Table 9.13 and the total effects of the project on nationals will then be those shown in the column *Total at Efficiency Prices*. This table is the same as 9.10, except that the column *Foreigners* has been included, and the *Financing* row has been replaced by the results obtained in Table 9.12. We can now see that the present value of the project at efficiency prices has increased, compared to the case with long-term financing from national sources (Table 9.10), in the value at efficiency prices of the foreign exchange transfer received from the "foreigners" ($38,000 \times 1.1 = 41,800$).

Finally, we should consider the possibility of the project being carried out with foreign investment. For example, let us consider the case described in Table 9.14, in which total fixed investment will be financed by long-term loans granted by the National Bank (86,000) and the remainder by contributions from national (60%) and foreign (40%) shareholders.[8] The latter will make their contribution in foreign exchange and will receive profits in proportion to their contributions, i.e. 40%. The effects of this financing on profitability at efficiency prices and the distributional effect can be recorded by including an additional column in Table 9.10 for foreign investors, as shown in Table 9.15. To begin with, we would assume that the foreign investors bring their share in cash and send the income obtained from their investments abroad as they receive it. Thus, they deposit foreign exchange for a domestic currency equivalent of $23,600. In addition, over the useful life of the project, they remit the capital invested that they have recovered, plus profits equivalent to a profitability rate equal to the discount rate, so that at the end of the useful life of the project they will have remitted a *present value* equal to their original investment. Now, as the project's profitability is greater than the discount rate, the foreign investors receive (and remit) 40% of these "excess profits". As both the capital contribution and subsequent remittances constitute flows of foreign exchange, these flows have been corrected by the APRFE and the corresponding transfers allocated to the Government. Note that, assuming that the change in the source of financing has no effect on

---

7. The fact that the "transfer" could be compensated by a higher price for equipment or by payments for technology, does not change this because these payments have already been entered as project costs.

8. The reader should keep in mind that working capital will be financed by short-term credit from the national banking system.

Table 9.13 Distribution of Income Changes from the Project When Long-Term Financing Is External and "Tied" to the Project (In $)

Source	Project	Purchasers of A	Unskilled Workers	Government	Depositors	Total at Efficiency Prices	Foreigner
Sales	630,000	4,200	—	70,754	—	704,954	—
Current Costs and Stocks	−462,200	—	16,512	−19,944	—	−465,632	—
Investment Costs	−145,000	—	1,720	−11,217	—	−154,497	—
Financing							
• Long-term	38,000	—	—	3,800	—	41,800	−38,000
• Short-term	6,500	—	—	—	−6,500	—	—
Direct Taxes	−6,730	—	—	6,730	—	—	—
Total	60,570	4,200	18,232	50,123	−6,500	126,625	−38,000

Source: Tables 9.10 and 9.12.

146

Table 9.14 Financing the Project with Direct Foreign Investment (In $)

Source	Amount	Percentage
Long-term Credits	86,000	59.3
National Shareholders	35,000	24.4
Foreign Shareholders	23,600	16.3
Total	$-145{,}000$	100.0

production and costs, the result is a reduction in benefits at efficiency prices. This reduction is equal to the share of foreign investors in the "excess profits" of the project multiplied by the APRFE.

It could be argued that the investors would not remit all of their income but would reinvest at least part of it instead. Let us assume initially that a certain sum I is invested for a year at profitability rate after taxes q, and that afterwards it will be remitted. Consequently, instead of remitting I_t the foreign investor remits

$$I_{t+1} = I_t(1+q)$$

one year later. The present value of this remittance (R_{t+1}) will be

$$PV(R_{t+1}) = \frac{I_t(1+q)}{(1+d)}$$

in which it can clearly be seen that the present value of the remittance at $t+1$ will be equal to what was not remitted at t when private profitability q is equal to the discount rate. If q were greater than d, the present value of the future remittance would be even greater than the present one and this would even further reduce the benefits at efficiency prices.[9] When reinvestment takes place at profitability q *lower* than the discount rate, it will reduce the foreign exchange cost of remittances. Given the unlikelihood of this situation for plausible discount rate values, the criterion followed in Table 9.15 appears conservative.

Although the aim is not cost-benefit analysis of direct foreign investment, the example given here may cast light on some key variables to be borne in mind during the negotiating process that normally precedes an investment from abroad.[10] Firstly, there is the problem of the so-called "transfer prices" in international transactions. If that were the case, it is obvious that the

---

9. The total effect of re-investment on benefits at efficiency prices will also depend on its profitability at efficiency prices.

10. The interested reader may consult Sen (1971), Weiss (1980) and Kumar (1984).

Table 9.15 Distribution of Income Changes from the Project Financed with Foreign Capital (In $)

Source	Project	Purchasers of A	Unskilled Workers	Government	Depositors	Total at Efficiency Prices	Foreign Investors
Effects of the Project with 100% Domestic Capital	60,570	4,200	18,232	8,323	−6,500	84,825	—
Effect of 40% Foreign Ownership							
• Capital Contribution	23,600	—	—	2,360	—	25,960	23,600
• Capital Recovery	−23,600	—	—	−2,360	—	−25,960	−23,600
• Excess Profits	−24,228	—	—	−2,423	—	−26,651	24,228
Total	36,342	4,200	18,232	5,900	−6,500	58,174	24,228

Source: Tables 9.10 and 9.14.

148

project's purchases or sales should be valued at such prices and not at the "world market" prices, since it is the former that determine effective flows of foreign exchange. Secondly, there is the problem of the valuation of the equipment that may constitute the capital contribution. It is logical to expect the foreign investor to try to overvalue it, since it is the book value (and not the real market value) that becomes the legal basis for the distribution of private profits from the project. Finally, in the example shown, it can clearly be seen that an important part of net income to investors comes from the transfers implicit in financing, this point being of greater importance the lower the real interest rate and the greater the proportion of financing from the national banking system.

CHAPTER 10

SELECTING EXPANSION PLANS FOR ELECTRICITY GENERATION: A COST-BENEFIT APPROACH

10.1 Introduction

The analysis of expansion plans for electricity generating systems is a field in which examples of applied cost-benefit analysis are scarce. In an effort to contribute to discussion, therefore, part of this chapter will deal with this topic.

Cost-benefit analysis, in its traditional form, takes as its point of departure the comparison of situations with and without the project in order to estimate costs and benefits attributable to the course of action consisting in carrying out the project. When the "output" of the project is sold on the market, the price will change by the amount required for the transition from one situation to another, and that price change constitutes the starting point for estimating income changes. Price changes will bring about changes in the production plans of the remaining production units, and in the quantities demanded by

The author is grateful to T. Powers, G. Westley, L. Gutierrez Santos and J. Millan for their comments on a preliminary version of this chapter.

consumers. In particular, changes in production plans are forecast on the basis of the knowledge available concerning the demand function for the product, the respective cost functions and the expected reactions of producers who seek to maximize profits.

In the field of electricity production and distribution, the situation is somewhat different. Production is normally in the hands of very few firms, generally one or two, and there is no market that determines prices equating supply and demand. Prices are fixed by the Government and the firms endeavour to supply the quantity requested at that price, i.e. they are responsible for designing and implementing the expansion plan. Individual projects are part of these plans, and the plans are normally designed to meet expected demand at the lowest possible cost. Since investment, particularly that for generation, features lengthy gestation and maturity periods, long-term planning is practically unavoidable.

If the projection of the quantity demanded is a datum, designing the expansion plan is restricted to seeking a solution that minimizes the economic cost. Conversely, if the objective is to maximize the economic benefits that can be obtained from the resources available, it is necessary to compare the costs and benefits of alternative expansion plans for different projections of the quantity of electricity demanded, and to define the instruments to be used for reaching each projection. When the tariff level is the instrument used, each course of action to be analyzed includes the combination between a tariff level and the associated expansion plans[1] (see Section 10.2). Once the alternatives have been defined, it is possible to compare the economic costs (benefits) resulting from increasing (reducing) the level of tariffs, in order to reduce (increase) the consumption of electricity, with the resulting benefits (costs) in terms of lower (greater) costs associated with expansion of the system. Changes in the forecast of the quantity to be supplied (demanded) normally affect *all* the projects incorporated in the expansion plan. Section 10.3 is therefore devoted to the selection of expansion plans in the framework of cost-benefit analysis when the tariff level is used to adjust the quantity demanded. Connecting new users to the network, or not doing so, as an alternative mechanism, is better dealt with in the analysis of distribution projects.[2] The reliability aspects of the generating sub-system also require separate treatment, although they can be included in the analysis through supply costs (Munasinghe and Gellerson, 1979) or the costs (benefits) to users (Westley, 1981).

The reader will note that in the example presented, some drastic assumptions have been made, particularly with respect to the electricity demand function. This is due to the lack of detailed studies on the topic, which

---

1. See Turvey and Anderson (1977, Chapter 10).
2. Castagnino (1980).

explains why in many cases, the data used reflect the minimum desired, rather than those actually available. As a result, the analysis indicates areas where further research would be desirable.

To determine the expansion plan and the generating costs for each projection of the quantity demanded, the simulation model known as WASP II is used.[3] A simulation model is used because it is a practically irreplaceable tool for the type of results it provides and because many countries in the region have some model of this type. The WASP II model was used because it was the one available to the author at the time the work was carried out.[4] It is a dynamic programming model designed to find the expansion plan for generating capacity that minimizes the present value of the respective investment and operating costs within a set of constraints imposed by the user.

The user has to provide the model with the following main data, among others:

(a) the power and energy requirements as well as the shape of the corresponding load duration curves that the solution has to meet for each period;
(b) the description of the existing generating system, the additions already decided on and the dates on which some plants will be retired;
(c) the type of units that the model has to consider as candidates for the expansion plan, and their characteristics;
(d) the minimum reliability acceptable for the generating system.

The model will produce the configurations (sets of plants) that meet the desired requirements, will calculate the costs associated with each of the possible expansion plans within the constraints imposed, and will select the least cost expansion plan, indicating on what date each of the plants in it has to enter into service.[5] These costs will be calculated at prices (for example, market or accounting prices) that the analyst has used to value the data required by the model.

Based on the results of the analysis described above, Section 10.4 provides an estimate of the distributional effect of the alternative courses of action. For this purpose, beneficiaries have been classified as "low-income persons" and "other private beneficiaries". A person is here said to belong to the low-income group when his per capita disposable income does not exceed a certain limit known as the "low-income level". When a person does not belong to the low-income group, he belongs to the group of "other private beneficiaries".

---

3. The acronym stands for Wien Automatic System Planning Package, a model developed by Jenkins and Joy (1974). See also IAEA (1976).

4. There is now a later version of the model known as WASP III. See IAEA (1980).

5. Readers interested in a more detailed description of the model may consult Jenkins and Joy (1974).

However, it is not only the private sector that receives the impact of the flows of income changes generated by a project or investment program; the public sector is also affected. What matters is how the public sector uses its funds, and how this use affects people's situations. It is nevertheless useful to treat it in the analysis as a separate beneficiary and analyze at the end the distributional impact of the use of its funds. Consequently, we will offer some criteria for quantifying the distribution of income changes between: (i) the low-income group; (ii) the other private beneficiaries; and (iii) the public sector.

Whether to treat the public sector as a single unit or differentiate between some of its parts will have to be decided in each case. However, a crucial element for this type of decision is whether the project or program gives rise to flows of funds from or to the public sector whose use is ear-marked, that is, funds that will only be spent on a defined subset of public activity. The distributional effect of a variation in the availability of funds for use in this subset may differ from the distributional effect of the public sector activity as a whole, and this is a reason for distinguishing between ear-marked public funds and those that are freely disposable. The electricity system whose expansion plan is being analyzed is administered by a public enterprise (henceforth ELEC), responsible for generating, transmitting and distributing electricity. ELEC is the owner of all the generating plants as well as the transmission and distribution grid. The public sector will therefore be subdivided initially into ELEC and the Central Government.

The low-income level is defined here as the annual disposable income *per person* needed to reach a certain per capita consumption level, assuming that all income is spent. Each person whose disposable income (assumed equal to his consumption expenditure) is equal to or less than this level will be considered as "low-income". Furthermore, it should be considered that a person does not necessarily spend for his own consumption all the disposable income that he obtains per given period. He usually puts his earnings into a family budget, and it is from the expenditure of that budget that the consumption level of each of its members is derived. That consumption level is compared with the low-income level established, assuming that each member of the family spends the same amount on consumption.

Consequently, to determine whether or not a person belongs to the low-income group, the income available to his family is divided by the number of members. If this value is less than or equal to the low-income level established, then the person belongs to the low-income group. The relevant disposable income for the classification is the one in the without project situation at the time of the analysis, even if the recipient were above the low-income level in the situation with the project, or in the future. In either of the last two cases, the total increase in his disposable income would be considered as accruing to the low-income group.

153

10.2 Formulating Alternative Expansion Plans

An expansion plan selected by a cost-minimization model involves a set of data that are extraneous to the model itself, such as the projects to be considered, the system's minimum acceptable reliability and the projection of the quantity demanded. However, the results do not show that the benefits resulting from executing the selected expansion plan are higher than the respective costs, since the (WASP II) model does not calculate benefits. Moreover, its use implicitly assumes that, given a level of reliability, the additional benefits from supplying electricity at the pace required by the projection of the quantity demanded instead of at a lower (higher) one are greater than the additional (reduction) costs resulting from supplying the difference between the projection used and a lower (greater) alternative.[6] Cost-benefit analysis, conversely, begins with the following question: are the benefits resulting from supplying an additional amount of electricity at a certain level of reliability greater than the costs required for such a purpose?[7] For this purpose, it is necessary to quantify these benefits and then compare them with the costs of supplying the additional amount of electricity. At the same time, we must specify the means that the electricity firm will use to change the quantity demanded.

The projection of the quantities demanded of power and energy corresponds to certain assumptions concerning the evolution of the tariff level, the expected growth of the population connected to the grid and its per capita income, the pace of urban development, and so on. Although these variables are exogenous to the simulation model, at least one of them is not exogenous to the decision making "model" for expanding the system. This variable is the tariff. An increase in the tariff level will in fact bring about a reduction in the quantity of electricity demanded, which will modify the expansion plan by bringing forward, postponing, replacing or eliminating projects, thus giving rise to an alternative expansion plan at lower cost. Accordingly, it is reasonable to ask whether it is worth implementing the expansion plan initially selected by the simulation model, as opposed to the alternative of raising tariffs, executing the second lowest-cost plan, and thus releasing resources to carry out for example, other projects which have been marginally displaced from the budget. The effect that a given reduction in the quantities demanded of power and energy has on the alternative expansion plan will determine the savings in investment and operating costs associated with the tariff increase,

---

6. The same type of assumption is present in comparisons between hydro-electric power stations and "equivalent" thermal developments, as explained in van der Tak (1966).

7. In this analysis, the reliability level was imposed as an exogenous variable, which is equivalent to assuming that the cost to the user of increasing it is equal to the cost of avoiding the increase. For an approach that includes the cost of unserved energy, see Munasinghe (1979) and Munasinghe and Gellerson (1979).

Table 10.1   Main Effects of a Tariff Increase

Source	ELEC	Customers	Total
ELEC Cost Savings	$+ \Delta FCEP$	$-$	$+ \Delta FCEP$
Market Value of Reduction $G_0 - G_1$	$- G_1ACG_0$	$+ G_1ACG_0$	$-$
Increase in the Market Value of G_1	$+ p_1BAp_0$	$- p_1BAp_0$	$-$
Willingness to Pay for $G_0 - G_1$	$-$	$- G_1BCG_0$	$- G_1BCG_0$

Source: Figure 10.1.

which can be compared with the losses experienced due to the reduction in electricity consumption. In other words, a tariff level p_0 over a period of time is associated with a projection of the quantity demanded $G(p_0)$, which corresponds to a least cost expansion plan EP_0 whose total economic cost (including investment and operating costs until the user is reached) is CEP_0. If the tariff level increases to $p_1 > p_0$, the projection of the quantity of electricity demanded will diminish to $G(p_1) < G(p_0)$, for which there will exist an associated expansion plan EP_1 with economic cost CEP_1. In schematic form

$$\left.\begin{array}{l} p_0 \rightarrow G(p_0) \rightarrow EP_0 \rightarrow CEP_0 \\ p_1 \rightarrow G(p_1) \rightarrow EP_1 \rightarrow CEP_1 \end{array}\right] CEP_0 > CEP_1$$

the increase in the tariff $\Delta p = p_1 - p_0$ gives rise to a reduction in consumption $\Delta G = G(p_0) - G(p_1)$ and consequently to a fall in the economic cost of expansion plan ΔCEP.

It will now be useful to analyze the main effects of a tariff increase, concentrating on the flows valued at the prices paid by the two main parties directly affected: ELEC and its customers. It has already been pointed out that an increase in tariff levels will bring about a reduction in the quantity of electricity demanded, which in turn will give rise to a new expansion plan. The reduction in the financial cost of the expansion plan ($\Delta FCEP = FCEP_0 - FCEP_1$) will be a saving of funds for ELEC.[8] For this reason, a positive value for ELEC equal to $\Delta FCEP$ is shown in Table 10.1, which outlines the effects of the tariff increase. For the remaining flows brought about by the tariff increase, Figure 10.1 is used. In addition to the reduction in costs $\Delta FCEP$, ELEC will stop receiving (the present value of) annual income G_1ACG_0 due to lower sales, but will receive p_1BAp_0 due to higher prices. The consumers undergo a loss measured by the CV of the tariff increase and estimated by the area p_1BCp_0. This can be broken down into the additional cost of energy G_1, which they consume with the tariff increase (p_1BAp_0), plus the difference between their willingness to pay for the energy

---

8. "Financial costs" is the term used for cost valued at the prices actually paid by ELEC.

Figure 10.1 Electricity Demand

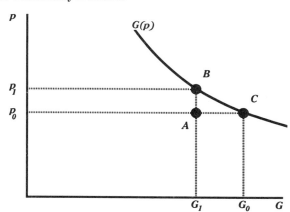

that they stop consuming (G_1BCG_0) and what is actually paid for it (G_1ACG_0). According to efficiency analysis distributional value judgments, the net economic effect of the project is the present value of the sum of the CVs of effects on ELEC and consumers each year, plus the net balance of transfers explaining the discrepancy between prices paid and efficiency prices. The tariff increase will be appropriate if this present value is positive, that is, if the loss resulting from increasing the tariff by $p_1 - p_0$ is less than the saving in costs ΔCEP.

For the above layout, we need to know the form of demand function $G(p)$ and to have a method for calculating the costs CEP associated with each expansion plan. The second problem is solved by the WASP II model as regards the generating sub-system, but needs to be completed with estimates for transmission and distribution costs.

The following presents what proved to be possible regarding the demand function $G(p)$. A tariff increase does not only affect the maximum power demanded each day but also off-peak demand. Consequently, it is possible that the tariff change, in this case one that does not distinguish the time at which a Kwh is consumed, will modify the shape of the daily load curve and consequently the annual load duration curve.[9] Very few studies exist on the effect on hourly demand of changing a tariff that makes no distinction between hours of the day. Those that do exist do not seem to offer decisive conclusions on whether or not there are important differences in price elasticity for the peak, middle and the bottom of the load curve. In this example, it is assumed that a variation of $X\%$ in the tariff affects the power demand by $Y\%$

---

9. In other words power demand functions $DMW_h = f_h(p)$ exist for each hour h of the day.

whatever the time of day and, consequently, the tariff changes do not affect the shape of the load duration curve.

The next problem to be solved can be expressed in two questions: (a) what is the effect of an increase of $X\%$ in the tariff on the quantity demanded? and (b) given that the adjustment of the quantity demanded to the tariff change is not immediate, how soon is it necessary to increase the tariff to achieve the desired reduction in demand ($Y\%$) on the date required? The first question refers to the long-run price elasticity of demand and the second to the transitional period between the short-run and long-run adjustments, matters that will be discussed below.

Most of the studies on electricity demand functions that have been carried out up to now deal with developed countries.[10] While conducting a recent study by the Bank, Westley (1981) found that with the exception of a study for a Colombian city, there were no detailed econometric studies on electricity demand functions for countries in the region. Until the results of such studies become available and, hopefully, some conclusions can be drawn from them on a plausible range of values for price elasticity,[11] the lack of data leaves us no alternative but to abandon attempts to carry out a cost-benefit analysis or base them on tentative judgments on the value of price elasticity. Here the second alternative has been adopted, since the objective is to illustrate the estimation of the distribution of costs and *benefits*.

According to estimates by Westley (1981), the long-run price elasticity of demand for electric energy by the residential and commercial sectors of Paraguay is between -0.40 and -0.60, the author leaning towards the top end of the range. A subsequent study on Costa Rica (Westley, 1984) found values between -0.45 and -0.55 for the price elasticity of residential demand and between -0.40 and 0.60 for commercial demand. Given the lack of a specific study for the country corresponding to the case examined, a value of -0.60 will be used for the demand of each of these sectors in this study and, for the same reason, for the industrial sector.[12]

Both the results of econometric studies and common sense indicate that price elasticity in the short run is considerably lower than that in the long run. In the first case, the consumer can only vary the utilization rate of a given stock of electricity-consuming equipment, whereas he requires more time to adjust the stock of equipment to changes in the relative prices of available

---

10. The interested reader may consult Taylor (1975) and Bohi (1981).

11. In the United States, the results obtained in recent studies for the long-run price elasticity of residential demand generally fall within the range -0.45 to -1.20. Bohi (1981) sets forth arguments for tending towards an absolute value of less than one.

12. According to Bohi (1981), the studies on commercial demand are less numerous and reliable than those on residential demand. As regards industrial demand, studies seem to show that it is more price elastic than residential demand, although this author presents arguments on possible upward biases in the estimation of the price elasticity of industrial demand.

energy sources. Accordingly, it is logical to expect that in response to a tariff increase, in the first year, the quantity demanded will be reduced by a lesser quantity than that indicated by long-run elasticity. The difference between the short-run and the long-run adjustment will take place gradually over the following years. This raises the problem of the length of time required for the adjustment, which will depend on the useful life of the electricity-consuming equipment and on the possibility of replacing it by other equipment that uses alternative energy sources. This aspect is analyzed later where an alternative projection of the quantity demanded is given.

We will assume that the Government's consumption is insensitive to tariff changes. This appears reasonable considering that the consumption of public enterprises is included in that corresponding to the industrial tariff, and that reductions are not expected in electricity consumption for public lighting or in public offices, hospitals, schools and so on.

As for the tariff, this consists of a fixed (f) and a variable (p) charge. In this case, the total cost to the user of the electricity consumed (C) will be

$$C(Kwh) = f + p \, Kwh$$

while in simplified form, $B(Kwh)$ will be the total benefits that the user obtains from the Kwh consumed. The net benefits $B-C$ that the customer obtains from electricity consumption will be at a maximum when $B' = C'$, (in which $'$ indicates the first derivative with respect to Kwh) that is,

$$B'(Kwh) = C'(Kwh) = p$$

This simplified formulation is presented in Figure 10.2(a), where it can be observed that a change in the fixed charge from f_0 to f_1 (parallel displacement of C) does not change the Kwh demanded by the client, which depend on variable charge p (Figure 10.2(b)), although it does reduce the customer's total benefits and increases the electricity firm's revenue.[13] However, a substantial increase in the fixed charge—such as to f_2 in Figure 10.2(a)—could result in the customer ceasing to demand electricity, because the total benefit he obtains is less than the total respective cost. In the case in hand, the objective is to reduce customers' demand for energy (and power) and not to increase the income of the firm or restrict the number of customers. Consequently, only the variable component of the tariff will be increased. In other words, the "marginal" price or rather the marginal cost of a Kwh for the user will increase.

---

13. This is valid only for small changes in the fixed charge since it ignores the income effect caused by increasing it.

Figure 10.2 Effects on Consumption of Changes in the Fixed and Variable Charges

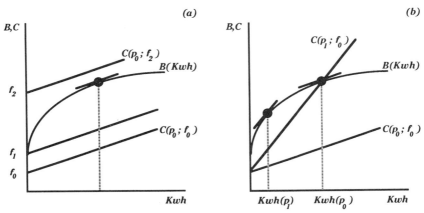

The above applies to tariffs for the residential and commercial sectors. In the industrial sector, the tariff includes a charge for the maximum power demanded during the day plus a charge per Kwh consumed. An increase in the charge per Kwh does not take into account at what time of the day this Kwh is demanded and will tend to reduce the energy (and power) demand at all times. Conversely, the effect of an increase in the charge for power can be broken down into two parts: (a) hourly reallocation of daily consumption; and (b) a reduction in daily consumption due to inflexibility in the hourly consumption pattern. In this case, it is assumed that only the energy charge of the industrial tariff would be increased.

Table 10.2 presents data on the variable component in tariffs according to class of customer. For residential customers, the variable component changes according to the consumption block the user is in. For this reason, and in order to facilitate subsequent estimation of the distributional effect, a distinction has been made between two groups: (a) low-income residential customers; and (b) other residential customers. The first group was defined in the

Table 10.2 Variable Charges by Group of Customers (In $/Kwh)

Customers	Tariff in Effect
Low-Income Residential	0.043
Remainder of Residential	0.049
Commercial	0.063
Industrial	0.052

159

following way. The electricity consumption of people at the low-income level was determined on the basis of the Kwh/year consumption by income brackets according to data from a household survey on income and expenditure. Then, anyone whose consumption was less than or equal to that of the low-income level according to the survey data, was defined as a low-income customer. The rest of the energy consumed by the residential sector was allocated to the "remainder of residential customers" group. Note that this approach has some weaknesses. A vacation home will have a low annual consumption, even though its owner is not a low-income person. In the same way, a low-income person who has a small business or workshop at home that makes intensive use of electricity will have high consumption and will not appear in the low-income group. A better procedure would be to use the survey to estimate the percentage of residential consumption corresponding to low-income customers, which was not possible in this case.

The average variable charge ($\bar{p}$) per group of customers (c) was calculated as

$$\bar{p}_c = \frac{\sum_i p_{ci} g_{ci}}{\sum_i g_{ci}}$$

in which p_{ci} is the variable charge paid by consumer i from class c and g_{ci} is the energy purchased by this consumer.[14] It is to these tariffs that the projection of the quantity demanded corresponds. That projection, presented in Table 10.3, is the one that determines the expansion plan being analyzed.

For the purposes of comparing the existing expansion plan with alternative courses of action consisting of reducing the quantity demanded by increasing the variable tariff charge, four alternative projections were worked out. Each of these will give rise to alternative expansion plans, called alternative plans (AP). The tariff increases considered and their effects on the quantity demanded are shown in Table 10.4.

The long-run effect of the tariff increase on the quantity of electricity consumed can be calculated on the basis of the formula for long-run price elasticity of demand

$$E^t = \frac{p_0}{G^t(p_0)} \frac{G^t(p_1) - G^t(p_0)}{p_1 - p_0} \qquad [10.1]$$

---

14. Appendix C presents the assumptions implied in the use of this average.

Table 10.3 Projection of Energy Demanded by Group of Customers (Gwh at the plant)

Year	Residential		Commercial	Industrial	Government		Total
	Low-Income	Remainder			Public Lighting	Remainder	
1981	91.1	820.1	306.9	948.3	33.0	246.0	2,445.4
1982	98.8	889.5	334.8	1,044.1	34.2	266.9	2,668.3
1983	107.5	967.4	366.3	1,152.7	35.4	290.4	2,919.7
1984	116.8	1,051.3	400.7	1,272.5	36.6	316.0	3,193.9
1985	128.2	1,153.9	442.4	1,417.6	38.1	345.1	3,525.3
1986	140.7	1,266.3	488.4	1,579.2	39.6	376.8	3,891.0
1987	154.6	1,390.9	539.2	1,759.2	41.2	411.5	4,296.6
1988	169.5	1,525.6	595.3	1,959.8	42.8	449.3	4,742.3
1989	186.4	1,677.4	657.2	2,183.2	44.5	490.7	5,239.4
1990	204.3	1,838.2	725.5	2,432.1	46.3	535.8	5,782.2
1991	223.8	2,014.6	801.0	2,709.4	48.2	585.1	6,382.1
1992	245.9	2,213.1	884.3	3,018.2	50.1	639.0	7,050.6
1993	269.4	2,424.1	976.3	3,362.3	52.1	697.7	7,781.9
1994	294.8	2,653.3	1,077.8	3,745.6	54.2	761.9	8,587.6
1995	323.4	2,910.4	1,189.9	4,172.6	56.3	832.0	9,484.6
1996	354.4	3,189.5	1,313.6	4,648.3	58.6	908.6	10,473.0
1997	387.7	3,489.3	1,450.3	5,178.2	60.9	992.2	11,558.6
1998	424.8	3,823.0	1,601.1	5,768.5	63.4	1,083.4	12,764.2
1999	464.7	4,182.4	1,767.6	6,426.1	65.9	1,183.1	14,089.8
2000	508.2	4,573.5	1,951.4	7,158.7	68.6	1,292.0	15,552.4

161

Table 10.4 Tariff Increases and Their Effects
on the Quantity Demanded

Expansion Plans	Tariff Increase[a] (in percentages)	Long-run Reduction in Consumption[b]	
		Mwh	MW
AP_1	4.4	57,193	10
AP_2	8.8	114,387	20
AP_3	13.2	171,579	30
AP_4	17.6	228,771	40

a. At the beginning of 1981.
b. Mwh and MW at the plant.

in which $G^t(p)$ is the long-run demand function in year t. Assuming that the long-run demand function is linear, and that it shifts parallel over time[15] (Figure 10.3), the long-run effect of the tariff increase on the quantity of electricity consumed will be constant and can be estimated on the basis of [10.1] as

$$G(p_1) - G(p_0) = \frac{(p_1 - p_0) E^t G^t(p_0)}{p_0}$$

bearing in mind that consumption $G^t(p_0)$ corresponds to the same year t as the estimation of E^t.

To prepare the alternative projections of the quantity demanded, we should first consider the short-run adjustment and the process of transition to the long-run position. To do this, it is useful to break down the electricity demanded by a consumer in period t, which begins with the tariff increase. Without the tariff increase, the quantity demanded will be given by:

(a) the previous year's stock of electrical equipment $Kw_{t-1}(p_0)$, the volume and composition of which is adjusted to tariffs p_0, and the use $H_{t-1}(p_0)$ of this equipment in the previous period;
(b) the increase in the utilization of old stock $\Delta H(p_0)$ due to, for example, an increase in consumer's income;
(c) the increase in the stock of equipment $\Delta Kw(p_0)$ during year t and its utilization $H^n(p_0)$.

15. It is assumed that the shift of the demand function for a given price brings together the effects of the increases in consumption per customer and the number of customers. Results for other assumptions on the shape and displacement of the demand function can be obtained by using the SIMOP model. See Powers and Valencia (1978).

Figure 10.3 Electricity Demand Function and Its Displacement

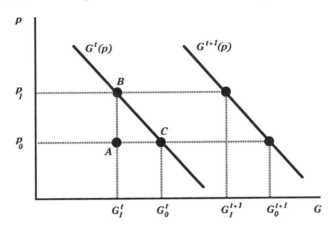

Thus, consumer's demand for electricity in year t (G_t) will be:

$$G_t(p_0) = Kw_{t-1}(p_0)\, H_{t-1}(p_0) + Kw_{t-1}(p_0)\, \Delta H(p_0)$$
$$+ \Delta Kw(p_0)\, H^n(p_0)$$

[10.2]

In response to a tariff increase, the consumer would like to be able to:

(a) adjust his old stock of equipment $Kw_{t-1}(p_0)$ to the new tariff level;
(b) adjust the use he made of his stock of old equipment $H_{t-1}(p_0)$ to one that reflects the effect of the tariff increase $H_{t-1}(p_1)$;
(c) reduce partially or totally the planned increase in this use to $\Delta H(p_1) < \Delta H(p_0)$;
(d) reduce partially or totally the planned increase in his stock of equipment to $\Delta Kw(p_1) < \Delta Kw(p_0)$;
(e) If $\Delta Kw(p_1)$ is not nil, adjust use $H^n(p_0)$ to $H^n(p_1)$.

Although the above outline is a simplification that leaves aside interaction between use and stock, it enables us to discuss possible adjustments in response to a tariff increase. The old stock of equipment cannot be adjusted rapidly and it is likely that the change in its composition will occur gradually as it is renewed; in other words, this is an adjustment that will take time. Conversely, the use of this stock can be adjusted rapidly. In this regard, the consumer may reduce both the use he made the previous year and the respective planned increase $\Delta H(p_0)$. It is only the first of these effects that is shown

163

by the short-run price elasticity, since the demand function assumes that all other variables (such as income) that give rise to ΔH remain constant. The latter (ΔH) will be one of those most drastically reduced, since it is to be expected that these are less "valuable" Kwh than the previous ones. Finally, the additional stock of equipment (ΔKw) and its planned use (H^n) can be adjusted to the new tariff level. Here too drastic reductions ought to be expected since the consumer would be including equipment whose services would be less "valuable" than those he obtains from the old stock.

Since there are no data on the aspects mentioned above, we will have to make some assumptions on the type of adjustment expected. In the case of residential demand, we assume that:

(a) short-run price elasticity is half that in the long-run;
(b) the consumption of old customers grows by 2% per year;[16]
(c) the increase in the consumption of old customers is reduced by two-thirds.
(d) new consumers adjust in accordance with long-run elasticity.

From the above, we can conclude that in the first year, approximately 60% of the long-run effect takes place. Since an important part of the previous adjustment will come from changes in the composition of equipment stocks, it is to be expected that subsequent reductions will be considerably smaller. These reductions are assumed to be 20% of the long-run effect in each of the following two years. In the commercial sector, there are no major possibilities for replacing energy sources. Adjustment will be determined by the effect of the tariff increase, through the prices of goods and services, on the volume of commercial transactions, and by the reduction in the utilization level of the stock of equipment for a given volume of sales, effects which will soon be felt. If this is the case, the adjustment pattern in the commercial sector should not differ much from the residential sector and would probably even be shorter. We will assume here that it is equal to that of the residential sector.

The industrial tariff increase will result in an increase in prices. The consequent reduction in the quantities of products demanded will reduce the expected use of installed capacity from the previous year, $H_{t-1}(p_0) + \Delta H(p_0)$ in expression [10.2], and that of the capacity introduced in the year of the increase $(H^n(p_0))$ since investments were decided on beforehand. In other words, the impossibility of postponing increases in capacity whose entry into operation was decided for the year in which the tariff increase is effected will be compensated by a reduction in the planned utilization levels $(H_{t-1}, \Delta H$ and $H^n)$ imposed by the reduction in the quantities demanded of products. Given

---

16. Consumption growth rate for a given tariff level when the customer is in a long-run equilibrium position.

that the average useful life of industrial equipment is longer than that of residential equipment, adjusting the composition of the stock to adapt to the new prices will take longer. However, it must be noted that this substitution will only be important for those industries in which electrical energy is a significant proportion of costs. Considering that almost all industry in the country in question is light industry, we will assume that the adjustment is completed in five years in the following sequence: 50% of the long-run adjustment in the first year, followed by 20% the next year, and 10% in each of the three remaining years.

The basic information for preparing alternative projections is given in Table 10.5. In that table, the reduction in the quantity of electricity demanded is expressed in Mwh consumed, while the WASP model has to be provided with the energy demanded at the plants. In other words, the data must be adjusted for transmission and distribution losses. In the case in hand, 1.16 net Mwh has to be generated for each Mwh consumed by the residential and commer-

Table 10.5 Data Used to Estimate the Effects of the Tariff Increase

| | ELEC Customers | | | | |
| | Low-Income Residential | Remainder of Residential | Commercial | Industrial | Total |
Data Used					
E (absolute value)	0.60	0.60	0.60	0.60	
$(1 + tdl)G_0^{81}$ (In Mwh at the plant)[a]	91,100	820,100	306,900	946,900	2,166,400
G_0^{81} (Mwh consumed)	78,535	706,983	264,569	839,204	1,889,291
p_0 (in \$/Mwh)	43	49	63	52	
Increase of 4.4%					
$p_1 - p_0$	1.892	2.156	2.772	2.288	
$G_0 - G_1$[b]	2,073	18,664	6,985	22,155	49,877
Increase of 8.8%					
$p_1 - p_0$	3.784	4.312	5.544	4.576	
$G_0 - G_1$[b]	4,147	37,329	13,969	44,310	99,755
Increase of 13.2%					
$p_1 - p_0$	5.676	6.468	8.316	6.864	
$G_0 - G_1$[b]	6,220	55,993	20,954	66,465	149,632
Increase of 17.6%					
$p_1 - p_0$	7.568	8.624	11.088	9.152	
$G_0 - G_1$[b]	8,293	74,657	27,938	88,620	199,508

a. tdl = transmission and distribution losses as a proportion of energy consumed.
b. Final long-run effect, in Mwh consumed.

Table 10.6 Effects of an 8.8% Tariff Increase on Quantity Demanded

Effects on	1981	1982	1983	1984	1985
Consumption (in Mwh)	−55,421	−75,373	−90,893	−95,324	−99,755
Generation (in Mwh)[a]	−63,624	−86,502	−104,372	−109,380	−114,387
Power (in MW)[b]	−11.1	−15.1	−18.3	−19.1	−20.0

a. Net generation required from plants.
b. Net power required from plants.

cial sectors and 1.13 Mwh for each Mwh consumed by the industrial sector.[17] Finally, Table 10.6 shows the annual reductions expected in the quantity demanded in the case of an 8.8% increase in the tariff level.

Each of the alternative projections for the quantity demanded gives rise to its corresponding expansion plan, presented in Table 10.7, which shows that the main immediate effect of plans AP_2, AP_3 and AP_4 is to postpone the entry into operation of a 120-Mw thermal power station and to advance by a year the entry into operation of the first hydro-electric project.[18] Conversely, the tariff increase in AP_1 (4.4%) is small enough not to introduce changes in the expansion plan until 1994. In the following section, we will consider the comparison of expansion plans for the purposes of selecting the best one according to the assumptions and value judgments of efficiency analysis.

10.3 Comparison of Expansion Plans

We now have the expansion plans corresponding to five projections of the quantity demanded. The first is the original projection, which led to the expansion plan being analyzed. The remainder correspond to alternative projections, resulting from the tariff increases shown in Table 10.5.

Table 10.8 shows the present value of the investment, fuel, operating and maintenance costs of the generating sub-system for each of the projections of the quantity demanded, expressed at efficiency prices. Note that the alternative expansion plans result in considerable savings in relation to the original expansion plan. However, these are not all the cost savings that can be expected since there will also be savings in the transmission and distribution sub-systems. The total cost savings valued at efficiency prices for each alternative to replace the existing expansion plan are presented in Table 10.9.

As Section 10.2 pointed out, the tariff increase affects customers and ELEC as indicated in Table 10.1. That level of disaggregation of the effect of the

---

17. The smaller losses for industrial consumption are due to the fact that part of the energy is supplied at medium voltage.
18. The entry into operation of a 125-Mw thermal power station in 1982 corresponds to a project already being carried out and its entry date was imposed on the model as a constraint.

166

Table 10.7 Alternative Expansion Plans
(In number of accumulated units)

Year	Existing Plan				AP₁				AP₂				AP₃				AP₄			
	VP2H	VP1H	GA25	VHYD	VP2H	VP1H	GA25	VHYD	VP2H	VP1H	GA25	VHYD	VP2H	VP1H	GA25	VHYD	VP2H	VP1H	GA25	VHYD
2000	14	6	1	2	15	4	1	2	15	4	1	2	15	3	0	2	14	5	2	2
1999	12	6	0	2	13	4	0	2	13	4	0	2	14	2	0	2	12	5	1	2
1998	10	6	0	2	11	4	0	2	11	4	0	2	12	2	0	2	10	5	1	2
1997	8	6	0	2	10	3	0	2	9	4	0	2	11	1	0	2	8	5	1	2
1996	7	5	0	2	8	3	0	2	8	3	0	2	9	1	0	2	7	4	1	2
1995	6	4	0	2	7	3	0	2	7	2	0	2	8	1	0	2	6	3	1	2
1994	6	2	0	2	5	3	0	2	6	2	0	2	6	1	0	2	5	3	0	2
1993	5	1	0	2	5	1	0	2	5	1	0	2	5	1	0	2	4	3	0	2
1992	4	1	0	2	4	1	0	2	4	1	0	2	4	1	0	2	3	2	0	2
1991	3	1	0	2	3	1	0	2	3	1	0	2	3	1	0	2	2	2	0	2
1990	2	1	0	2	2	1	0	2	2	1	0	2	2	1	0	2	2	2	0	2
1989	2	1	0	2	2	1	0	2	2	1	0	2	2	1	0	2	1	2	0	2
1988	2	1	0	2	2	1	0	1	2	1	0	2	2	1	0	2	1	2	0	2
1987	2	1	0	1	2	1	0	1	2	1	0	1	2	1	0	1	1	2	0	1
1986	2	0	0	1	2	0	0	0	1	1	0	1	1	1	0	1	1	1	0	1
1985	2	0	0	0	2	0	0	0	1	0	0	1	1	0	0	1	1	0	0	1
1984	2	0	0	0	2	0	0	0	1	0	0	0	1	0	0	0	1	0	0	1
1983	1	0	0	0	1	0	0	0	1	0	0	0	1	0	0	0	1	0	0	0
1982	1	0	0	0	1	0	0	0	1	0	0	0	1	0	0	0	1	0	0	0
1981	0	0	0	0	0	0	0	0	0	0	0	0	0	0	0	0	0	0	0	0

VP2H: Thermal steam plants of 125 Mw.
VP1H: Thermal steam plants of 75 Mw.
GA25: Gas turbines of 25 Mw.
VHYD: Hydroelectric power stations.

Table 10.8   Investment and Operating Costs of the Generating Sub-System for Alternative Expansion Plans, at Efficiency Prices (In thousands of $)

Expansion Plan	Investment Costs[a]	Fuel, Operation & Maintenance Costs	Total
Existing	336,008	808,297	1,144,305
AP_1	334,645	795,665	1,130,310
AP_2	329,481	780,384	1,109,865
AP_3	327,812	768,065	1,095,877
AP_4	324,521	756,887	1,081,408

a. Net of residual values of the plants after the year 2000.

Table 10.9   Present Value of Savings at Efficiency Prices for Alternative Expansion Plans (In thousands of $)

Savings in Costs	AP_1	AP_2	AP_3	AP_4
Generation				
• Investment	1,363	6,527	8,196	11,487
• Fuel, Operation & Maintenance Costs	12,632	27,913	40,232	51,410
Transmission and Distribution				
• Investment	4,057	8,114	12,172	16,229
• Operation & Maintenance Costs	2,131	4,261	6,392	8,522
Total	20,183	46,815	66,992	87,648

tariff increase is useful for distributional analysis. For the selection of the expansion plan according to the efficiency criterion, it is sufficient to value energy $G_0^t - G_1^t$ (see Figure 10.1) in accordance with willingness to pay for the reduction in consumption in each year t.[19] This willingness to pay will be measured according to the customers' actual substitution, reflected in the slope of the demand curve resulting from the adjustment they were able to make in their stock of equipment during the previous period.

---

19. If the market prices of the alternative sources of energy differed considerably from their efficiency prices, the use of willingness to pay would include an error; the bigger this price difference and the bigger the substitution brought about by the tariff change, the bigger this error would be.

Figure 10.4 Adjustment to a Tariff Increase

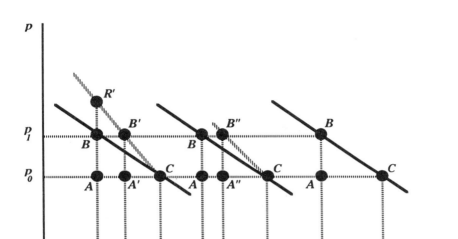

The example of Figure 10.4, which reflects the adjustment of a residential customer over a period of three years, will clarify the above. At time $t = 1$, when tariff increase $p_1 - p_0$ occurs, if the consumer could adjust his stock of equipment immediately, he would be prepared to forego the consumption of other goods up to a maximum of $G_1^1 ABCG_0^1$, provided that he did not do without $G_0 - G_1$ units of energy. However, he does not adjust his stock of equipment immediately and this stock will initially be higher than desired at the new tariff p_1. Until he adjusts his stock to the desired level (for example, by replacing his refrigerator with one that consumes less for the same cooling capacity), the reduction $G_0^1 - G_1^1$ in energy consumption will be more valuable than it would be if the adjustment had already been made (and with the more efficient refrigerator, he could chill to the same degree with less energy consumption). This is why, if it were necessary, in year $t = 1$ he would forego as much as $G_1^1 R' C G_0^1$ of other goods before doing without $G_0 - G_1^1$. Given that for $G_1' - G_1^1$ he has to pay less ($G_1^1 BB' G_1'$) than what he is willing to pay, he consumes these units and substitutes only those ($G_0^1 - G_1'$) whose value in terms of other goods that year ($G_1' A' B' C G_0^1$) is less than the new price p_1. In the following period ($t = 2$) the consumer has been able to partially adjust his

Table 10.10 Comparison of Alternative Expansion Plans[a]
(In thousands of $)

Present Value of Effects of the Tariff Increase	AP_1	AP_2	AP_3	AP_4
Value of the Reduction in Electricity Consumption	−20,164	−41,203	−63,097	−85,866
Cost Savings	20,183	46,815	66,992	87,648
Total	19	5,612	3,895	1,782

a. Plans AP_i correspond to increases in the tariff level of 4.4%, 8.8%, 13.2% and 17.6%, respectively.

stock of equipment, which improves his substitution possibilities. For this reason, he substitutes some additional units of electricity. Thus, in year $t = 2$ he reduces his electricity consumption by $G_0^2 - G_1''$ units for a total value of $G_1'' B'' CG_0^2$ in terms of other goods. In other words, the value the consumer attributes to a unit less of energy depends on the adjustment he actually made in his stock of equipment, and that adjustment takes time. As a result, the value of the energy no longer consumed can be calculated in the following way:

Year 1 $\frac{1}{2}(p_1 + p_0)(G_0^1 - G_1')$
Year 2 $\frac{1}{2}(p_1 + p_0)(G_0^2 - G_1'')$
Year 3 $\frac{1}{2}(p_1 + p_0)(G_0^3 - G_1^3)$

This has been the method used in this study. Values $p_1 + p_0$ for each alternative and the respective annual reductions in energy consumption come from Tables 10.5 and 10.6. On the basis of these data, we calculated the present value of the flows corresponding to willingness to pay for the difference between the electricity that would be used under the existing plan and the electricity that would be used with the tariff increases described above. The results appear in the first row of Table 10.10 as the value of the reduction in electricity consumption. The second row shows the savings in generating, transmission and distribution costs for each alternative brought about by the supply of a smaller quantity of electrical energy. These savings exceed customers' willingness to pay for that energy in any of the four alternatives studied. It is therefore advisable, on the basis of the "efficiency" criterion, to increase the tariff and modify the existing expansion plan. However, AP_2 is better than the three remaining plans in terms of this criterion, in that the tariff level can be increased by 9% with advantages in relation to increases of 4%,

13% and 18%. The estimate of the distributional effect, which will be made in the following section, will be based on plan AP_2.[20]

10.4 Distributional Effect of Tariff Increases

The distributional effect generated by the saving in investment and operating costs of the generating, transmission and distribution sub-systems can be traced to two main points:

(a) who stops paying (saves) these costs, valued at the prices actually paid; and
(b) who receives or grants the transfers that explain the difference between market and efficiency prices.

For the corresponding allocation, it is necessary, therefore, to know the cost saving (corresponding to the tariff increase being analyzed) valued at the prices paid, these savings valued at efficiency prices and the transfers that explain the difference.

The valuation criteria used for costs can be summarized as follows:

(a) traded goods and services were broken down into foreign exchange, which was corrected by the respective APRFE, and other domestic costs, which were added to non-traded goods (as a public enterprise, ELEC is exempt from the payment of import taxes);
(b) non-traded goods and services were valued at their market prices;
(c) unskilled labor was valued at its wages in alternative employment; and
(d) skilled labor was valued at its market wages.

The APRFE was calculated on the basis of expression [3.33] already presented in Section 3.5, that is

$$\text{APRFE} = \frac{M + T_m + X - T_x}{M + X}$$

in which M is the CIF value of imports, X is the FOB value of exports, T_m is revenue from import taxes and T_x is the revenue from taxes (net of subsidies) on exports. The resulting APRFE was 1.15.

The investment cost at efficiency prices of the generating sub-system for

---

20. Appendix D shows the relation between the approach followed in this section and the long-run marginal cost tariff.

each expansion plan is provided by the WASP II model, but no simple method exists for obtaining this cost at the prices paid. Furthermore, there is no way of identifying transfers.[21] For this reason, in this case we could only make a rough estimate of the breakdown of investment costs at efficiency prices, and from there, estimate costs valued at prices paid, bearing in mind that purchases by ELEC are exempt from import tariffs. In the case of fuel, operating and maintenance costs, the main source of discrepancies lies in the price of fuel. However, it is possible here to estimate transfers by using data provided by the WASP II model. For fuel, operating and maintenance costs, the model provides the annual expenditure flow classified as external and internal expenditure. Since the model treats operating and maintenance costs as domestic expenditures, these components can be separated by entering in the data files expenditure on fuel as foreign expenditure.

The results are shown in Table 10.11, where the savings in investment costs, like the others, have been broken down into foreign exchange, unskilled labor and other domestic costs. The first have been corrected in accordance with the APRFE, while for the other domestic costs, market prices have been accepted as being equal to their efficiency prices. In the case of unskilled labor, no detailed estimate is available of its accounting price. So, the wages paid were compared with the prevailing wages in the informal sector for similar activities, the latter proving to be approximately 60% of the wages paid for project activities. This wage in the informal sector was interpreted as the CV of the corresponding job or minimum income required to accept a job in project work, so the remaining 40% is additional income for these workers.

The Government pays a 10% subsidy on the fuel used by ELEC, which is imported at the margin. This subsidy is paid directly to the refinery according to its sales to ELEC. For this reason, Table 10.11 shows a present value of 2,141 for the Government for the subsidies that it will not have to pay due to the fuel saving.

The estimated breakdown of the savings in investment, transmission and distribution costs was based on data from projects being carried out. The components were then valued at efficiency prices, recording the respective transfers. The operating and maintenance costs of the generating sub-system have been broken down into foreign exchange and other internal costs (the unskilled labor element is practically nil) and valued in the same way as the previous cases.

To choose between the alternative expansion plans, the analysis concen-

---

21. Costs at prices paid could be obtained by replacing the unit costs ($/Kw, $/Kwh) in the WASP data files and making the model consider only the sequence of plants integrating each plan. It would be possible in this way to quantify the total of transfers but not to identify them.

Table 10.11   Breakdown of the Present Value of Cost Savings Valued at Efficiency Prices (In thousands of $)

Cost Savings	ELEC	Government	Unskilled Workers	Total at Efficiency Prices
Generation				
Investments	6,146	553	−172	6,527
• Foreign Exchange	3,688	553	—	4,241
• Unskilled Labor	430	—	−172	258
• Other Domestic Costs	2,028	—	—	2,028
Fuel	21,414	5,626	—	27,040
• Foreign Exchange	23,235	3,485	—	26,720
• Subsidies	−2,141	2,141	—	—
• Other Domestic Costs	320	—	—	320
Operation and Maintenance	821	52	—	873
• Foreign Exchange	346	52	—	398
• Other Domestic Costs	475	—	—	475
Transmission and Distribution				
Investment	7,615	743	−244	8,114
• Foreign Exchange	4,950	743	—	5,693
• Unskilled Labor	609	—	−244	365
• Other Domestic Costs	2,056	—	—	2,056
Operation and Maintenance	4,153	324	−216	4,261
• Foreign Exchange	2,160	324	—	2,484
• Unskilled Labor	540	—	−216	324
• Other Domestic Costs	1,453	—	—	1,453
Total	40,149	7,298	−632	46,815

trated on ELEC's cost savings and users' willingness to pay for the reduction in electricity consumption. Since estimating the distributional effect means estimating the income changes of the main parties involved, the appropriate starting point is a table that shows not only users' willingness to pay for electricity, but also the income changes that they and ELEC experience as a consequence of the tariff increase. This set of data for the tariff increase in question, excluding ELEC's cost savings, is provided by Table 10.12 and constitutes the starting point for the subsequent analysis.

The effects on residential consumers already constitute a final effect on their incomes. Thus, for example, in the case of low-income consumers, 5,502 is the estimate of the sum of the CVs of the tariff increase. In turn, part of the loss to these consumers (5,434−1,388) is additional income for ELEC. The algebraic sum of the CVs of the customers and ELEC, equal to the total willingness to pay, indicates the minimum cost savings necessary to make compensation *possible*.

In the case of the Government, the reader should remember that its consumption was assumed to be insensitive to small tariff changes. Consequently, the tariff increase results only in a transfer to ELEC equal to the present value of the increase in the corresponding payments.

For industrial consumers, the effect of the tariff increase appears initially as an increase in costs, which firms will try to transfer through prices. The outcome of doing this will depend on market characteristics. If electricity is used to produce imported or exported goods at the margin, whose domestic prices are determined by international prices, the tariff increase cannot be transferred and in the short run will have to be absorbed by producers as a reduction in profits. As producers adjust to the new situation (higher costs), they will cut back production and, consequently, the supply of foreign exchange will be reduced (less exports), and/or its demand will increase (less production of imported goods). This will give rise to an increase in the price of foreign exchange (the EER), thus increasing the prices of traded goods, which will directly or indirectly increase the prices of consumer goods. Given that, in the long run, it is unlikely that the tariff increase will significantly affect the people's relative nominal income, the basic effect will be to reduce, through price increases, their real incomes in proportion to expenditure and thus transfer the equivalent income to the electricity firm. In the case of the production of non-traded goods, the expected effect is similar. Although initially, part of the tariff increase could result in reduced profits, in the long run, the prices of consumer goods will increase, reducing consumers' real incomes and increasing the electricity firm's real income.

The restructuring of production resulting from the tariff increase may bring about some changes in relative incomes, for example by resulting in relative less employment of unskilled labor in the formal sector.[22] However, due to the minor relative importance of electricity costs in the total cost of each firm, the long-run adjustment is made basically through an increase in the prices of consumer goods, which reduces consumers' real incomes by an amount approximately equal to the increase in real income of the electricity firm.

This should make it clear how difficult it is to identify the distributional effect of the tariff increase on the industrial sector. However, considering that in the first few years, short-run considerations take priority, i.e. part of the effect could result in reduced profits, it is likely that the present value of the

----

22. See Mishan (1968).

Table 10.12 Direct Effects of a Tariff Increase on Customers and ELEC Income, Excluding Cost Savings (In thousands of $)

Direct Effects	ELEC Customers					Government	ELEC	Total at Market Prices
	Low-Income Residential	Remainder of Residential	Commercial	Industrial				
Willingness to Pay	−1,456	−14,870	−7,155	−17,722		—	—	−41,203
Paid	1,388	14,244	6,853	16,975		—	−39,460	—
Increase in the Market Value of G_1	−5,434	−55,730	−28,393	−78,837		−16,862	185,256	—
Total	−5,502	−56,356	−28,695	−79,584		−16,862	145,796	−41,203

total effect on the final purchasers will be less than its share of consumption. For this reason, and in order to obtain a reasonable range for the distributional effect of the industrial tariff increase, the following two extreme hypotheses were considered:

(a) the industrial firms succeed in transferring a minimum of 60% of the effects of the tariff increase to domestic final consumers; and
(b) the firms succeed in transferring 100% of the effects of the tariff increase to domestic final consumers.

In the case of commercial customers, it is reasonable to expect that a higher percentage of the tariff increase will be passed on to consumers through prices for three basic reasons: (a) the vast majority of commercial establishments operate in the consumer goods markets, where there are fewer transactions until the final purchaser is reached, reducing the instances in which part of the increase cannot be transferred in the short-run and has to be absorbed as smaller profits; (b) adjustments due to substitution will be expected to be more rapid than in the industrial sector; and (c) entry and exit of firms will take place more quickly than in the industrial sector. For these reasons, we will assume that a minimum of 80% and a maximum of 100% of the tariff increase is transferred to the final consumers through prices.

Now that a range has been estimated for the distribution of the effects of the industrial and commercial tariff increases, between profit reductions and increases in the prices of goods and services, we need to consider how the groups of beneficiaries considered (the Government, low-income people and the remainder of the private sector) absorb these effects. Assume that the reductions in profits are in the private sector, and that only those persons with incomes above the low-income level are owners of firms.[23] With regard to the price increase, not only is the private sector affected, but the Government will also see the real value of its expenditure on goods and services (excluding wage payments) reduced. According to a recent household survey, low-income people account for 38% of total private expenditure on consumption, and general Government expenditure on goods and services (excluding wages) is 9% of private expenditure on consumption. Given those percentages, the effects of the price increase can be distributed among the groups considered as follows:

---

23. This includes an error for public enterprises, which represent a small percentage of industrial demand.

Government	8.2
Low-incomes	34.9
Remainder	56.9
Total	100.0

The final results for the two hypotheses appear in Table 10.13 for industrial customers, and in Table 10.14 for commercial customers.

The various aspects of the distributional effect of the tariff increase can now be brought together. Tables 10.15 and 10.16 summarize the data obtained in the previous sections for each of the two hypotheses for transfer to the final consumers. Hypothesis (a) corresponds to the assumption that 60% of the increase in the industrial tariff and 80% of the commercial tariff is transferred. Hypothesis (b) is that 100% of the increase in both tariffs is transferred. As for Government consumption of electricity, it was assumed that its demand is totally inelastic with respect to tariff changes, so that only a transfer between the Government and ELEC occurs. The remaining cost savings come from the estimates made in the two previous sections.

In order to simplify the presentation, it will be useful to group the various sectors affected according to our purposes. Thus, since both low-income final consumers and unskilled workers are low-income people, they can be combined into a single category. Similarly, neither the owners of firms nor the remainder of the final consumers belong to the low-income group and are listed separately. As for ELEC, this is an enterprise that is running a deficit and whose investment plans depend to a large extent on compensatory transfers from the Government. Consequently, the greater availability of funds that the tariff increase will produce for ELEC will in reality be a reduction in Government transfers. Consequently, both values can be added together into a single one under the heading *Government*.

Table 10.17, which provides the results after the consolidation mentioned, shows that those on low incomes will absorb between 19% and 27% of the effect of the tariff increase on the private sector. However, this does not measure the net effect on these people, since it does not consider the benefits that they will receive from the additional income accruing to the Government when it reduces the compensating transfers to ELEC. If it were possible to know the distribution of the income changes generated by the use of additional funds for the Government, it would be possible to calculate the *net* effect on low-income people. This information is not available, which is why the analysis limits itself to what has been explained up to now.

Table 10.13 Effects of the Industrial Tariff Increase (In thousands of $)

Effects of the Tariff Increase	Firms	Final Consumers		Public Sector		Total at Efficiency Prices
		Low Income	Remainder	Government	ELEC	
Hypothesis (a)						
Willingness to Pay	−7,089	−3,711	−6,050	−872	—	−17,722
Paid	6,790	3,555	5,795	835	−16,975	—
Increase in the Market Value of G_1	−31,535	−16,509	−26,915	−3,878	78,837	—
Total	−31,834	−16,665	−27,170	−3,915	61,862	−17,722
Hypothesis (b)						
Willingness to Pay	—	−6,185	−10,085	−1,452	—	−17,722
Paid	—	5,924	9,659	1,392	−16,975	—
Increase in the Market Value of G_1	—	−27,514	−44,858	−6,465	78,837	—
Total	—	−27,775	−45,284	−6,525	61,862	−17,722

Source: Prepared on the basis of Table 10.12, as presented in Section 10.4.

Table 10.14 Effects of the Commerical Tariff Increase (In thousands of $)

Effects of the Tariff Increase	Firms	Final Consumers		Public Sector		Total at Efficiency Prices
		Low Income	Remainder	Government	ELEC	
Hypothesis (a)						
Willingness to Pay	-1,431	-1,998	-3,257	-469	–	-7,155
Paid	1,371	1,913	3,119	450	-6,853	–
Increase in the Market Value of G_1	-5,679	-7,927	-12,924	-1,863	28,393	–
Total	-5,739	-8,012	-13,062	-1,882	21,540	-7,155
Hypothesis (b)						
Willingness to Pay	–	-2,497	-4,071	-587	–	-7,155
Paid	–	2,392	3,899	562	-6,853	–
Increase in the Market Value of G_1	–	-9,909	-16,156	-2,328	28,393	–
Total	–	-10,014	-16,328	-2,353	21,540	-7,155

Source: Prepared on the basis of Table 10.12, as presented in Section 10.4.

Table 10.15 Summary of the Distributional Effects of a Tariff Increase. Hypothesis (a)
(In thousands of $)

Source	Private Sector				Public Sector		Total at Efficiency Prices
	Firms	Final Consumers		Unskilled Workers	ELEC	Govern- ment	
		Low Income	Remainder				
Customers							
• Residential	—	-5,502	-56,356	—	45,532	—	-16,326
• Industrial	-31,834	-16,665	-27,170	—	61,862	-3,915	-17,722
• Commercial	-5,739	-8,012	-13,062	—	21,540	-1,882	-7,155
• Government	—	—	—	—	16,862	-16,862	—
ELEC Cost Savings							
1. Generation							
• Investment				172	6,146	553	6,527
• Fuel				—	21,414	5,626	27,040
• Operation & Maintenance				—	821	52	873
2. Transmission & Distribution							
• Investment	—	—	—	-244	7,615	743	8,114
• Operation & Maintenance	—	—	—	-216	4,153	324	4,261
Total	-37,573	-30,179	-96,588	-632	185,945	-15,361	5,612

Source: Tables 10.11, 10.12, 10.13(a) and 10.14(a).

Table 10.16 Summary of the Distributional Effects of a Tariff Increase. Hypothesis (b) (In thousands of $)

Source	Private Sector				Public Sector		Total at Efficiency Prices
	Firms	Final Consumers		Unskilled Workers	ELEC	Government	
		Low Income	Remainder				
Customers							
• Residential	—	−5,502	−56,356	—	45,532	—	−16,326
• Industrial	—	−27,775	−45,284	—	61,862	−6,525	−17,722
• Commercial	—	−10,014	−16,328	—	21,540	−2,353	−7,155
• Government	—	—	—	—	16,862	−16,862	—
ELEC Cost Savings							
1. Generation							
• Investment	—	—	—	−172	6,146	553	6,527
• Fuel	—	—	—	—	21,414	5,626	27,040
• Operation & Maintenance	—	—	—	—	821	52	873
2. Transmission & Distribution							
• Investment	—	—	—	−244	7,615	743	8,114
• Operation & Maintenance	—	—	—	−216	4,153	324	4,261
Total	—	−43,291	−117,968	−632	185,945	−18,442	5,612

Source: Tables 10.11, 10.12, 10.13(b) and 10.14(b).

181

Table 10.17 Consolidation of the Distributional Impact of the Tariff Increase
(In thousands of $)

| | Private Sector | | | |
Hypothesis	Persons on Low Incomes	Remainder of Private Sector	Government	Total at Efficiency Prices
Hypothesis (a)	−30,811	−134,161	170,584	5,612
Hypothesis (b)	−43,923	−117,968	167,503	5,612

Source: Tables 10.15 and 10.16.

10.5 Data Requirements

The analysis presented in the preceding sections rests on a set of assumptions, not all of them explicit, on the values of certain key variables for the outcome of distributional analysis. The objective of this section will be to explain the main assumptions and provide guidance on alternatives to improve approximations.

Let us begin with the projections of the quantity of electricity demanded according to the type of customer. Given that the quantity of electricity demanded for type of customer i in year t depends on the price p_i^t and on other variables x_{ij}^t

$$G_i^t = f(p_i^t; x_{ij}^t)$$

projection G_i^t requires exogenous projections of the tariff and the remaining variables x_{ij}^t. The tariff was assumed to be constant throughout the planning period, since it is considered the signal that encourages or discourages electricity consumption. Given that, as discussed in Section 10.2, adjustments in consumption require adjustments in equipment stocks, which take time, the system of signals should ideally not change from year to year. This does not exclude the possibility of short-run adjustments in response to exceptional situations (for example, rainfall far below the average in a predominantly hydro-electric system) provided the users are aware that the change is a short-run change, and that decisions on equipment have to be taken on the basis of the long-run tariff. Consequently, the quantity of electricity demanded can be presented as a function of a price, which is constant over time

$$G_i^t = f(p_i; x_{ij}^t)$$

182

The breakdown of residential demand by income groups and its separate projection is an important element in estimating the distributional effect. This projection can be conceptualized as the number of residential clients of type i in year t (N_i^t) times the average consumption per customer (g_i^t)

$$G_i^t = N_i^t(p_i; x_{ij}^t) \times g_i^t(p_i; x_{ij}^t)$$

It should be borne in mind that in most Latin American countries, customers who have no *access* to the grid are mainly low-income people, and that this access is determined principally by the electricity firm's connection policy. Furthermore, elasticity of consumption per customer with respect to variables x_{ij}^t will in general be different for different income levels. Consequently, projections per type of customer should ideally take account of these effects. All this will result in different annual growth rates for the quantity demanded for each group. This of course requires an effort in the estimates of functions N_i^t and g_i^t which did not exist for the case in hand, in which a uniform growth rate was used for each group (see Table 10.3).

As a result of the above, there will be different price elasticities of demand for each group. In particular, price elasticity is expected to diminish (in absolute value) as the customer's income level increases.[24] This aspect was not taken into account either in the analysis carried out, in which price elasticity was assumed to be equal for both groups of residential customers. Lack of data also made drastically simplifying assumptions necessary with regard to the price elasticity of industrial and commercial demand.

In summary, the application of cost-benefit analysis to the field of selecting expansion plans and, in particular, estimating the distribution of income changes, requires a considerable effort with regard to estimating electricity demand functions, an effort that has scarcely begun.[25]

A second set of problems concerns the transfer and final effect of the change in industrial and commercial tariffs. In the case of relatively small tariff increases, which do not give rise to strong substitution effects, it is very likely that assuming a transfer (in the long run) to the final consumers of 100% of the effect will be a reasonable approximation. However, the dearth of studies on this subject makes it advisable to use a second transfer hypothesis, as in the case presented. This approach will provide a range that is likely

---

24. See Westley (1981).
25. Westley (1981 and 1984) gives estimates for residential and commercial demand in Paraguay and Costa Rica.

to include the real effect, but hopefully not too wide as to make the results useless.

Finally, there is the problem of which part of the increase in the industrial and commercial tariffs will be absorbed by the final consumers. In section 10.4, we assumed that it was proportional to the expenditure on consumption of each group. However, the indirect content of electricity in consumer baskets, i.e. the direct and indirect requirements for electricity of the goods making up the basket, will not be identical for all groups. Using the input-output model presented in section 7.4, the indirect requirements for electricity in the consumption basket can be approximated. To simplify presentation, let us assume that there is a simple model with only three sectors corresponding to the "products" agriculture (X_1), industry (X_2) and electricity (X_3), and that the final demand matrix D can be broken down into the following vectors: consumption by low-income people (C^b), consumption by the rest of the private sector (C^r), Government consumption (C^g) and the remainder of final demand (D^r). Thus, according to expression [7.2], production values can be expressed as

$$
\begin{bmatrix} X_1 \\ X_2 \\ X_3 \end{bmatrix} = \begin{bmatrix} T_{11} T_{12} T_{13} \\ T_{21} T_{22} T_{23} \\ T_{31} T_{32} T_{33} \end{bmatrix} \times \begin{bmatrix} C_1^b C_1^r C_1^g D_1^r \\ C_2^b C_2^r C_2^g D_2^r \\ C_3^b C_3^r C_3^g D_3^r \end{bmatrix}
$$

Total direct and indirect requirements for electricity corresponding to the low-income group's consumption basket will be

$$
X_3(C^b) = T_{31} C_1^b + T_{32} C_2^b + T_{33} C_3^b
$$

which can be interpreted in the following way. To supply one peso's worth of industrial output (1) it is necessary to produce T_{31} pesos of electricity, so that $T_{31} C_1^b$ indicates the value of electricity production "contained" in C_1^b pesos' worth of consumption. Thus, $X_3(C^b)$ will be the electricity "content" of the low-income group's consumption basket, made up of its direct consumption C_3^b and its indirect consumption through the electricity needed to produce basket C_j^b. Direct consumption of electicity C_3^b is low-income residential consumption, the effect of which has been dealt with separately (see Table 10.12), while indirect consumption will be

$$
X_3(C^b) - C_3^b = T_{31} C_1^b + T_{32} C_2^b + (T_{33} - 1) C_3^b
$$

184

Similarily, the indirect consumption of electricity by the rest of the private sector and Government consumption could be calculated, thus yielding the indirect requirements of each group of consumers

$$X_3(C^b) - C_3^b$$
$$X_3(C^r) - C_3^r$$
$$X_3(C^g) - C_3^g$$

Then the share of the tariff increase that the industrial and commercial sectors are assumed to transfer to the final consumers through prices, can be distributed in proportion to the share of indirect consumption of each group of final consumers in total indirect consumption.

PART II

THE USE OF INPUT-OUTPUT TECHNIQUES

CHAPTER 11

THE USE OF INPUT-OUTPUT TECHNIQUES FOR ESTIMATING ACCOUNTING PRICES

11.1 Accounting Prices for Non-Traded Goods

We have assumed up to now that the market prices of non-traded goods are equal to their efficiency prices. Part II is an introductory presentation on the procedures for correcting these market prices by using input-output techniques, and on their use in estimating distributional effects.

As the reader will recall from the analysis of the industrial project in Chapter 9, the value of construction at market prices was not accepted as being equal to its value at efficiency prices. Instead, the corresponding cost structure was revalued on the assumption that the market prices of non-traded inputs were equal to their efficiency prices, but with imported inputs and unskilled labor valued at their efficiency prices. This allowed for the value at efficiency prices of construction to be approximated. The same backwards breakdown procedure following the output-input chain could have been con-

---

This chapter is only an introduction to the topic. The reader can find more detailed presentations in Powers (1981) and Scott, et al. (1976).

tinued, in order to reduce even more the influence of market prices of non-traded goods in the valuation. For example, the value of bricks could, in turn, have been broken down into non-traded inputs, foreign exchange, taxes on foreign trade, wages for unskilled labor, etc. and all these valued at their efficiency prices. The procedures presented in this chapter for the valuation of non-traded goods follow the logic of this backwards breakdown along the output-input chain.

To simplify presentation, suppose initially that: (a) the long-run supply of all non-traded goods and services is infinitely elastic, i.e. that any additional demand will be met by expanding production at approximately constant long-run marginal costs; (b) foreign exchange is in fixed supply, so that what was presented in Section 3.2 on the APRFE applies; (c) there is only one type of labor, the supply of which is perfectly elastic at the wages in force, which are above the corresponding "willingness to receive," i.e. the information presented in Table 6.5 applies; and (d) there are no "capital costs."

Changes in the "production" of foreign exchange by changing the production of imported or exported goods are beyond the scope of this chapter, as this would require a more extensive treatment of the preparation and use of input-output matrices.[1] As for labor, Chapter 13 discusses unskilled labor in detail, which is, in most cases, where the most important distributional effects are to be found. Finally, considering "capital costs" may also lead to identifying significant distributional effects, but taking them into account would require an explanation of how long-run marginal costs may be represented in a matrix. For this reason, some of these aspects are only mentioned, but not fully developed, in sections 11.2, 11.3 and 11.4.

To calculate the value at accounting prices of a certain additional quantity ΔQ of a non-traded good valued at market prices, we need to know the long-run marginal cost of producing this additional quantity and the accounting (and market) prices of the inputs comprising these costs. To know the accounting prices of these inputs, we also need to know those of the inputs that go into the production of the inputs of ΔQ, and so on. In other words, it is necessary to break down the market value of ΔQ backwards in successive stages following the output-input chain. At each step back, the prices paid for inputs can be broken down into the following four main categories:

(a) the market value of other non-traded inputs, the additional demand for which is met by additional production;
(b) the market value of foreign exchange, which by being in fixed supply is withdrawn from other alternative uses;
(c) the value of taxes on foreign trade; and
(d) the market value of labor.

---

1. See Londero (1994).

Table 11.1   Breakdown of a Value at Market Prices, Iterative Procedure

	Non-Traded	Foreign Exchange	Wages	Taxes	Value at Market Prices
First Round	40.0	30.0	25.0	5.0	100.0
Second Round	10.0	20.0	9.0	1.0	40.0
Third Round	2.0	4.0	3.6	0.4	10.0
Fourth Round	0.5	0.6	0.8	0.1	2.0
Total After Four Rounds	0.5	54.6	38.4	6.5	100.0

Since foreign exchange has been assumed to be in fixed supply, the increase in the exchange rate brought about by the additional demand for foreign exchange, caused by the additional production of non-traded goods, will not lead to an increase in the production of exports. Furthermore, neither un-skilled labor nor taxes are "produced," so that the backwards breakdown is done only for non-traded items, while successive requirements for foreign exchange, labor and taxes build up. In this way, at each step backwards in the output-input chain, a higher proportion of the market value of ΔQ is decomposed into categories (b), (c) and (d), yielding a lower one in (a). It is then possible to take a sufficient number of steps in order for the percentage of the value of ΔQ that still remains as the market value of non-traded inputs to be as small as desired. Through a sufficient number of steps, it can be brought down practically to zero; in other words, the remainder of inputs in categories (a) tends towards zero when the number of steps backwards tends towards infinity.

An example will help to clarify the procedure. In Table 11.1, the first row shows the cost of providing a production value of 100 at market prices of, for example, construction in the industrial project in Chapter 9. This cost is broken down into 40 of additional production costs for non-traded inputs (category (a)) and 60 of what will be called non-produced inputs (foreign exchange and labor) and transfers.[2] In turn, the 40 of non-traded inputs (for example, cement, bricks, etc.) can also be broken down backwards, yielding 10 of additional production of inputs and 30 of non-produced inputs and transfers, and so on. After only four steps back along the chain, 99.5% of the original value of 100 at market prices is expressed as direct requirements (first row) and indirect requirements (total of the following rows) for foreign exchange, wages and taxes.

Once 100% of the value at market prices has been broken down in such a way, foreign exchange, labor and taxes can be valued at efficiency prices, as set forth in Part I. Thus, in the first column of Table 11.2, the value at market

---

2. Foreign exchange, although obtained from the production of exported goods, is not pro-duced *at the margin,* since it is assumed to be in fixed supply.

Table 11.2 Valuation of a Non-Traded Input

	Project	Workers	Government	Total
Non-Traded Inputs	−0.50	—	—	−0.50
Foreign Exchange	−54.60	—	−5.46	−60.06
Wages	−38.40	23.04	—	−15.36
Taxes	−6.50	—	6.50	—
Total	−100.00	23.04	1.04	−75.92

prices of non-traded inputs is given in accordance with the results of the backwards decomposition obtained in Table 11.1. Foreign exchange has been valued in accordance with the corresponding APRFE ($APRFE = 1.1$) and the wages of unskilled labor broken down into willingness to receive ($WR = 15.36$) and transfer $w - WR = 23.04$ on the assumption that all this labor was previously unemployed. The error implied in accepting the market price of the non-traded good as being equal to its accounting price has been reduced to a minimum since it now represents only 0.5% of total. However, this does not imply that the entire effect of market prices has been eliminated. The reader will recall from Chapter 3, that an APRFE calculated on the basis of a weighted average of taxes on foreign trade includes assumptions of equality between market and efficiency prices.

If at this stage, the reader feels skeptical about the practical possibility of effecting the backwards breakdown by manual methods even for a single non-traded input, his skepticism is well grounded. Although the long-run marginal cost structures can be estimated, the breakdown process by manual methods is a gigantic task and consequently impractical. However, there are simple algebraic procedures for calculating these total (direct and indirect) requirements for non-produced inputs and transfers using input-output techniques. This will be the topic of the following section.

11.2 Calculating Accounting Price Ratios for Non-Traded Goods: Some Formulas

Let us begin by recalling that the accounting price ratio of good j (APR_j) was defined as the quotient between its accounting price (p_j^c) and its market price (p_j), i.e.

$$APR_j = \frac{p_j^c}{p_j}$$

The following explanation will show a way of calculating APRs for non-traded intermediate goods, on the basis of the long-run marginal costs of these goods expressed at market prices. For this purpose, it is useful to begin by writing these marginal costs as

$$\sum_{j=1}^{n} \Delta Q_{ij} p_j + \sum_{h=1}^{k} \Delta F_{ih} p_h + \sum_{h=k+1}^{m} \Delta T_{ih} \gtreqless \Delta Q_i p_i \qquad [11.1]$$

in which

ΔQ_{ij} = physical quantity of non-traded good or service j required to produce ΔQ_i additional units of intermediate good or service i

ΔF_{ih} = quantity of non-produced input h ($h = 1, \ldots, k$; for the moment foreign exchange and unskilled labor) required to produce ΔQ_i additional units of intermediate good or service i

ΔT_{ih} = value of transfers h ($h = k + 1, \ldots, m$; for the moment taxes on foreign trade) brought about by the production of ΔQ_i.

Ideally, these marginal costs will be the present value of the cost of expanding production of good i by ΔQ_i annual units, i.e.

$$\Delta Q_{ij} p_j = PV(\Delta Q_{ijt} p_j)$$

$$\Delta Q_i p_i = PV(\Delta Q_{it} p_i)$$

in which PV indicates present value and t the period.[3] Consequently, the respective investment costs will be included in $\Delta Q_{ij} p_j$, $\Delta F_{ih} p_h$ and ΔT_{ih}. Those costs that correspond to non-traded goods will be included in $\Delta Q_{ij} p_j$, while traded goods will be broken down into foreign exchange (included in $\Delta F_{ih} p_h$), taxes on foreign trade (ΔT_{ih}) and other non-traded intermediate goods and services such as port, transport and trading costs (included in the respective $\Delta Q_{ij} p_j$). Since these present values will be calculated using the discount rate, we can rewrite equation [11.1] as

$$\sum_{j=1}^{n} \Delta Q_{ij} p_j + \sum_{h=1}^{k} \Delta F_{ih} p_h + \sum_{h=k+1}^{m} \Delta T_{ih} + \Delta B_i = \Delta Q_i p_i \qquad [11.2]$$

in which ΔB_i is the difference between the present value of the value of additional production and the present value of long-run marginal costs. This difference (ΔB_i) will be positive if the present value of the value of additional

---

3. Note that prices do not have subscript t because it is assumed that the relative prices remain constant.

production ΔQ_i at market prices is greater than the present value of the long-run marginal costs, also at market prices, that is, if the internal rate of return on investment, *at market prices* and before direct taxes (q), is greater than the discount rate (d).

Dividing both sides of [11.2] by ΔQ_i yields

$$\sum_{j=1}^{n} \frac{\Delta Q_{ij}}{\Delta Q_i} p_j + \sum_{h=1}^{k} \frac{\Delta F_{ih}}{\Delta Q_i} p_h + \sum_{h=k+1}^{m} \frac{\Delta T_{ih}}{\Delta Q_i} + \frac{\Delta B_i}{\Delta Q_i} = p_i$$

The accounting price of good i ($p_i^c = APR_i p_i$) will be equal to the corresponding marginal cost valued at accounting prices, that is,

$$\sum_{j=1}^{n} \frac{\Delta Q_{ij}}{\Delta Q_i} p_j APR_j + \sum_{h=1}^{k} \frac{\Delta F_{ih}}{\Delta Q_i} p_h APR_h^f + \sum_{h=k+1}^{m} \frac{\Delta T_{ih}}{\Delta Q_i} APR_h^t$$

$$+ \frac{\Delta B_i}{\Delta Q_i} APR_i^b = APR_i p_i$$

from which the accounting price ratio of i can be expressed as

$$\sum_{j=1}^{n} \frac{\Delta Q_{ij} p_j}{\Delta Q_i p_i} APR_j + \sum_{j=1}^{k} \frac{\Delta F_{ih} p_h}{\Delta Q_i p_i} APR_h^f + \sum_{h=k+1}^{m} \frac{\Delta T_{ih}}{\Delta Q_i p_i} APR_h^t$$

$$+ \frac{\Delta B_i}{\Delta Q_i p_i} APR_i^b = APR_i$$

If we now assume that the coefficients for inputs ($\Delta Q_{ij}/\Delta Q_i$; $\Delta F_{ih}/\Delta Q_i$), transfers ($\Delta T_{ih}/\Delta Q_i p_i$) and net benefits at market prices per unit of production value ($\Delta B_i/\Delta Q_i p_i$) are independent of the *size* of ΔQ_i, the above expression can be written in simpler form as

$$\sum_{j} a_{ij} APR_j + \sum_{h} f_{ih} APR_h^f + \sum_{h} t_{ih} APR_h^t + b_i APR_i^b = APR_i \qquad [11.3]$$

in which a_{ij}, f_{ih}, t_{ih} and b_i are value coefficients of the inputs or transfers per additional unit of production value and b_i are the net benefits at market prices per additional unit of production value. Expression [11.3] indicates that to calculate the APR of non-traded good i (APR_i) it is necessary to know not only APR_h^f, APR_h^t and APR_i^b, but also the APRs of its non-traded inputs $j = 1, ..., n$. The APRs of the non-traded inputs of good i ought also to be calculated on the basis of their respective expressions [11.3]. It will thus be necessary to have a complete system of equations [11.3] for all the non-traded intermediate goods. For this purpose, and to simplify notation, t_{ih}, b_i and their respective APRs can be included within the common notation f_{ih} and APR_h^f. In this way, the complete system of equations for non-traded goods $j = 1, \ldots, n$ can be written as

$$\sum_{j=1}^{n} a_{1j} APR_j + \sum_{h=1}^{m} f_{1h} APR_h^f = APR_1$$

$$\vdots \qquad\qquad \vdots$$

$$\sum_{j=1}^{n} a_{nj} APR_j + \sum_{h=1}^{m} f_{nh} APR_h^f = APR_n$$

The same system can also be written using matrix notation

$$\begin{bmatrix} a_{11} \cdots a_{1n} \\ \vdots \quad\quad \vdots \\ a_{n1} \cdots a_{nn} \end{bmatrix} \begin{bmatrix} APR_1 \\ \vdots \\ APR_n \end{bmatrix} + \begin{bmatrix} f_{11} \cdots f_{1m} \\ \vdots \quad\quad \vdots \\ f_{n1} \cdots f_{nm} \end{bmatrix} \begin{bmatrix} APR_1^f \\ \vdots \\ APR_m^f \end{bmatrix} = \begin{bmatrix} APR_1 \\ \vdots \\ APR_n \end{bmatrix}$$

and, more concisely still, as

$$A \times APR + F \times APR^f = APR$$

from which the vector of the APRs of the non-traded intermediate goods can be obtained as

$$APR = (I - A)^{-1} \times F \times APR^f \qquad\qquad [11.4]$$

Expression [11.4] can be interpreted in the following way. Each row of the matrix $[f_{ih}^*] = (I - A)^{-1} \times F$ provides the total requirements, direct and indirect, of non-produced inputs and transfers per unit of production value. Thus, in the case of non-traded good k,

$$\sum_{h=1}^{m} f_{kh}^* = 1$$

Table 11.3 Hypothetical Intersectoral Relations Matrix

Outputs	(1)	(2)	(3)	fe	uw	sw	t	bp	bg	Total
(1)	—	0.37	0.05	0.30	0.15	0.10	0.03	—	—	1.00
(2)	0.14	—	0.06	0.40	0.20	0.15	0.03	0.02	—	1.00
(3)	0.09	0.14	—	0.70	0.05	0.15	—	—	−0.13	1.00

(column group header: Inputs)

Then the product $[f_{ih}^*]\, APR^f = (I - A)^{-1} \times F \times APR^f$, which in the case of non-traded good k corresponds to

$$\sum_{h=1}^{m} f_{kh}^* APR_h^f = APR_k \qquad [11.5]$$

will be these total requirements multiplied by their respective APR_h^f. If we now make the comparison with the example of Table 11.1, the f_{kh}^* correspond to the last row of this table in which the remainder of non-traded goods has been reduced to zero. When the assumptions and value judgments of efficiency analysis are adopted, [11.5] is equivalent to the total of the last column of Table 11.2 per unit of production value, since taxes and benefits above the discount rate are transfers and, consequently, their APR_h^f are zero.

11.3 A Numerical Example

Let us assume there is a simplified system in which there are only three non-traded intermediate goods. The first (1) is machinery and the other two (2 and 3) are current inputs. The long-run marginal cost structures are those shown in Table 11.3. All the sectors use the machinery as well as the other two inputs. However, the elements in the main diagonal (the a_{ii}) in the transactions matrix $A = [a_{ij}]$ are nil because consumption in the sector has been subtracted from production. In addition to the non-traded inputs, the sectors purchase foreign exchange (fe), unskilled (uw) and skilled (sw) labor, and pay import duties (t). In sector (1) the market price is equal to the long-run marginal cost, so that there are no excess profits ($bp_1 = 0$). Conversely, in sector (2) the price of the product is higher than these costs ($bp_2 > 0$), a difference resulting from the discount rate being lower than the minimum total profitability (at market prices) necessary for firms in the sector to expand production. Finally, sector (3) is the responsibility of a public firm, which charges a tariff lower than the long-run marginal cost, so that $bg_3 < 0$.[4] On the basis of Table 11.3, equations system [11.4] can be set out as

---

4. Note that, due to interest in the distributional aspects, a distinction has been made between excess profits in the private sector and for the Government.

$$\begin{bmatrix} APR_1 \\ APR_2 \\ APR_3 \end{bmatrix} = \begin{bmatrix} 1.00 & -0.37 & -0.05 \\ -0.14 & 1.00 & -0.06 \\ -0.09 & -0.14 & 1.00 \end{bmatrix}^{-1} \begin{bmatrix} 0.30 & 0.15 & 0.10 & 0.03 & - & - \\ 0.40 & 0.20 & 0.15 & 0.03 & 0.02 & - \\ 0.70 & 0.05 & 0.15 & - & - & -0.13 \end{bmatrix} \begin{bmatrix} APR_{fe} \\ APR_{uw} \\ APR_{sw} \\ APR_t \\ APR_{bp} \\ APR_{bg} \end{bmatrix}$$

$$APR = (I - A)^{-1} \times F \times APR^f$$

By now solving $(I - A)^{-1}$ total direct and indirect requirements for foreign exchange, unskilled and skilled labor wages, taxes and excess profits can be calculated as

$$F^* = [f^*_{ih}] = (I - A)^{-1} F$$

$$\begin{bmatrix} F^*_{1h} \\ F^*_{2h} \\ F^*_{3h} \end{bmatrix} = \begin{bmatrix} 1.0636 & 0.4044 & 0.0774 \\ 0.1560 & 1.0678 & 0.0719 \\ 0.1176 & 0.1859 & 1.0170 \end{bmatrix} \begin{matrix} fe_i & uw_i & sw_i & t_i & bp_i & bg_i \\ \begin{bmatrix} 0.30 & 0.15 & 0.10 & 0.03 & - & - \\ 0.40 & 0.20 & 0.15 & 0.03 & 0.02 & - \\ 0.70 & 0.05 & 0.15 & - & - & -0.13 \end{bmatrix} \end{matrix}$$

in which h indicates the type of non-produced input or transfer. By working out the product $(I - A)^{-1} F$ we obtain

$$\begin{bmatrix} F^*_{1h} \\ F^*_{2h} \\ F^*_{3h} \end{bmatrix} = \begin{matrix} fe^*_i & uw^*_i & sw^*_i & t^*_i & bp^*_i & bg^*_i \\ \begin{bmatrix} 0.535 & 0.244 & 0.179 & 0.044 & 0.008 & -0.010 \\ 0.524 & 0.241 & 0.187 & 0.036 & 0.021 & -0.009 \\ 0.821 & 0.106 & 0.192 & 0.009 & 0.004 & -0.132 \end{bmatrix} \end{matrix} \qquad [11.6]$$

which is the matrix of total requirements sought. The reader can check that the sum of total requirements of non-produced inputs and transfers in each sector $(\Sigma_h f^*_{ih})$ verifies that

$$fe^*_i + uw^*_i + sw^*_i + t^*_i + bp^*_i + bg^*_i = 1$$

It is now possible to value, for example, the machinery produced by sector (1) in accordance with the criteria already presented. Assuming that the present value of the purchases of this machinery for a project is 100, this cost can be broken down into its total requirements by using the corresponding vector F^*_{1h} and thus obtaining the first column of Table 11.4. Then, the income changes created by producing and selling the machinery can be calculated on the basis of total requirements for non-produced inputs and transfers. Thus using an APRFE = 1.1, valuing unskilled labor at its alternative wages in the informal sector and accepting the wages of skilled labor as equal to their

Table 11.4   Breakdown of the Present Value of Purchases of Machinery (1)

	Project	Unskilled Workers	Other Firms	Government	Total
Foreign Exchange	−53.50	—	—	−5.35	−58.85
Unskilled Labor	−24.40	14.64	—	—	−9.76
Skilled Labor	−17.90	—	—	—	−17.90
Taxes	−4.40	—	—	4.40	—
Excess Profits (Private)	−0.80	—	0.80	—	—
Excess Profits (Government)	1.00	—	—	−1.00	—
Total	**−100.00**	14.64	0.80	−1.95	−86.51

accounting price, we obtain the results in Table 11.4. While the first four columns do not require further explanation, since this is simply what we have done up to now, the last two deserve at least a brief discussion. For the moment, this will be in the framework of efficiency analysis and on the assumption of equality between the marginal rate of return on investment and a common discount rate for all persons.[5] The entrepreneurs receive, through the expansion of machinery production by 100, profits of 0.80 in excess of those strictly necessary to compensate their investment, given the common discount rate d. This private net benefit is the result of the project paying 0.80 for the machinery above its long-run marginal production cost. However, the Government grants a transfer of 1.00 to the project by charging a lower tariff than the respective long-run marginal cost. The final result is that the cost at market prices exceeds the cost at efficiency prices by approximately 15%, and that this difference is explained mainly by the difference between the cost to employers and the efficiency wage of unskilled labor.

11.4 Cost Structures for Non-Traded Goods

In preceding sections, it was simply taken for granted that the long-run marginal cost structures for non-traded goods $[a_{ij}, f_{ih}]$ were available. In this section, we will briefly consider the type of data desirable in order to calculate these cost structures, and move towards the type of data most frequently encountered in practice.

Strictly speaking, the rows of the matrix ought to contain the structure of the

---

5. With all the problems that this implies, already discussed in Chapter 8. Interpretations based on other assumptions and distributional value judgments will be given in Part III.

difference between the present value of the production costs of projection Q_{it} of the supply of output i, and the present value of those for projection $Q_{it} + \Delta Q_{it}$, i.e.

$$[a_{ij}; f_{ih}] = \left[\frac{PV(\Delta Q_{ijt}p_j)}{PV(\Delta Q_{it}p_i)} ; \frac{PV(\Delta F_{iht}p_h)}{PV(\Delta Q_{it}p_i)} \right]$$

in which one of the F_{iht}, let us say F_{ibt}, captures the difference between the present value of production value and the present value of private costs.[6] Since the costs in each year t include investment costs, F_{ibt} will be what are sometimes called net benefits at market prices. However, in practice, this ideal approach can only be pursued in a few cases. One of these is electricity, in which the use of simulation models can provide an approximation of the long-run marginal cost by means of a procedure similar to that used in Chapter 9.

However, in most cases the above procedure will not be feasible. A close substitute would be to construct cost structures based on investment projects, which can provide a good approximation when the main long-run effect of the increase in the quantity demanded of a non-traded input is to advance execution of the project. Table 11.5 shows an outline of a cost structure obtained in this way, which corresponds to the case of the industrial project analyzed in Chapter 9 on the assumption now that it produces non-traded goods. The disadvantage of this procedure in relation to the previous one is that it leaves aside the effects resulting from changes in the use of already installed capacity, which are taken into account by simulation models of the electrical systems type. The main advantage in relation to other procedures is that it allows for the composition of investment costs to be dealt with better.

Finally, the third alternative is to use the cost structures that can be calculated on the basis of industrial censuses or surveys, or their equivalent for other sectors. These data usually provide a good description of current costs, but are incomplete as regards investment costs, since they only provide data on the gross operating surplus.[7] Normally this leaves no alternative but to consider the gross operating surplus as the capital cost, but it does not solve the problem of breaking that cost down at least into traded and non-traded goods. The latter can be worked out only in a very approximate way on the

---

6. Note the assumption that p_i, the p_j and the p_h^f are constant over time.

7. Although some surveys ask for data on capital stock, these correspond to the accounting valuation, which raises problems not only because of the tax aspects involved but also because of the effects of inflation, which are not always properly corrected by the procedures for revaluing assets.

Table 11.5 Example of a Long-Run Marginal Cost Structure for the Preparation of the Matrix (Producer Prices)

Source	In $	Coefficients
Non-Traded Input 1		
Non-Traded Input 2	167,625	0.266
.		
.		
.		
Non-Traded Input n		
Construction	30,000	0.048
Transport	10,002	0.016
Trade	15,229	0.024
Foreign Exchange	310,176	0.492
Taxes on Foreign Trade	2,223	0.003
Skilled Labor	39,558	0.063
Unskilled Labor	32,387	0.051
Long-Term Loan	−38,000	−0.060
Short-Term Loan	−6,500	−0.010
Direct Taxes	6,730	0.011
Indirect Taxes	18,900	0.030
Excess Profits	41,670	0.066
Total	630,000	1.000

Note: The reader may reconstruct the data in this table by using those in Tables 9.1, 9.3, 9.5 and 9.9 and the following additional information: (a) sales from the project are non-traded goods subject to an indirect tax of 3%; (b) in Table 9.5, the $350 of imported inputs are composed of $328 of foreign exchange and $22 of import taxes; and (c) to value the cost structure at producer prices, 1% for transport and 6% for trade were deducted from non-traded inputs and added to the respective entries.

basis of secondary information or through an average breakdown according to the composition of industrial investment. This procedure has the obvious disadvantage of blurring the differences between sectors and can give rise to significant errors when the import substitution process in the area of machinery and equipment has advanced to a considerable degree.

CHAPTER 12

COST-BENEFIT ANALYSIS OF AN IRRIGATION PROJECT

12.1 The Project

This chapter has two main objectives: (a) to present the cost-benefit analysis of a project in which various types of participants intervene and between whom various transfers take place; and (b) to illustrate the use of total requirements of non-produced inputs and transfers calculated using input-output techniques. The simplified version of a real irrigation project used is but an example, and not a complete presentation of cost-benefit analysis of this type of project. Nevertheless, a short discussion is included on the characteristics of the project and of the steps followed to draw up the data that will provide the basis for analysis.

The project consists of the introduction of gravity irrigation in an area where dry farming is practiced. The Government, through the National Irrigation Institute (NII), will be responsible for the construction, operation and

The author is grateful to Alejandra Masís for her assistance on the preparation of the financial flows of the project.

maintenance of the system.[1] Since new agricultural technology is being introduced, the NII will provide the necessary agricultural extension services. Furthermore, it will be responsible for training and organizing producers in order to set up an agricultural co-operative that will provide three main services: (a) leasing machinery and equipment to farms of up to 10 hectares; (b) storing and marketing produce; and (c) marketing seed, pesticides and fertilizers. Table 12.1 shows the costs for these activities valued at the prices actually paid.

The Government finances investment with budget funds and with a loan from a multilateral financing organization. However, since this loan would have been available and would have been used even in the absence of this specific project, the transfers between lender and borrower to which it gives rise are not *attributable* to the project, i.e. they would have existed without it. As for the co-operative, it will receive credits from the National Agricultural Bank (NAB) to finance its investment, including replacement. In addition, it will receive short-term finance, particularly during the first few years. Since these credits are granted at a real interest rate below the discount rate, the co-operative will receive a transfer equal to the difference between the present value of the credits received and the present value of the repayment flow.

Finally, the NII will receive revenue for water charges and the co-operative income for the leasing of machinery and equipment, for storage and marketing services and for the trade margins on seed, fertilizer and pesticides. This revenue is the counterpart of the respective payments in the farmers' cost accounts which are shown below.

In agricultural production, the introduction of irrigation leads to major changes in agricultural technology and crop composition. The situation without the project is extensive dry farming, with little use of industrial inputs and yielding only one crop a year. In the situation with the project, there will be intensive farming, with abundant use of fertilizers and pesticides, which will result in two, and in some cases as many as three, crops per year. Table 12.2 presents the budgets of a typical two-hectare farm, with and without the project, for the first year of operations of the irrigation system. These farm budgets can be broken down into three large groups. The first is the cash flow from farming, the total of which is shown in row (e). To this income is added that from other activities, in this case paid work away from the farm, giving the total monetary income shown in row (g). Finally, the net balance of the CVs of other costs and benefits attributable to the project, which do not appear directly as monetary flows are added together. The result is the

---

1. The real project also includes improvements to access roads leading to the area, which also benefit farmers not affected by the irrigation itself. Since inclusion of this aspect would complicate analysis without increasing its instructional value, it was excluded.

Table 12.1 Present Value of Costs and Revenues of Irrigation, Extension and Marketing Systems
(In $)

		Government	Co-operative	Total
I.	COST OF IRRIGATION SYSTEM			
	Infrastructure Works	−1,045,655	−	−1,045,655
	Imported Machinery & Equipment	−700,589	−	−700,589
	Skilled Labor	−41,826	−	−41,826
	Unskilled Labor	−62,739	−	−62,739
	Non-Traded Inputs	−94,109	−	−94,109
	Imported Inputs	−146,392	−	−146,392
	Operation & Maintenance	−142,991	−	−142,991
	Skilled Labor	−102,472	−	−102,472
	Unskilled Labor	−19,009	−	−19,009
	Imported Machinery & Equipment	−14,586	−	−14,586
	Non-Traded Inputs	−6,924	−	−6,924
II.	COST OF SUPPORT SERVICES			
	Commercial Infrastructure	−	−49,540	−49,540
	Construction	−	−7,257	−7,257
	Silos	−	−13,404	−13,404
	Equipment	−	−28,879	−28,879
	Agricultural Machinery	−	−36,130	−36,130
	Vehicles	−15,020	−36,074	−51,094
	Current Costs	−48,475	−31,767	−80,242
	Skilled Labor	−43,740	−10,935	−54,675
	Unskilled Labor	−	−3,443	−3,443
	Imported Inputs	−1,508	−7,092	−8,600
	Non-Traded Inputs	−3,227	−10,297	−13,524
III.	COSTS SUB-TOTAL (I + II)	−1,252,141	−153,511	−1,405,652
IV.	REVENUE			
	Water Charges	185,983	−	185,983
	Machinery & Equipment Services	−	47,946	47,946
	Storage & Marketing	−	126,568	126,568
	Sales	−	987,623	987,623
	Less Purchases Of:			
	Seed	−	−158,317	−158,317
	Fertilizer	−	−573,177	−573,177
	Pesticide	−	−206,749	−206,749
V.	FINANCE			
	Credit from the NAB	−	222,836	222,836
	Repayments	−	−191,422	−191,422
VI.	**TOTAL (III + IV + V)**	−1,066,158	101,797	−964,361

Table 12.2 Comparison of Income and Costs, Monetary and Non-Monetary, of a Typical 2-ha Farm, With and Without the Project. Year 2 (In $)

	Without the Project	With the Project	Incremental
(a) Sales	16,611	47,997	31,386
Dry Maize	942	819	−123
Production	(5,064)	(5,880)	(816)
Home Consumption	(−3,890)	(−4,945)	(−1,055)
Seed	(−232)	(−116)	(116)
Soft Maize	585	3,700	3,115
Wheat	412	—	−412
Barley	251	—	−251
Beans	—	—	—
Peas	5,168	16,876	11,708
Potatoes	9,253	26,602	17,349
Vegetables	—	—	—
(b) Production Costs	−8,598	−24,246	−15,648
Hired Labor	—	—	—
Purchased Seed	−1,713	−3,173	−1,460
Machinery & Equipment Services	−3,711	−4,776	−1,065
Fertilizers	−1,017	−7,145	−6,128
Pesticides	−51	−2,031	−1,980
Materials & Tools	2,106	−2,596	−490
Water Costs	—	−4,525	−4,525
(c) Storage & Marketing	—	−1,108	−1,108
(d) Finance	−249	5,219	5,468
Credit Received	10,872	22,472	11,600
Repayments	−11,121	−17,253	−6,132
(e) Monetary Income of the Farm [(a) + (b) + (c) + (d)]	7,764	27,862	20,098
(f) Wages away from the Farm	20,000	8,000	−12,000
(g) Total Monetary Income [(e) + (f)]	27,764	35,862	8,098
(h) Non-Monetary Income	−16,922	−9,469	7,453
Home Consumption	12,600	15,900	3,300
CV of Family Work	−9,522	−17,369	−7,847
CV of Work away from the Farm	−20,000	−8,000	12,000
(i) Total Income [(g) + (h)]	10,842	26,393	15,551

farmer's total "real" income. The third column of Table 12.2 is the farm's incremental budget, that is, the difference *for the farmer* between the situations with and without the project. These effects are *attributable* to the project and constitute the starting point for quantifying the benefits of introducing irrigation and the technological package that goes with it. Consequently, it would be useful to discuss in greater detail the way data are presented.

Sales, as the name indicates, record the monetary income for that part of production that is for the market. In the case of small farms, and as seen in Table 12.2 for dry maize, sales are equal to production minus home consumption and minus the part kept as seed for the next sowing season. Since home consumption is income in kind for the producer, total home consumption of all produce is shown as part of non-monetary income. Agricultural costs include wages for hired labor, and therefore not the cost attributable to family labor, since the upper part of Table 12.2 refers only to monetary flows. The CV of the work performed by members of the family is included as a cost in non-monetary income. Agricultural costs also include payments to the NII for the irrigation water used, which were referred to above. When farmers' accounts are consolidated with those of the others affected by the project, these payments will be revenue for the NII. Payments to the co-operative for storage and marketing services (i.e. sales are valued at the co-operative gate) are included separately, and when added to revenues for the leasing of machinery and equipment will constitute co-operative income. As for financing, the credits that the NAB will provide to farmers and their repayments are shown. The algebraic total of sales, agricultural costs, payments for storage and marketing services and financing is monetary income for the farm as a unit of agricultural production.

The project will be carried out in an area where there is a large number of family small holdings, of which only some will receive irrigation. The incomes of the farmers on these small holdings in the situation without the project are insufficient to finance a minimum level of consumption due to the low agriculture yields per surface unit and the high ratio between the labor available per family and the area that can be cultivated. For these reasons, these farmers supplement their income by working for a salary on the bigger farms. However, the widespread nature of this situation in the region results in smallholders and landless farmers being unemployed or under-employed practically the entire year and being willing to work for a market wage equal to the CV of this job. Consequently, a family's monetary income is equal to that for agricultural work on the farm, plus wages for work away from the farm. The latter is equal to the respective CV, so that this CV is shown as a cost under the heading "non-monetary income." Since the project will increase income from the farm and employment of farmers on their smallholdings, wages received for work away from the farm in the situation with the project will fall as the project develops and the CV of family work rises (see Table 12.3 below).

On the basis of farm budgets for situations with and without the project for the various years, a table such as 12.3 can be prepared for each typical farm, which shows the flow of *additional* monetary and non-monetary income for the estimated useful life of the project. Each column in this table corresponds

Table 12.3 Additional Income and Costs, Monetary and Non-Monetary, of a Typical 2-ha. Farm (In $)

	Present Value	Year 0	1	2	3	4	5	6	7	8	9-27
(a) Sales	507,862	—	—	31,386	71,387	91,842	97,380	100,450	103,550	103,550	103,550
Dry Maize	9,832	—	—	-123	993	2,109	2,117	2,117	2,117	2,117	2,117
Soft Maize	39,713	—	—	3,115	5,618	7,821	7,821	7,821	7,821	7,821	7,821
Wheat	-2,315	—	—	-412	-412	-412	-412	-412	-412	-412	-412
Barley	-1,411	—	—	-251	-251	-251	-251	-251	-251	-251	-251
Beans	3,277	—	—	—	357	696	696	696	696	696	696
Peas	114,927	—	—	11,708	17,238	22,120	22,120	22,120	22,120	22,120	22,120
Potatoes	175,110	—	—	17,349	25,604	33,859	33,859	33,859	33,859	33,859	33,859
Vegetables	168,729	—	—	—	22,240	25,900	31,430	34,500	37,600	37,600	37,600
(b) Production Costs	-221,932	—	-1,320	-15,648	-29,175	-38,644	-42,083	-43,981	-45,222	-45,222	-45,222
Hired Labor	-5,325	—	—	—	—	-402	-630	-1,010	-1,450	-1,450	-1,450
Purchased Seed	19,990	—	—	-1,460	-2,473	-3,140	-3,720	-4,160	-4,160	-4,160	-4,160
Machinery & Equip. Services	-19,563	—	—	-1,065	-2,739	-3,924	-3,924	-3,924	-3,924	-3,924	-3,924
Fertilizers	-103,233	—	—	-6,128	-13,364	-17,834	-19,898	-20,684	-21,402	-21,402	-21,402
Pesticides	-32,600	—	—	-1,980	-4,119	-6,111	-6,323	-6,615	-6,698	-6,698	-6,698
Materials & Tools	-15,710	—	-1,320	-490	-1,955	-2,708	-3,063	-3,063	-3,063	-3,063	-3,063
Water Costs	-25,430	—	—	-4,525	-4,525	-4,525	-4,525	-4,525	-4,525	-4,525	-4,525
(c) Storage & Marketing	-16,169	—	—	-1,108	-2,308	-2,921	-3,088	-3,180	-3,273	-3,273	-3,273
(d) Finance	11,409	—	15,000	5,468	6,614	77	-792	-3,527	-304	-1,326	-1,326
Credit Received	154,704	—	15,000	11,600	22,420	26,250	28,650	27,840	28,650	28,650	28,650
Repayments	-143,296	—	—	-6,132	-15,806	-26,173	-29,442	-31,367	-28,954	-29,976	-29,976
(e) Monetary Income of the Farm [(a)+(b)+(c)+(d)]	281,169	—	13,680	20,098	46,518	50,354	51,417	49,762	54,751	53,729	53,729
(f) Wages away from the Farm	-111,029	—	-10,000	-12,000	-14,000	-20,000	-20,000	-20,000	-20,000	-20,000	-20,000
(g) Total Monetary Income [(e)+(f)]	170,141	—	3,680	8,098	32,518	30,354	31,417	29,762	34,751	33,729	33,729
(h) Non-Monetary Income	4,545	—	-5,000	7,453	1,327	730	574	574	574	574	574
Home Consumption	26,855	—	—	3,300	4,200	4,800	5,100	5,100	5,100	5,100	5,100
CV of Family Work	-133,339	—	-15,000	-7,847	-16,873	-24,070	-24,526	-24,526	-24,526	-24,526	-24,526
CV of Work away from the Farm	111,029	—	10,000	12,000	14,000	20,000	20,000	20,000	20,000	20,000	20,000
(i) Total Income [(g)+(h)]	174,686	—	-1,320	15,551	33,845	31,084	31,991	30,336	35,325	34,303	34,303

to a comparison between the situations with and without the project similar to that made for year 2 in Table 12.2. Only the column corresponding to year 1 deserves any particular explanation. In that year, the farmers will have to prepare the farm land for the beginning of irrigated farming the following year. They will therefore have additional expenditures on materials and tools ($-1,320$). They will also have to use labor available in the family unit ($-15,000$) and they will have to reduce their paid work away from the farm. The latter will reduce their income under this heading ($-10,000$), a reduction that is equal to the corresponding CV. Since this would involve a reduction in monetary income, which small farmers could not afford, they would receive a loan from the NAB (15,000) with a grace period of a year and a half which, as a result, they will start repaying once they begin to receive additional income from irrigated farming.

Finally, Table 12.4 shows the consolidation of the present value of the incremental budgets of all the farms affected by the project. Thus, for example, the column for farms of zero to five hectares corresponds to the *present value* column of Table 12.3 multiplied by the equivalent number of farms of that size. This table is the starting point for quantifying the income changes brought about by the project.

12.2 Breakdown of the Value of Inputs into Non-Produced Inputs and Transfers

The results of the preceding section, Tables 12.1 and 12.4, summarize the flows of additional income of the three main groups affected: the Government, the co-operative and the farmers. To identify the income changes of others affected as a result of purchases from the project, it is necessary to have the total requirements, direct and indirect, of non-produced inputs and transfers attributable to supplying the inputs required for the project. These requirements can be obtained by a method similar to that followed in Chapter 11. Those for non-traded inputs are given in simplified form in Table 12.5 and are conceptually equivalent to the results obtained in expression [11.6]. The gross value of production to which they correspond is at producer prices, that is at the factory gate, and therefore excludes the transport and trading costs necessary to put them where they will be used (the project). This is because these costs vary from project to project.

Consequently, in order to value the inputs delivered to the project, these total requirements first have to be corrected. This can be done by one of two equivalent procedures. The first is to break down the value of the project inputs into

Table 12.4 Present Value of the Incremental Income and Costs, Monetary and Non-Monetary, of All Farms According to Size (In $)

	Size in Hectares				
	0–5	5–10	10–50	50 or More	Total
(a) Sales	7,150,620	639,309	1,357,345	1,228,143	3,975,417
Dry Maize	14,532	60,618	135,243	123,990	334,383
Soft Maize	58,696	98,364	114,898	227,763	499,721
Wheat	−3,422	−7,843	−18,729	−69,963	−99,957
Barley	−2,085	−9,948	31,796	96,289	116,052
Beans	4,843	83,572	195,563	163,170	447,148
Peas	169,862	75,198	356,641	426,783	1,028,484
Potatoes	258,813	−2,118	541,933	260,111	1,058,739
Vegetables	249,381	341,466	—	—	590,847
(b) Production Costs	−328,013	−350,123	−723,357	−664,013	−2,065,506
Hired Labor	−7,870	−102,660	−226,095	−226,811	−563,436
Purchased Seed	−29,545	−7,808	−76,908	−52,388	−166,649
Machinery & Equipment Services	−28,914	−19,032	—	—	−47,946
Machinery & Equipment	—	—	−83,464	−102,466	−185,930
Fertilizers	−152,578	−112,612	−189,123	−149,031	−603,344
Pesticides	−48,301	−40,546	−64,912	−63,871	−217,630
Materials & Tools	−23,219	−36,779	−20,417	−14,173	−94,588
Water Costs	−37,586	−30,686	−62,438	−55,273	−185,983
(c) Storage & Marketing	−23,898	−20,354	−43,215	−39,101	−126,568
(d) Finance	16,862	21,624	59,967	62,197	160,650
Credit Received	228,653	240,267	522,820	498,856	1,490,596
Repayments	−211,791	−218,643	−462,853	−436,659	−1,329,946
(e) Monetary Income of the Farm [(a)+(b)+(c)+(d)]	415,571	290,456	650,740	587,226	1,943,993
(f) Wages away from the Farm	−164,101	−18,196	—	—	−182,297
(g) Total Monetary Income [(e)+(f)]	251,470	272,260	650,740	587,226	1,761,696
(h) Non-Monetary Income	6,718	−27,810	−37,477	—	−58,569
Home Consumption	39,692	8,604	—	—	48,296
CV of Family Work	−197,075	−54,610	−37,477	—	−289,162
CV of Work away from the Farm	164,101	18,196	—	—	182,297
(i) Total Income [(g)+(h)]	258,188	244,450	613,263	587,226	1,703,127

$$\frac{\text{price of the input}}{\text{delivered to the project}} = \frac{\text{producer}}{\text{price}} + \frac{\text{transport}}{\text{margins}} + \frac{\text{trade}}{\text{margins}}$$

and then value each component *as if* it were a specific input. In other words, when the project demands an input delivered to the site, in reality it demands the input at the factory gate plus the necessary transport and trade to deliver it to the site. An equivalent procedure is to recalculate the total requirements of Table 12.5 at purchasers' prices. The latter procedure will be simpler since a

Table 12.5 Unitary Total Requirements of Non-Traded Inputs at Producer Prices

Outputs	Foreign Exchange	Skilled Labor	Unskilled Labor	Taxes	Total
Non-Traded Inputs	0.50	0.17	0.20	0.13	1.00
Construction	0.35	0.33	0.22	0.10	1.00
Silos	0.60	0.14	0.17	0.09	1.00
Transport	0.65	0.13	0.02	0.20	1.00
Wholesale Trade	0.32	0.39	0.21	0.08	1.00
Seed	0.38	0.40	0.20	0.02	1.00
Fertilizers	0.70	0.05	0.08	0.17	1.00
Pesticides	0.68	0.08	0.07	0.17	1.00

number of them will be used in different parts of the project. By way of example, the one corresponding to non-traded inputs will be recalculated.

Converting total requirements at producer prices to purchasers' prices also involves starting from the breakdown of the price of the good at the project site. This breakdown for non-traded inputs is as follows:

$$\frac{\text{at-project-site}}{\text{price}} = \frac{\text{producer}}{\text{price}} + \text{transport} + \frac{\text{wholesale}}{\text{trade}}$$

$$1.00 = 0.88 + 0.02 + 0.10$$

On this basis, the breakdown into total requirements of the price at the project site can be calculated, using the transport and trade total requirements (Table 12.5), as follows:

	Foreign Exchange	Skilled Labor	Unskilled Labor	Taxes	Total
Producer Price	0.50×0.88	0.17×0.88	0.20×0.88	0.13×0.88	0.88
Transport	0.65×0.02	0.13×0.02	0.02×0.02	0.20×0.02	0.02
Wholesale Trade	0.32×0.10	0.39×0.10	0.21×0.10	0.08×0.10	0.10
Total	0.49	0.19	0.20	0.12	1.00

In other words, total requirements of non-produced inputs and transfers will be a weighted average of the requirements for the good valued at producer prices, of transport and of trade requirements respectively, in which the weights are the share of each one in the purchasers' price. The results obtained for the purchasers' price structures given in Table 12.6 are shown in Table 12.7. A comparison of Tables 12.7 and 12.5 will show that, up to the second decimal place, the breakdowns vary only to a very small degree.

Table 12.6 Composition of Purchasers' Prices (Project) of Non-Traded Inputs

Outputs	Producer Price	Transport	Trade	Total
Non-Traded Inputs	0.88	0.02	0.10	1.00
Construction	0.97	0.03	0.00	1.00
Silos	0.95	0.05	0.00	1.00
Transport	1.00	0.00	0.00	1.00
Wholesale Trade	1.00	0.00	0.00	1.00
Seed[a]	0.97	0.03	0.00	1.00
Fertilizer[a]	0.98	0.02	0.00	1.00
Pesticides[a]	0.99	0.01	0.00	1.00

a. Trade margins are not included in seed, fertilizers and pesticides since they are included in the co-operative's costs (Table 12.1).

A similar situation arises with imported goods. If these were simply valued at their foreign exchange prices, expressed in the national currency plus import taxes, breakdown would be simple. However, they are valued at the prices actually paid by the purchaser and, consequently, include the respective domestic transport and trade margins.

$$\frac{\text{at-project-site}}{\text{price}} = \frac{\text{foreign}}{\text{exchange}} + \text{taxes} + \text{transport} + \text{trade}$$

In the same way as for non-traded goods, two alternative procedures may be followed. The first consists in considering expenditure as being payment for four different components: foreign exchange, taxes, transport and trade. The second, simpler one is to recalculate total requirements for non-produced goods and transfers at the appropriate purchasers' prices.

Let us consider the case of imported inputs purchased by the Government. Their price includes the transport and trade margins of the national distribu-

Table 12.7 Unitary Total Requirements of Non-Traded Goods, at Purchasers' Prices (Project)

	Foreign Exchange	Skilled Labor	Unskilled Labor	Taxes	Total
Non-Traded Inputs	0.48	0.19	0.20	0.13	1.00
Construction	0.36	0.33	0.21	0.10	1.00
Silos	0.60	0.14	0.16	0.10	1.00
Transport	0.65	0.13	0.02	0.20	1.00
Wholesale Trade	0.32	0.39	0.20	0.08	1.00
Seed	0.39	0.39	0.20	0.02	1.00
Fertilizers	0.70	0.05	0.08	0.17	1.00
Pesticides	0.68	0.08	0.07	0.17	1.00

Source: Calculated on the basis of Tables 12.5 and 12.6.

tors from whom they are purchased but not import taxes, since Government purchases are brought in free of taxes, or they are refunded in the case of products purchased on the domestic market. Thus, the breakdown of the purchasers' price is as follows,

$$\frac{\text{at-project-site}}{\text{price}} = \frac{\text{foreign}}{\text{exchange}} + \text{taxes} + \text{transport} + \text{trade}$$

$$1.00 \quad = \quad 0.89 \quad + 0.00 + \quad 0.01 \quad + 0.10$$

and the total requirements sought can also be calculated by using those for transport and trade (Table 12.5) in the following way:

	Foreign Exchange	Skilled Labor	Unskilled Labor	Taxes	Total
Foreign Exchange	0.89	0.00	0.00	0.00	0.89
Transport	0.65×0.01	0.13×0.01	0.02×0.01	0.20×0.01	0.01
Trade	0.32×0.10	0.39×0.10	0.21×0.10	0.08×0.10	0.10
Total	0.93	0.04	0.02	0.01	1.00

In the case of the project analyzed, Table 12.8 shows the breakdown of the prices paid by those affected by the project, with a distinction between the Government and the private sector (co-operative and farmers), because of the former's special tax treatment. The resulting total requirements are shown in Table 12.9 and a comparison of them with Table 12.8 indicates that they are substantially different from those that would result from assuming that the valuation of imported inputs merely corresponded to foreign exchange plus import taxes.

Once total requirements are available, it is possible to break down the costs incurred by the Government and the co-operative. Thus, for example, pur-

Table 12.8   Composition of Purchasers' Price (Project) of Imported Inputs

	Foreign Exchange	Taxes	Transport	Trade	Total
Inputs (govt.)	0.89	0.00	0.01	0.10	1.00
Mach. & Equip. (govt.)	0.88	0.00	0.03	0.09	1.00
Equipment (private)	0.83	0.06	0.02	0.09	1.00
Agricultural Mach. (co-op.)	0.82	0.06	0.03	0.09	1.00
Vehicles (govt.)	0.85	0.00	0.00	0.15	1.00
Vehicles (private)	0.80	0.05	0.00	0.15	1.00
Inputs (private)	0.81	0.10	0.01	0.08	1.00

Table 12.9   Unitary Total Requirements of Imported Inputs, at Purchasers' Prices (Project)

	Foreign Exchange	Skilled Labor	Unskilled Labor	Taxes	Total
Inputs (govt.)	0.93	0.04	0.02	0.01	1.00
Mach. & Equip. (govt.)	0.93	0.04	0.02	0.01	1.00
Equipment (private)	0.87	0.04	0.02	0.07	1.00
Agricultural Mach. (private)	0.87	0.04	0.02	0.07	1.00
Vehicles (govt.)	0.90	0.06	0.03	0.01	1.00
Vehicles (private)	0.85	0.06	0.03	0.06	1.00
Inputs (private)	0.84	0.03	0.02	0.11	1.00

Source: Calculated on the basis of Table 12.5 and 12.8.

chases of non-traded inputs by the Government for infrastructure works ($94,109) are broken down using the first row of Table 12.7. This shows that to increase production by $1.00 at purchasers' prices involves using $0.48 of foreign exchange, so that the Government's demand for non-traded inputs will mean a use (direct and indirect) of foreign exchange equal to $94,109 \times 0.48 = \$45,172$. In the same way, the remaining total requirements for non-produced inputs and transfers can be obtained:

Foreign Exchange	$94,109 \times 0.48 =$	45,172
Skilled Labor	$94,109 \times 0.19 =$	17,881
Unskilled Labor (FS)	$94,109 \times 0.20 =$	18,822
Taxes	$94,109 \times 0.13 =$	12,234
Total		$= 94,109$

The same procedure allows for the breakdown of the remaining inputs demanded by the Government and the co-operative to be calculated in order to obtain the results shown in Tables 12.10 and 12.11. It should be noted that in these tables, the *Income* figures are kept as they were since this income is financial transfers between farmers, the Government and the co-operative, whose costs are already considered in the remaining accounts. For example, Government revenue from water charges is equal to payments by farmers, and the costs of providing it are those of the irrigation system. The same occurs with co-operative revenue for machinery and storage services, in which the respective costs are included in the support services as expenditure on construction, silos, machinery, labor, etc. As regards the sales of seed, fertilizers and pesticides by the co-operative, income is equal to the payments to farmers for these items and it is the purchase of these inputs by the co-operative, which has been broken down into its total requirements for non-produced inputs and transfers. Finally, it should be noted in Table 12.10 that when the

Table 12.10 Breakdown of the Present Value of Government Costs in the Irrigation System (In $)

	Government	Foreign Exchange	Labor Skilled	Labor Unskilled FS	Labor Unskilled RS	Taxes	Total
I. COST OF THE IRRIGATION SYSTEM	−1,188,646	−849,753	−197,957	−119,186	—	−21,750	−1,188,646
Infrastructure Works	−1,045,655	−832,865	−93,586	−98,500	—	−20,704	−1,045,655
Imported Machinery & Equipment	−700,589	−651,548	−28,024	−14,012	—	−7,006	−700,589
Skilled Labor	−41,826	—	−41,826	—	—	—	−41,826
Unskilled Labor	−62,739	—	—	−62,739	—	—	−62,739
Non-Traded Inputs	−94,109	−45,172	−17,881	−18,822	—	−12,234	−94,109
Imported Inputs	−146,392	−136,145	−5,856	−2,928	—	−1,464	−146,392
Operation & Maintenance	−142,991	−16,889	−104,371	−20,686	—	−1,046	−142,991
Skilled Labor	−102,472	—	−102,472	—	—	—	−102,472
Unskilled Labor	−19,009	—	—	−19,009	—	—	−19,009
Imported Machinery & Equipment	−14,586	−13,565	−583	−292	—	−146	−14,586
Non-Traded Inputs	−6,924	−3,324	−1,316	−1,385	—	−900	−6,924
II. COST OF SUPPORT SERVICES	−63,495	−16,469	−45,315	−1,126	—	−585	−63,495
Marketing Infrastructure	—	—	—	—	—	—	—
Construction	—	—	—	—	—	—	—
Silos	—	—	—	—	—	—	—
Equipment	—	—	—	—	—	—	—
Agricultural Machinery	—	—	—	—	—	—	—
Vehicles	−15,020	−13,518	−901	−451	—	−150	−15,020
Current Costs	−48,475	−2,951	−44,413	−676	—	−435	−48,475
Skilled Labor	−43,740	—	−43,740	—	—	—	−43,740
Unskilled Labor	—	—	—	—	—	—	—
Imported Inputs	−1,508	−1,402	−60	−30	—	−15	−1,508
Non-Traded Inputs	−3,227	−1,549	−613	−645	—	−420	−3,227
III. TOTAL COSTS (I + II)	−1,252,141	−866,223	−243,272	−120,312	—	−22,335	−1,252,141

Source: Calculated on the basis of Tables 12.1, 12.7 and 12.9.

Table 12.11 Breakdown of the Present Value of Co-Operative Costs (In $)

	Co-Operative	Foreign Exchange	Labor Skilled	Labor Unskilled FS	Labor Unskilled RS	Taxes	Total
I. COST OF IRRIGATION SYSTEM	–	–	–	–	–	–	–
II. COST OF SUPPORT SERVICES	-153,511	-108,775	-22,140	-8,252	-3,443	-10,900	-153,511
Trading Infrastructure	-49,540	-35,780	-5,427	-4,246	–	-4,088	-49,540
Construction	-7,257	-2,613	-2,395	-1,524	–	-726	-7,257
Silos	-13,404	-8,042	-1,877	-2,145	–	-1,340	-13,404
Equipment	-28,879	-25,125	-1,155	-578	–	-2,022	-28,879
Agricultural Machinery	-36,130	-31,433	-1,445	-723	–	-2,529	-36,130
Vehicles	-36,074	-30,663	-2,164	-1,082	–	-2,164	-36,074
Current Costs	-31,767	-10,900	-13,104	-2,201	-3,443	-2,119	-31,767
Skilled Labor	-10,935	–	-10,935	–	–	–	-10,935
Unskilled Labor	-3,443	–	–	–	-3,443	–	-3,443
Imported Inputs	-7,092	-5,957	-213	-142	–	-780	-7,092
Non-Traded Inputs	-10,297	-4,943	-1,956	-2,059	–	-1,339	-10,297
III. TOTAL COSTS (I + II)	-153,511	-108,775	-22,140	-8,252	-3,443	-10,900	-153,511
IV INCOME							
Water Payments	47,946	–	–	–	–	–	–
Mach. & Equip. Services	126,568	–	–	–	–	–	–
Storage & Marketing	987,623	–	–	–	–	–	–
Sales							
Less Purchases Of:							
Seed	-158,317	-61,744	-61,744	-31,663	–	-3,166	-158,317
Fertilizer	-573,177	-401,224	-28,659	-45,854	–	-97,440	-573,177
Pesticide	-206,749	-140,589	-16,540	-14,472	–	-35,147	-206,749
V FINANCING							
Credit from the NAB	222,836	–	–	–	–	–	–
Repayments	-191,422	–	–	–	–	–	–
VI.TOTAL (III + IV + V)	101,797	–	–	–	–	–	–

Source: Calculated on the basis of Tables 12.1, 12.7 and 12.9.

214

Government purchases, for example, non-traded inputs for infrastructure works for \$94,109, \$12,234 correspond to taxes included in the value at purchasers' prices of those inputs. These are taxes paid by the manufacturers of the inputs and constitute Government *revenue*.

It now remains for us to break down the value of additional agricultural production attributable to the project. First we need to consider separately the three parts making it up, viz: seed, home consumption and sales. In turn, this will help justify the particular way in which the farm budgets were prepared (Tables 12.2, 12.3 and 12.4). Seed from the previous period's production (as opposed to that purchased) needs to be valued at its production cost *at the farm* since this is what actually happens, especially in the situation without the project.[2] As these costs have already been calculated in *Farming costs*, their breakdown and subsequent valuation takes into account the additional production intended for consumption on the farm as seed. A similar situation arises with home consumption. Since the small farmers, the only ones for whom increased home consumption exists, do not purchase those products that they themselves produce, but instead only sell the surpluses, greater home consumption merely reflects a better diet. Any effect on additional supply takes place through changes in sales. The net effect of greater production for home consumption is calculated as the difference between the value of home consumption and its *production* costs (as opposed to those for *sales*). The former has to be valued at the CV of the additional consumption, estimated here by the difference between the sales value for the co-operative and payments for storage and marketing services, since these are a percentage on sales. In other words, it is assumed that at the margin, farmers value additional home consumption at what for them is the opportunity cost. The corresponding production costs are already included in the farm budget under that title.

Soft maize, wheat, barley and beans are imported at the margin, so the project will substitute imports in this regard. Consequently, purchaser's prices for imports and project output have to be compared, as well as their respective breakdowns. This comparison shows that the wholesale and retail trade margins are not affected by the source of outputs and that differences in domestic transport costs are insignificant. As a result, the sales price of the co-operative, which sells at the co-operative gate, will be equivalent to the CIF value plus taxes paid for the imports replaced. The breakdown of prices appears in Table 12.12, and using those figures to break down the additional supply of imported agricultural outputs enables us to obtain the results in Table 12.13.

---

2. Note that this is valid regardless of whether the output in question could have been imported at the margin. The effect of keeping a larger or smaller proportion of production as seed *will affect supply through sales*.

Table 12.12   Breakdown of the Sales Price of Agricultural Outputs Imported at the Margin

	Foreign Exchange	Taxes	Total
Dry Maize	0.95	0.05	1.00
Wheat	0.90	0.10	1.00
Barley	0.90	0.10	1.00
Beans	0.95	0.05	1.00

The remaining outputs are non-traded and, according to Section 7.3, we need to ascertain whether the technical change introduced by the project changes production conditions *at the margin* and, consequently, prices, or whether it merely displaces marginal producers to other activities without discernible effects on prices. The project is in the latter category, so that the additional supply of non-traded goods ought to be valued according to what was presented in Table 7.3. However, no information is available on the production costs of marginal producers, so that additional production is valued at its market price. As pointed out in Section 7.3, this amounts to assuming that this price is equal to the production cost at efficiency prices of the displaced producers.

The lower part of Table 12.13 provides a breakdown of purchases of inputs. There the reader will see that those purchases whose breakdown is already included in Tables 12.10 and 12.11 for the Government and the co-operative have been omitted. This is the case for seed purchased, machinery and equipment services, fertilizers, pesticides and water.

12.3 Consolidation of the Income Changes Brought About by the Project

All the information needed to consolidate the income changes generated by the project is now available. The first seven columns of Table 12.14 correspond to the consolidation of the income changes already presented in preceding sections. Six of these columns are for the Government, the co-operative and the four sizes of farms. The seventh is for the National Agricultural Bank (NAB) and is included to complete the entries for the income flows between the co-operative, the farmers and the bank. The eighth column, *Government (taxes)*, is included to record the changes in Government revenue from the taxes included in the prices of the goods purchased and sold as well as those that account for the difference between the exchange rate and the APRFE. The Government thus appears twice. The first time is as the source of expenditure on the irrigation system and support services, as well as the recipient of

Table 12.13 Breakdown of Present Value of Sales of Imported Outputs and Purchases of Inputs (In $)

	Total	Foreign Exchange	Skilled Labor	Unskilled Labor, FS	Taxes	Total
SALES OF IMPORTED OUTPUTS						
Farms of 0 – 5 ha.	13,868	13,450	—	—	418	13,868
Dry Maize	14,532	13,805	—	—	727	14,532
Wheat	-3,422	-3,080	—	—	-342	-3,422
Barley	-2,085	-1,877	—	—	-209	-2,085
Beans	4,843	4,601	—	—	242	4,843
Farms of 5 – 10 ha.	126,399	120,969	—	—	5,430	126,399
Dry Maize	60,618	57,587	—	—	3,031	60,618
Wheat	-7,843	-7,059	—	—	-784	-7,843
Barley	-9,948	-8,953	—	—	-995	-9,948
Beans	83,572	79,393	—	—	4,179	83,572
Farms of 10 – 50 ha.	343,873	326,026	—	—	17,847	343,873
Dry Maize	135,243	128,481	—	—	6,762	135,243
Wheat	-18,729	-16,856	—	—	-1,873	-18,729
Barley	31,796	28,616	—	—	3,180	31,796
Beans	195,563	185,785	—	—	9,778	195,563
Farms of 50 or more ha.	313,486	296,495	—	—	16,991	313,486
Dry Maize	123,990	117,791	—	—	6,200	123,990
Wheat	-69,963	-62,967	—	—	-6,996	-69,963
Barley	96,289	86,660	—	—	9,629	96,289
Beans	163,170	155,012	—	—	8,159	163,170
PURCHASES OF INPUTS						
Farms of 0 – 5 ha.	-23,219	-11,145	-4,412	-4,644	-3,018	-23,219
Machinery & Equipment	—	—	—	—	—	—
Materials & Tools	-23,219	-11,145	-4,412	-4,644	-3,018	-23,219
Farms of 5 – 10 ha.	-36,779	-17,654	-6,988	-7,356	-4,781	-36,779
Machinery & Equipment	—	—	—	—	—	—
Materials & Tools	-36,779	-17,654	-6,988	-7,356	-4,781	-36,779
Farms of 10 – 50 ha.	-103,881	-82,414	-7,218	-5,753	-8,497	-103,881
Machinery & Equipment	-83,464	-72,614	-3,339	-1,669	-5,842	-83,464
Materials & Tools	-20,417	-9,800	-3,879	-4,083	-2,654	-20,417
Farms of 50 or more ha.	-116,639	-95,948	-6,792	-4,884	-9,015	-116,639
Machinery & Equipment	-102,466	-89,145	-4,099	-2,049	-7,173	-102,466
Materials & Tools	-14,173	-6,803	-2,693	-2,835	-1,842	-14,173

Source: Calculated on the basis of Tables 12.4, 12.7 and 12.9.

Table 12.14 Consolidation of the Income Changes Brought About by the Project
(In $)

	Government	Co-Operative	NAB
I. GOVERNMENT & CO-OPERATIVE COSTS			
Cost of the Irrigation System			
Foreign Exchange	−849,753	−	−
Skilled Labor	−197,957	−	−
Unskilled Labor (FS)	−119,186	−	−
Taxes	−21,750	−	−
Cost of Support Services			
Foreign Exchange	−16,469	−108,775	−
Skilled Labor	−45,315	−22,140	−
Unskilled Labor (FS)	−1,126	−8,252	−
Unskilled Labor (RS)	−	−3,443	−
Taxes	−585	−10,900	−
Purchases of Seed, Fertilizers & Pesticides			
Foreign Exchange	−	−603,557	−
Skilled Labor	−	−106,943	−
Unskilled Labor (FS)	−	−91,989	−
Taxes	−	−135,753	−
Loan to the Co-Operative	−	222,836	−222,836
Repayments	−	−191,422	191,422
II. FARMERS			
Sales			
Foreign Exchange	−	−	−
Taxes	−	−	−
Soft Maize	−	−	−
Peas	−	−	−
Potatoes	−	−	−
Vegetables	−	−	−
Production Costs			
Foreign Exchange	−	−	−
Skilled Labor	−	−	−
Unskilled Labor (FS)	−	−	−
Taxes	−	−	−
Hired Labor	−	−	−
Purchased Seed	−	166,649	−
Machinery & Equipment Services	−	47,946	−
Fertilizers	−	603,344	−
Pesticides	−	217,630	−
Water Costs	185,983	−	−
Storage & Marketing	−	126,568	−
Loan Received	−	−	−1,490,596
Repayments	−	−	1,329,946
Wages away from the Farm	−	−	−
Non-Monetary Income	−	−	−
TOTAL ADDITIONAL INCOME	−1,066,158	101,799	−192,064

Farms Size (in hectares)				Government	Workers	
0–5	5–10	10–50	50 or more	(Taxes)	Unskilled	Total
—	—	—	—	−84,975	—	−934,728
—	—	—	—	—	—	−197,957
—	—	—	—	—	35,756	−83,430
—	—	—	—	21,750	—	—
—	—	—	—	−12,524	—	−137,768
—	—	—	—	—	—	−67,455
—	—	—	—	—	2,813	−6,565
—	—	—	—	—	—	−3,443
—	—	—	—	11,485	—	—
—	—	—	—	−60,356	—	−663,913
—	—	—	—	—	—	−106,943
—	—	—	—	—	27,597	−64,392
—	—	—	—	135,753	—	—
—	—	—	—	—	—	—
—	—	—	—	—	—	—
13,450	120,969	326,026	296,495	75,694	—	832,634
418	5,430	17,847	16,991	−40,686	—	—
58,696	98,364	114,898	227,763	—	—	499,721
169,862	75,198	356,641	426,783	—	—	1,028,484
258,813	−2,118	541,933	260,111	—	—	1,058,739
249,381	341,466	—	—	—	—	590,847
−11,145	−17,654	−82,414	−95,948	−20,716	—	−227,877
−4,412	−6,988	−7,218	−6,792	—	—	−25,410
−4,644	−7,356	−5,753	−4,884	—	6,791	−15,846
−3,018	−4,781	−8,497	−9,015	25,311	—	—
−7,870	−102,660	−226,095	−226,811	—	—	−563,436
−29,545	−7,808	−76,908	−52,388	—	—	—
−28,914	−19,032	—	—	—	—	—
−152,578	−112,612	−189,123	−149,031	—	—	—
−48,301	−40,546	−64,912	−63,871	—	—	—
−37,586	−30,686	−62,438	−55,273	—	—	—
−23,898	−20,354	−43,215	−39,101	—	—	—
228,653	240,267	522,820	498,856	—	—	—
−211,791	−218,643	−462,853	−436,659	—	—	—
−164,101	−18,196	—	—	—	—	−182,297
6,718	−27,810	−37,477	—	—	—	−58,569
258,188	244,450	613,262	587,226	50,736	72,957	670,396

the water charges paid by farmers. In both cases, flows originating directly in the financial statements of the project are involved. The second appearance relates to the effects on tax revenue, and is included separately to facilitate interpretation of the vertical totals of the columns, which, as can be seen, coincide with those of Tables 12.1 and 12.4. Finally, the *Unskilled Workers* column is included to record the additional income which, as will be seen, explains the difference between the wages paid to these workers in the formal sector of the economy and their income in the sector from which they come.

As regards the rows, the upper part of Table 12.14 contains irrigation and support services costs already broken down into their total requirements of non-produced inputs and transfers originating in Tables 12.10 and 12.11. These costs are classified according to whether they are paid by the Government or the co-operative. The costs for purchasing seed, fertilizers and pesticides by the co-operative are shown in the same way. Its income for machinery and equipment leasing, storage, marketing and sales of inputs to farmers is included as the counterpart of payments by the latter in the lower part of the table, which is merely a different way of presenting Table 12.4. The difference is that the sales of imported agricultural outputs and the purchases of the remaining inputs are shown broken down into their total requirements for non-produced inputs and transfers.

To complete the income changes brought about by the project, only the effects of the net production of foreign exchange on the collection of taxes and the additional income of unskilled workers need to be included. It is estimated that for each $1.00 of additional foreign exchange, the Government receives $0.10 in taxes as the net balance between greater receipts for imports and lower receipts for exports, i.e. the APRFE = 1.1. The change in tax receipts attributable to the use and production of foreign exchange is shown in the *Government (taxes)* column. As for unskilled labor, a distinction has been made between wages paid in the formal urban sector (FS) of the economy (or equivalent) and in the rural sector (RS). This is because in the formal urban sector, wages are considerably higher than those in the informal sector due to high unemployment and widespread under-employment. Since at the margin, unskilled labor comes from under-employment in the rural sector, the prevailing wages in this sector were taken as an approximation of the CV of additional employment, which turned out to be equal to 70% of the wages in the formal sector. Consequently, the difference between the two is shown as additional income for unskilled workers in the formal sector. In the rural sector, the wages paid are considered good approximations of the corresponding CV, and thus no additional income is entered under this heading.

12.4 Net Benefits and Their Distribution

The reader will recall from Part I of this study, that in order to obtain a measure of "total" benefits attributable to the project, an aggregation criterion or interpersonal distributional value judgment is needed. If this value judgment corresponds to that of the operational version of efficiency analysis, an additional unit of income is equally valuable whatever the income level of the recipient, and the sum of the *Total* column will be the net benefits from the project at efficiency prices each time there is equality between the discount rate and the rate of return on marginal investment. This last column is all that is required by the operational version of efficiency analysis. However, if the interpersonal distributional value judgment were different, or the discount rate and the rate of return on marginal investment were not equal, the calculation of "total" net benefits would require us to know, as we will see in Part III, the distribution of the *net* changes in income. As pointed out earlier, this is the difference between the distribution of income changes generated by the project and by the alternative course of action. Since the decision to construct the irrigation system is the element that gives rise to all the other income flows, and since the funds financing its construction are those on which a decision is being taken, the alternative course of action is what corresponds to the *other* use that would be made of these funds if the project were not carried out. The income changes that this alternative use of funds would lead to, and their distribution, constitute the *without* project situation.

CHAPTER 13

EXTENSIONS OF THE USE OF INPUT-OUTPUT TECHNIQUES: UNSKILLED LABOR

In Chapter 10, the APRs of non-produced inputs and transfers, elements of the APR^f vector, were treated as exogenous to the solution of the equation system [11.4]. Clearly this is not the case in reality, since estimating the APR^f_h relies on accepting, at some point in the analysis, the assumption that the market price is equal to the efficiency price. Remember that this took place, for example, in Chapter 3 in discussing the APRFE when there are imports of intermediate goods, and in Chapter 6 in discussing the valuation of skilled labor. To avoid it would require formulating a general equilibrium model and its adjustment rules for demand and supply changes of each of the goods and services involved. Since estimating a model of this type is considered beyond practical possibilities, this approach will not be attempted. However, in this chapter we will consider a type of extension of the model presented in Chapter 10, which could be applied provided the data are available. This type of extension uses input-output analysis logic to incorporate the effects of some changes in the production of goods and services resulting from changes in the demand for non-produced inputs. The procedure consists in treating the direct requirements for some non-produced inputs as endogenous to the system of equations

Table 13.1 Preparation of the Column "Producing" Unskilled Labor

Breakdown	General Notation	Cost to the Employer	Co-efficients	Notation in the Matrix
Increase in the Monetary Income of the Worker	Δw	13,712	0.43	f_{ih}
Increase in ISS Income	$w^t t_{ss}$	2,232	0.07	f_{ih}
Compensating Variation of Additional Work	d^f	9,566	0.30	f_{ih}
Income in Export Agriculture	w^x	6,377	0.20	a_{ij}
Total	w^t	31,887	1.00	

a. Values corresponding to the numerical example in Section 6.6.

[11.4]. As an illustration, the case of unskilled labor will be presented using the example from Section 6.6, in which the cost to the employer of unskilled labor was broken down into: (a) the increase in the worker's monetary income (Δw); (b) the increase in the income of the Institute of Social Security (ISS); (c) the compensating variation of the additional work (d^f); and (d) the wages earned in export agriculture (w^x).

13.1 Treatment in the Matrix

In order to estimate the APR of unskilled labor, we can start by treating it *as if* it were a produced input, incorporating into the matrix $[a_{ij}; f_{ih}]$ a row i that "produces" labor and from which other sectors demand according to their respective coefficients representing the cost to the employer of unskilled labor. This "labor-producing" row consists of the coefficients resulting from the breakdown of the cost to the employer mentioned above (see Table 13.1). Following the traditional criterion in cost-benefit analysis of ignoring the indirect effects resulting from expenditure of additional income, transfer Δw and the cost of the non-produced good d^f are assigned to the matrix $[f_{ih}]$. Income changes in export agriculture represent changes in exports, the results of which on foreign exchange and some non-traded services can be included in the matrix.

As indicated in preceding chapters (see [6.13]), if we accept that w^x is equal to the farm gate value of the marginal product, then

$$w^x = q^x p^{fob} - q^x p^{fob} t_x - q^x p^{fob} tra^x - q^x p^{fob} com^x$$

Namely, the salary paid is equal to the foreign exchange value (expressed in

Table 13.2 Preparation of the Column for the Reduction in Exports

	General Notation	Cost to the Employer	Co-Efficients	Notation in the Matrix
Reduction in the Supply of Foreign Exchange	$q^x p^{fob}$	7,873	1.23	f_{ih}
Export Taxes	$-q^x p^{fob} t_x$	−315	−0.05	f_{ih}
Savings in Transport Costs	$-q^x p^{fob} tra^x$	−79	−0.01	a_{ij}
Savings in Trading Costs	$-q^x p^{fob} com^x$	−1,102	−0.17	a_{ij}
Total	w^x	6,377	1.00	

the national currency at the EER) of the reduction in exports minus the corresponding export taxes, minus the savings in transport and trading costs.[1] The structure corresponding to w^x can be included in the matrix as indicated in Table 13.2, which uses the numerical example from Section 6.6. The reduction in the supply of foreign exchange and export taxes will be in the matrix of non-produced inputs and transfers $[f_{ih}]$ and the reduction in demand for transport and trading services will appear in the transactions matrix. Finally, contributions to the ISS appear as a transfer brought about by hiring unskilled workers, who would not have joined the social security system if not hired.

13.2 A Numerical Example

By way of example, the treatment of unskilled labor presented in the previous section will be included in the matrix used in Chapter 12, Table 12.3. To simplify the explanation, columns *bp* and *bg* in Table 11.3 have been incorporated into a single one as if sectors (2) and (3) were both private (or public). It will be useful to begin by repositioning column *wnc* as a column in the matrix $[a_{ij}]$. That is column (4) of Table 13.3. Next, it is necessary to include the corresponding row that "produces" unskilled labor whose coefficients are those from the *Coefficients* column in Table 13.2. This row "demands" $w^x = 0.20$ backwards to incorporate the effects of the reduction in exports q^x. It also contains transfers $\Delta w = 0.43\,q^x$ and $w\,t_{ss} = 0.07$, since these are workers who at the margin join the social security system, and the CV of additional work $d^f = 0.30$. Row (5) corresponds to the breakdown of w^x in its effects on foreign exchange (1.23), transport and trading costs (−0.18) and

---

1. If the exported output is processed to any degree, the respective costs would also have to be deducted.

Table 13.3 Numerical Example of an Intersectoral Relations Matrix Including Endogenous Treatment of Wages to Unskilled Labor

Outputs	Inputs												Total
	(1)	(2)	(3)	(4)	(5)	...	fe	Δw	wt_{ss}	d^f	wc	t	b	
(1)	–	0.37	0.05	0.15	–		0.30	–	–	–	0.10	0.03	–	1.00
(2)	0.14	–	0.06	0.20	–		0.40	–	–	–	0.15	0.03	0.02	1.00
(3)	0.09	0.14	–	0.05	–		0.70	–	–	–	0.15	–	–0.13	1.00
(4)	–	–	–	–	0.20		–	0.43	0.07	0.30	–	–	–	1.00
(5)	–	–	–0.18	–	–		1.23	–	–	–	–	–0.05	–	1.00

Source: Prepared on the basis of the matrix in Table 11.3.

225

Table 13.4 Matrix of Total Requirements for Non-Produced Inputs and Transfers

F_{ih}^*	fe^*	Δw^*	wt_{ss}^*	d^{f*}	wc^*	t^*	b^*	Total
F_{1h}^*	0.588	0.105	0.017	0.073	0.177	0.041	−0.001	1.000
F_{2h}^*	0.576	0.103	0.017	0.072	0.185	0.034	0.013	1.000
F_{3h}^*	0.844	0.045	0.007	0.032	0.192	0.008	−0.128	1.000
F_{4h}^*	0.215	0.428	0.070	0.299	−0.007	−0.010	0.005	1.000
F_{5h}^*	1.078	−0.008	−0.001	−0.006	−0.035	−0.051	0.023	1.000

Source: Calculated on the basis of the matrix in Table 13.3.

the collection of export taxes (−0.05). Now, using the new matrix of inter-sectoral relations, we can calculate the total requirements, direct and indirect, of non-produced inputs and transfers, which are shown in Table 13.4. Row (4) of the matrix,

$$[F_{4h}^*] = [0.215; 0.428; 0.070; 0.299; -0.007; 0.010; 0.005]$$

will be the total requirements of non-produced inputs and transfers associated with hiring unskilled labor per peso of cost to the employer. Thus, for example, the cost to the employer of unskilled labor hired for the industrial project in Chapter 9 ($31,887 in Table 9.3) can be broken down according to the first column of Table 13.5. The remaining columns contain the changes (direct and indirect) in the incomes of the others affected, calculated and allocated in the same way as in the previous cases, the total of which is equal to the value at efficiency prices. Note that the row for contributions to the ISS corresponds to the example in Table 6.7. There it is assumed that the benefit that the worker

Table 13.5 Breakdown of the Cost to the Employer and Valuation at Efficiency Prices of Unskilled Labor

	Project	Government	Unskilled Workers	Other Firms	Total
Foreign Exchange (fe^*)	−6,856	−686	—	—	−7,542
Increase in Income (Δw^*)	−13,648	—	13,648	—	—
Contributions to the ISS (wt_{ss}^*)	−2,232	−568	2,800	—	—
Compensating Variation (d^{f*})	−9,534	—	—	—	−9,534
Skilled Labor (wc^*)	223	—	—	—	223
Taxes (t^*)	319	−319	—	—	—
Excess Profits (b^*)	−159	—	—	159	—
Total (Cost to the Employer)	−31,887	−1,573	16,448	159	−16,853

Source: Table 6.7 and row (4) in Table 13.4, for APRFE = 1.1.

Table 13.6   Breakdown of Valuation at Efficiency Prices of Unskilled Labor (In percentages)

Project	Government	Unskilled Workers	Other Firms	Total
−100.00	−4.93	51.58	0.50	−52.85

Source: Table 13.5.

receives by belonging to the system is equal to the cost of providing it (valued at market prices) and that the difference between this cost and the contribution to the ISS is financed by the Government.

The breakdown of the valuation of unskilled labor shown in the rows in Table 13.5 does not pretend to suggest that this breakdown must be included when presenting the distributional effect of the project being analyzed. For our purposes, it will be sufficient for the project analyst to have the composition in percentages of the *Total* row, taking the cost to the employer as a base, since this will be the figure available in project documentation. This breakdown, derived from Table 13.5, appears in Table 13.6.

Finally, we should point out that a similar procedure can be used for foreign exchange. In fact, since foreign exchange has been treated as a non-produced input at the margin, total requirements fe_i^* must be interpreted as changes in demand. This can affect the exchange rate and, consequently, the production of traded goods. The effects of the latter can be included in the matrix, thus avoiding postulating equality between the market price and the long-run marginal cost of producing traded goods.[2]

---

2. See Section 3.5 and Londero (1994).

PART III

DIFFERENT
ASSUMPTIONS AND
VALUE JUDGMENTS

CHAPTER 14

ACCOUNTING PRICES OF INVESTMENT

The case studies presented so far correspond to the most frequently used version of "efficiency" analysis. As pointed out in Chapters 1 and 8, this operational version involves the assumption of equality between the discount rate and the rate of return at efficiency prices of marginally displaced investment. This chapter includes a brief presentation on the modifications required in this analysis when the above assumption is not valid, while the remaining value judgments on which efficiency analysis rests are maintained. In particular, we will try to highlight the importance acquired, in this case, by the quantification of income changes according to beneficiaries.

In general, the UNIDO (1972, Chapter 14) presentation, which can be referred to for a more detailed explanation of some of the topics considered, will be followed. Readers already familiar with the work of UNIDO will find in this chapter a simple presentation of accounting prices of investment (valued at efficiency prices) and of investment *funds*. In addition, the reader will see that in order to apply these accounting prices, it is necessary to have available the distribution of income changes brought about by the project analyzed and by the one marginally displaced.

14.1 The Concept

Let us assume that a project is being considered whose investment at efficiency prices is I, the profitability of which is q_m during the only period of useful life, and the benefits of which will be entirely for consumption. In this case the flow of costs and benefits at efficiency prices will be

$$- I; I (1 + q_m)$$

If the discount rate d is equal to q_m, the present value of the consumption generated by this investment will be equal to the consumption lost by investing I, that is,

$$I = \frac{I (1 + q_m)}{(1 + d)}$$

and in this sense, an additional unit of investment is said to be just as valuable as an additional unit of consumption. The situation does not change if, at the end of the first period, a proportion s_m of the benefits obtained is reinvested at q_m and the benefits of reinvestment are consumed in the second period. In this case, the flow of changes in consumption (costs and benefits) generated by the project and reinvestment will be

$$-I; I (1 + q_m) (1 - s_m); s_m I (1 + q_m)^2$$

In period zero, consumption I is lost in order to put it into investment. In period 1, benefits $I (1 + q_m)$ are obtained, of which only a proportion $(1 - s_m)$ is consumed and the remainder reinvested. Finally, in period 2 what is invested in period 1, $s_m I (1 + q_m)$ is recovered, plus additional benefits q_m per unit reinvested. Since $d = q_m$, the present value of the flow of consumption will be nil

$$-I + \frac{I (1 + q_m) (1 - s_m)}{(1 + d)} + \frac{s_m I (1 + q_m)^2}{(1 + d)^2} = 0$$

and consequently

$$I = \frac{I (1 + q_m) (1 - s_m)}{(1 + d)} + \frac{s_m I (1 + q_m)^2}{(1 + d)^2} \qquad [14.1]$$

the value of the reduction I in consumption in year zero is equal to the present value of the consumption generated by the project and reinvestment. Thus, when $d = q_m$, a unit of investment is said to be, at the margin, as valuable as one of consumption in the sense that the reduction in present consumption is equal to the present value of the future additional consumption generated by investment. The reader will also find the above referred to as follows: the accounting price of a unit of investment valued at efficiency prices, or accounting price of investment, is equal to one, i.e. an additional peso's worth of investment generates a flow of consumption whose present value is one. In the simplified example of expression [14.1], the accounting price of investment I will be the present value of consumption generated by the investment (right-hand side of expression [14.1]) expressed per unit, that is,

$$P^{inv} = \frac{(1 + q_m)(1 - s_m)}{(1 + d)} + \frac{s_m(1 + q_m)^2}{(1 + d)^2} \qquad [14.2]$$

which will be equal to one, since it was assumed that $d = q_m$. However, if q_m were greater than the discount rate, the present value of the flow of consumption generated by an additional peso's worth of investment would be more than one ($P^{inv} > 1$). In this simplified example, the accounting price of investment depends on the values of q_m and s_m. The bigger q_m is, the bigger P^{inv} will be for a given discount rate and a given marginal propensity to save. At the same time, given a positive difference between q_m and d, the greater the marginal propensity to save of the recipient of the income, the bigger the P^{inv} would be.

If the present value of consumption generated by an additional unit of investment is greater than one, that is $P^{inv} > 1$, the present value of the additional net consumption generated by a project will depend on how the *net* changes in income generated are distributed between consumption and investment. In other words, it will depend on the distribution between consumption and investment of the income changes brought about by the project and by the alternative course of action. Consequently, acceptance of the interpersonal distributional value judgment of efficiency analysis will not be enough to aggregate the *income* changes until they have been distributed between consumption and investment and the latter expressed in consumption units. Only then will it be possible to speak of contributions to "total economic welfare" or benefits. This procedure involves using consumption (whatever its distribution) as a numeraire, although nothing prevents investment from being selected as a unit of account and expressing additional consumption in such units.[1]

---

1. The reader may have encountered the recommendation in literature on the subject that when $q > d$ either q or a weighted average of q and d must be used as the discount rate (e.g. Harberger, 1973). UNIDO (1972, Section 13.4), Feldstein (1973) and Ray (1984) have shown that these approaches are generally incorrect and they are only mentioned here because they are, curiously enough, very widespread.

14.2 Some Simple Formulas for Calculating the Accounting Price of Investment

In the preceding section, the use of an example of only two periods enabled us to define the concept of the accounting price of investment and to work out a simple expression for it. In this section, some simple formulas will be deduced for the P^{inv} that are also based on simplifying, although less restrictive assumptions.

To start with, let us assume that a project is being analyzed whose investment, which is all effected in year zero, is I_0 valued at market prices and $I_0 - T_0$ valued at efficiency prices, where T_0 represents the transfers explaining the difference between the value at market prices and at efficiency prices. Beginning in year 1, the project will produce annual income Y_t ($t = 1, 2, \ldots$) in perpetuity, which is entirely devoted to consumption, so that it is expressed in the numeraire. The flow of income changes brought about by the project will then be

$$- (I_0 - T_0); Y_1; Y_2; \ldots; Y_n; \ldots \qquad [14.3]$$

The alternative course of action to the one analyzed is a different use of *funds* I_0, since this is the variable controlled by whoever takes decisions and which in turn gives rise to the income changes Y_t generated by the project. Let us suppose that this alternative use is another project, the investment in which is also I_0 valued at market prices and $I_0 - T_0^m$ valued at efficiency prices. This alternative investment produces a constant stream of income changes equal to $q (I_0 - T_0^m)$ per year in perpetuity, which is also entirely devoted to consumption. Consequently, the flow of income changes brought about by the alternative project will be

$$- (I_0 - T_0^m); q (I_0 - T_0^m); q (I_0 - T_0^m); \ldots \qquad [14.4]$$

in which q is the change in income, excluding transfer T_0^m, per unit of investment expressed at efficiency prices. Since in this example q is a yield in perpetuity, it is also the project's internal rate of return.[2] In fact, the present value of flow [14.4] will be

$$- (I_0 - T_0^m) + \sum_{t=1}^{\infty} \frac{q (I_0 - T_0^m)}{(1 + q)^t} = - (I_0 - T_0^m)$$

$$+ q (I_0 - T_0^m) \sum_{t=1}^{\infty} \frac{1}{(1 + q)^t}$$

---

2. See Appendix E for clarification of the difference between q and the rate of return.

and recalling that for all $i > 0$,

$$\sum_{t=1}^{\infty} \frac{1}{(1+i)^t} = \frac{1}{i} \qquad [14.5]$$

the present value of income changes from the alternative project will be zero at rate q.

It is now possible to calculate the present value of the *net* income changes brought about by the project being examined, as the present value of the difference between flows [14.3] and [14.4], i.e.

$$PV(\Delta Y) = (I_0 - T_0^m) - (I_0 - T_0) + \sum_{t=1}^{\infty} \frac{Y_t}{(1+d)^t} - \sum_{t=1}^{\infty} \frac{q(I_0 - T_0^m)}{(1+d)^t}$$

Using expression [14.5] and effecting the operations between the first two terms of the right-hand side, we arrive at

$$PV(\Delta Y) = (T_0 - T_0^m) + \sum_{t=1}^{\infty} \frac{Y_t}{(1+d)^t} - \frac{q}{d}(I_0 - T_0^m) \qquad [14.6]$$

Since the income changes generated (excluding investment) by both projects were assumed to be for consumption, if $T_0 - T_0^m$ is nil or also goes to consumption, expression [14.6] will be the present value of the net (efficiency) *benefits* attributable to the project analyzed. If we assume that the difference $T_0 - T_0^m$ is nil for all practical purposes, the above expression is identical to that provided by UNIDO (1972) for the case in which all the income generated by investment is consumed.[3] The reader should note here that the last term in [14.6] is the present value of consumption generated by investing, in the alternative project, goods and services for a value of $I_0 - T_0^m$ at efficiency prices. Since q/d expresses this present value per unit of investment valued at efficiency prices, it will be the value of the accounting price of investment, that is

$$P^{inv} = \frac{q}{d} \qquad [14.7]$$

---

3. See UNIDO (1972, Chapter 14, Section 14.1)

This expression enables us to compare the "recipes" for the operational version of efficiency analysis, that is when the $q = d$ equality is achieved, with the results of assuming that $q \neq d$ when all the income generated is consumed. If the approximation $T_0 = T_0^m$ is accepted and if $q = d$, expression [14.6] can be written as

$$PV(\Delta B) = - (I_0 - T_0) + \sum_{t=1}^{\infty} \frac{B_t}{(1 + d)^t}$$

which is the present value of the net benefits from the project calculated according to the operational version of efficiency analysis. Although there are no reasons to assume that the $T_0 = T_0^m$ equality is strictly verified, in most practical cases, the differences will be minimal and the problem can be disregarded. However, the $q = d$ equality cannot simply be assumed. It can only be the conclusion of a more detailed discussion on the discount rate and an empirical investigation into the profitability at efficiency prices of marginally displaced investment.

The presentation of the flow of income changes from the alternative project on the basis of investment valued at efficiency prices (expression [14.4]) made it possible to deduce the accounting price of investment as it is defined in UNIDO (1972), the most widespread version of this concept. However, as the reader will see below, it is more useful to present the flow of income changes from alternative investment in a slightly different way. Instead of using q, the income per unit of investment from the alternative project when flows are expressed at efficiency prices, a coefficient of income per unit of investment *funds* (q') can be used so that

$$q' I_0 = q (I_0 - T_0)$$

Consequently, the flow of income changes from the alternative project will be

$$- (I_0 - T_0); q' I_0; q' I_0; \ldots \tag{14.8}$$

and the present value of *net* income changes attributable to the project being analyzed will be

$$PV(\Delta Y) = - (I_0 - T_0) + (I_0 - T_0^m) + \sum_{t=1}^{\infty} \frac{Y_t}{(1 + d)^t} - \sum_{t=1}^{\infty} \frac{q' I_0}{(1 + d)^t} \tag{14.9}$$

Assuming now that $T_0 = T_0^m$ is also devoted to consumption, and following the same steps as in the previous case, [14.9] can be expressed as the present value of net benefits.

$$PV(\Delta B) = (T_0 - T_0^m) + \sum_{t=1}^{\infty} \frac{B_t}{(1 + d)^t} - \frac{q'}{d} I_0 \qquad [14.10]$$

in which

$$P^{finv} = \frac{q'}{d}$$

is the accounting price of investment *funds* I_0.

14.3 The Accounting Price of Investment Funds When Part of the Benefits is Reinvested

In the preceding section, an accounting price of investment funds was deduced for the case in which all income generated by both projects, the one being examined and the alternative, is devoted to consumption. However, part of the investment will be reinvested so that the expression for the P^{finv} will also have to take into account the present value of consumption coming from *reinvesting* the income generated. Suppose initially that the marginal propensities to save on the changes in income brought about by both projects are both equal to s and that these savings are reinvested in both cases at rate q', from which in turn a proportion $(1 - s)$ is consumed and a part s is reinvested, also at rate q', and so on. In this case, the present value of the additional flow of consumption (benefits) attributable to the project analyzed will be

$$PV(\Delta B) = (T_0 - T_0^m)\,[(1 - s) + s\,P^{finv}] + \sum_{t=1}^{\infty} \frac{Y_t\,[(1 - s) + s\,P^{finv}]}{(1 + d)^t}$$

$$- q'\,I_0\,[(1 - s) + s\,P^{finv}] \sum_{t=1}^{\infty} \frac{1}{(1 + d)^t} \qquad [14.11]$$

The difference between this way of expressing net benefits and that used in [14.10] is that each change in income has been broken down into consumption $(1 - s)$ and investment (s) and the latter has been expressed in units of consumption through the P^{finv} or present value of consumption generated per

237

unit of investment funds. If ΔC is used to indicate the present value of consumption generated by the use of I_0 in the alternative project, then

$$\Delta C = q' I_0 [(1 - s) + s P^{finv}] \sum_{t=1}^{\infty} \frac{1}{(1 + d)^t}$$

Using identity [14.5] and dividing both sides by I_0 yields

$$P^{finv} = \frac{\Delta C}{I_0} = \frac{q' [(1 - s) + s P^{finv}]}{d} \qquad [14.12]$$

from which P^{finv} becomes

$$P^{finv} = \frac{(1 - s) q'}{d - s q'} \qquad [14.13]$$

This expression is similar to the accounting price of investment deduced in UNIDO (1972), except that the latter is a corrector of investment valued at efficiency prices whereas P^{finv} is a corrector of investment *funds*. The expression for the P^{inv} of UNIDO (1972) can be deduced by the same procedure used here —expressing the income flows generated by the projects (the one analyzed and the alternative) according to the value at efficiency prices of the goods and services that are "invested."

Now, on the basis of [14.12] the present value of consumption generated by investing funds I_0 in the alternative marginal project can be obtained as follows:

$$\Delta C = I_0 P^{finv}$$

Consequently, the present value of additional consumption attributable to the project being analyzed (expression [14.11]) can now be written as

$$PV(\Delta B) = (T_0 - T_0^m) [(1 - s) + s P^{finv}]$$

$$+ \sum_{t=1}^{\infty} \frac{Y_t [(1 - s) + s P^{finv}]}{(1 + d)^t} - I_0 P^{finv} \qquad [14.14]$$

If we now assume that the alternative use of funds I_0 is only partially investment, the previous expression for $PV(\Delta B)$ has to be modified. For example, if in the absence of the project analyzed, only a proportion a of the funds would have been invested and the remainder $(1 - a)$ devoted to consumption, expression [14.14] would become

$$PV(\Delta B) = (T_0 - a\, T_0^m)\,[(1 - s) + s\, P^{finv}] - (1 - a)\, T_0^m$$
$$+ \sum_{t=1}^{\infty} \frac{Y_t\,[(1 - s) + s\, P^{finv}]}{(1 + d)^t} - I_0\,[a\, P^{finv} + (1 - a)] \qquad [14.15]$$

In these formulations, the reader should note that the marginal propensities to save on total benefits are assumed to be equal for both projects, the one being analyzed and the alternative. Given that the savings produced on income changes Y_t can be expressed as

$$s\, Y_t = \sum_i s^i\, Y_t^i$$

in which i indicates the individual or group of individuals, and those of the alternative project as

$$s_a\, q'\, I_0 = \sum_i s_a^i\, (q'\, I_0)^i$$

the assumption that the marginal propensities to save $(s = s_a)$ are equal implies, from a practical point of view, either a coincidence or an identical distribution of income changes per group defined according to their marginal propensities to save. This explains why the results in expression [14.14] and [14.15] are independent of the distribution of the income changes brought about by the alternative project. This and other simplifying assumptions can be discarded without significant complications. In the first place, the projects being compared do not need to have an infinite useful life, which is why from now on they will have a useful life of n years. Secondly, we will now assume that the marginal propensities to save on the income changes generated by each of the two projects are different since the distributions of these incomes according to those affected (gainers and losers) are different for each project. The assumption that investment is made in the first year and starts to generate benefits in the second will also be discarded. Finally, the assumption that the marginally displaced project yields constant annual income will be discarded. However, the assumptions of a single marginal propensity to save on income generated by reinvestment and a coefficient q' of benefits in perpetuity per

Table 14.1 Income Flows Generated by the Marginally Displaced Project

	h	$h+1$	$\cdots$	t	$\cdots$	n
Consumption	$(1-s_m)\,Y_h^m$	$(1-s_m)\,Y_{h+1}^m$	$\cdots$	$(1-s_m)\,Y_t^m$	$\cdots$	$(1-s_m)\,Y_n^m$
Savings	$s_m\,Y_h^m$	$s_m\,Y_{h+1}^m$	$\cdots$	$s_m\,Y_t^m$	$\cdots$	$s_m\,Y_n^m$

unit of reinvested funds will be retained. With these changes, expression [14.14] can be rewritten as

$$PV(\Delta B) = (T - T^m)\,[(1 - s_g) + s_g\,P^{finv}] + \sum_{t=k}^{n} \frac{Y_t^a\,[(1 - s_a) + s_a\,P^{finv}]}{(1 + d)^t}$$

[14.16]

$$- \sum_{t=h}^{n} \frac{Y_t^m[(1 - s_m) + s_m\,P^{finv}]}{(1 + d)^t}$$

in which the subscripts or superscripts represent the following:

m: the marginally displaced project

g: the recipients of transfers T. No distinction is made between recipients of transfers from one project or the other to avoid complicating notation even more

a: the project being analyzed

It is now easy to demonstrate that P^{finv} depends only on the coefficient of benefits from reinvestment (q') and on the marginal propensity to save on the income generated by these reinvestments. For that purpose any of the flows included in expression [14.16], for example the one for the marginally displaced investment, can be considered. This will generate the consumption and savings flows shown in Table 14.1. Each one of these savings $Y_t^m\,s_m$ will be invested at rate q', producing a present value in year t equal to

$$PV_t(\Delta C) = \sum_{j=1}^{\infty} \frac{s_m\,Y_t^m\,q'\,[(1 - s) + s\,P^{finv}]}{(1 + d)^j}$$

in which $j = (t + 1) - t$, i.e. the year after the one in which the savings (investment) are made. Following the same steps as in the previous cases we have

$$PV_t(\Delta C) = \frac{s_m\,Y_t^m\,q'\,[(1 - s) + s\,P^{finv}]}{d}$$

The present value of consumption generated per unit of investment funds or accounting price of these funds will then be

$$P^{finv} = \frac{PV_t(\Delta C)}{s_m \, Y_t^m} = \frac{q'(1-s) + q' s \, P^{finv}}{d}$$

from which we obtain

$$P^{finv} = \frac{(1-s) \, q'}{d - s \, q'}$$

This P^{finv} is the one that will now be used to calculate the present value of consumption originating in the reinvestments resulting from the flows of additional income in expression [14.16].

The reader may now go back to expression [14.16] and note that it can also be presented as a total of the *net* additions to consumption and savings (expressed in units of consumption) attributable to the project analyzed. However, the savings produced by each of the projects will depend on the marginal propensities to save of those affected, gainers or losers. For example, these propensities will depend on income levels, on whether the groups are urban or rural, and so on. In other words, in order to estimate the savings *attributable* to a project, the analyst needs to estimate not only the distribution, by group of beneficiaries, of income changes generated by the project but also that distribution generated by the alternative. In addition, given the objective, beneficiaries ought to be grouped together according to their marginal propensities to save. Since this distribution of additional income is the synthesis of the changes in *income* attributable to the project, the corresponding proportion of savings will have to be corrected by an accounting price for investment *funds*.

Finally, we should point out that different marginal propensities to save or different profitabilities q' between, for example, the public and private sectors, require sector-specific accounting prices of investment. The formulas for these prices depend on the income changes that reinvestments in one sector bring about for the other, a topic that lies beyond the scope of this study.[4]

14.4 An Example

The analysis of an industrial project in Chapter 9 was based on the assumption of equality between the discount rate and the rate of return at efficiency prices of marginally displaced investment. In fact, the present value of the displaced

---

4. See UNIDO (1972)

project was close to zero. In this section, the project will be analyzed under the assumption that the profitability of marginally displaced investments is greater than the discount rate. This analysis will be carried out first assuming that the distribution of income changes generated by the alternative project is not known, and second, assuming that it is.

The first step is to obtain an estimate of P^{finv}, i.e. to know the discount rate and to have estimates of the parameters q' and s. As an example, let

$$
\begin{aligned}
d &= 0.05 \\
q' &= 0.08 \\
s &= 0.28
\end{aligned}
$$

from which it follows that

$$P^{finv} = \frac{(1 - 0.38) \times 0.08}{0.05 - 0.28 \times 0.08}$$

$$P^{finv} = 2.09$$

The second step is to identify the distribution of the income changes generated by the project analyzed. This appears in Table 14.2 and corresponds to Table 9.10, with some changes in form to facilitate analysis. In particular, details of the project financing have been provided in order to make discussion of the alternative use of such funds possible. Investments valued at the prices paid by the project (145,000 + 11,600) are financed with long-term credit (86,000), a renewable line of short-term credit (11,600) and the investors' own funds (59,000).

The reader will remember from Chapter 9 that the project was one submitted to the National Development Bank (NDB) for financing, and that the objective of its cost-benefit analysis is to provide information on whether or not to finance the project, i.e. whether or not to grant the long-term loan for a present value of $86,000. Since the decision to carry out the project is not in the hands of the NDB, it can only consider the following alternatives; (a) grant the loan, which is equivalent to the situation *with* the project; and (b) not grant it, which is *not* necessarily equivalent to a *without* project situation since its sponsors can seek and obtain financing elsewhere.

Let us begin by assuming that the decision against financing it is equivalent to a without project situation since no alternative sources exist. Now, the specific nature of the without project situation requires that the alternative use of the funds be identified. The NDB knows that the alternative use of its $86,000 is the financing of other industrial projects, although it does not know which ones. The Bank also knows that if the loan is not granted, the $59,000 from the sponsors would also be invested through their participation

242

Table 14.2 Distribution of the Present Value of the Income Changes Generated by an Industrial Project (In $)

Source	Industrial Firms Project Investment	Industrial Firms Project Other	Other Firms	Unskilled Workers	Government Investment	Government Others	Total
Investment Costs	−156,600	—	—	2,139	—	−11,710	−166,171
• Fixed	−145,000	—	—	1,720	—	−11,217	−154,497
• Stock	−11,600	—	—	419	—	−493	−11,674
Financing	97,600	−53,100	−6,500	—	−38,000	—	—
• Long-term	86,000	−48,000	—	—	−38,000	—	—
• Short-term[a]	11,600	−5,100	−6,500	—	—	—	—
Current Income & Costs	—	172,670	4,200	16,093	—	58,033	250,996
• Sales	—	630,000	4,200	—	—	70,754	704,954
• Current Costs	—	−450,600	—	16,093	—	−19,451	−453,958
• Direct Taxes	—	−6,730	—	—	—	6,730	—
Total	−59,000	119,570	−2,300	18,232	−38,000	46,323	84,825

a. Assumes that the loss of the transfer from short-term financing (6,500) is completely absorbed by the firms, i.e. it is not passed on through prices of their products.
Source: Table 9.10.

243

in association with other industrial firms, thus reducing their demand for investment credit and allowing for additional investment to be financed for $59,000. Finally, as for short-term credit, we assume that the investments that would be undertaken in the without project situation would require an approximately equal volume of funds. Consequently, in the without project situation, the $156,600 would also be invested, although the Bank does not know on which specific projects. Thus, it follows that transfers within the *Industrial Firms* sector, and between this sector and the Government, would also take place in the without project situation, so that they cancel each other out when the "with minus without" net flow is calculated. With regard to the transfer to unskilled workers brought about by investment, this would vary between different projects, but as the alternative investments are not known, we assume that they would generate the same transfer, so that this too is cancelled when the net flows are calculated.

The only characteristic of the alternative investments that we know is their profitability, so the net benefits from the project (the additional consumption generated) can be calculated by using expression [14.14]:

$$PV(\Delta B) = (T_0 - T_0^m) \left[(1 - s) + s\, P^{finv} \right]$$

[14.14]

$$+ \sum_{t=1}^{\infty} \frac{Y_t \left[(1 - s) + s\, P^{finv} \right]}{(1 + d)^t} - I_0\, P^{finv}$$

Since in this case T_0 and T_m are assumed to be equal in amount and distribution, the expression for net benefits is reduced to

$$PV(\Delta C) = \sum_{t=k}^{n} \frac{Y_t \left[(1 - s) + s\, P^{finv} \right]}{(1 + d)^t} - I_0\, P^{finv}$$

in which the Y_t correspond to the row *Current Income & Costs* in Table 14.2. It is now necessary to break these income changes down into consumption and savings. For this purpose, the analyst must ensure that the distribution of income changes with which he is working is the final one, and that there are no transfers yet to be recorded. For example, in Chapter 9, the $4,200 received by the *Other Firms* as additional income originating in the *Current Income and Costs*, correspond to a reduction in prices which, we assume, these firms do *not* pass on through prices. If this transfer existed and had not yet been recorded in the distribution of income changes, it would have to be shown *before* the breakdown of these changes into consumption and invest-

244

ment. Otherwise, marginal propensities to save could be used that did not correspond to those of the real final recipients.

In accordance with the data available, the following marginal propensities to save have been estimated:

(a) the marginal propensity to save of firms, which includes the project and the other firms, is 0.35;
(b) that of unskilled workers is nil; and
(c) that of the Government on its current income is 0.20.

Consequently, the income changes in question can be broken down as shown in Table 14.3.

We can now calculate the present value of the net benefits generated by the project as

$$PV(\Delta C) = 177,484 + 73,512\ P^{finv} - 156,600\ P^{finv}$$

which for $P^{finv} = 2.09$ turns out to be

$$PV(\Delta C) = 3,830$$

This result shows that the present value of consumption generated by the project analyzed is greater than that resulting from using the investment funds on the financing of other projects, with a coefficient of benefits in perpetuity q' of 8%, on which 28% is reinvested.

It is thus evident that the distribution by beneficiary of the income changes generated by the project plays a vital role in the result, since the use of the funds for either consumption or investment depends on it. A redistribution of the income changes generated by the project changes the result. For example, the reader can check that a change in direct taxes affects the present value of net benefits because, in the hypothetical example used, the propensity to save of firms is different from that of the Government.

Let us now consider the case in which those projects that would be financed in the event that the loan to the project analyzed were not granted, are known

Table 14.3 Use of Current Net Income from the Industrial Project (In $)

	Consumption	Investment	Total
Firms	114,965	61,905	176,870
Workers	16,093	—	16,093
Government	46,426	11,607	58,033
Total	177,484	73,512	250,996

Source: Calculated on the basis of Table 14.2.

to the analyst. In order to compare the income changes of the projects, we also need to identify the distribution of these incomes for the alternative projects, which is shown in summary form in Table 14.4.

The expected result of the alternative use of the $86,000 yields a coefficient q practically identical to that of the project analyzed earlier, but differs considerably in the distribution of the income changes generated. This will affect the proportions of this income that will be devoted to consumption and to investment and, in that way, the outcome of comparing the alternatives. To make this comparison, we can begin by breaking down the income changes brought about by each alternative into: funds whose alternative uses are either consumption or investment; or funds that will end up being saved or spent on consumption. Next, we calculate the incremental consumption and investment balances resulting from executing the project being analyzed and, consequently, not carrying out the alternative project. Finally, we value the additional investment funds with the P^{finv} and add them to the respective additional consumption funds.

In the example analyzed (Table 14.2), the project uses funds whose alternative use is investment for a present value of $156,600, generating transfers to unskilled workers of $2,139 and to the Government for −$11,710. This investment will generate an income flow, the present value of which is $250,996, consisting of $177,484 of estimated expenditure on consumption and $73,512 of estimated expenditure on investment. Consequently, and according to the marginal propensities to save being used, the income generated by the project being analyzed can be broken down as shown in Table 14.5.

For the alternative projects, let us suppose, for example, that the alternative use for the investors' own funds and the short-term financing is also investment, and that the same marginal propensities to save of firms, unskilled workers and Government are applied. Now, since we know the alternative use of the financing and the propensities to save on current net income, we can follow the same procedure used for the project analyzed to calculate the distribution between consumption and investment of the income changes from the alternative projects. The results appear in Table 14.6.

To compare the project analyzed with the alternative course of action, we consider the difference between what is obtained from the former and what would be obtained from the latter. This amounts to calculating the difference between Tables 14.5 and 14.6, to come up with the following:

	Consumption	Investment	Total
Project Analyzed	170,255	−85,430	84,825
Alternative Project	−173,085	−(−88,210)	−84,875
	−2,830	2,780	−50

Table 14.4 Distribution of the Income Changes Brought About by the Alternative Projects (In $)

Source	Industrial Firms Project		Other Firms	Unskilled Workers	Consumers		Government		Total
	Investment	Other			Low-income	Remainder	Invest-ment	Other	
Investment Costs	−160,000	—	—	5,045	—	—	—	−11,220	−166,175
Finance	100,300	−54,300	−8,000	—	—	—	—	—	—
• Long-term	86,000	−48,000	—	—	—	—	−38,000	—	—
• Short-term	14,300	−6,300	−8,000	—	—	—	−38,000	—	—
Current Income & Costs	—	190,200	—	23,530	—	—	—	37,320	250,050
Total	−59,700	135,900	−8,000	28,575	—	—	−38,000	26,100	84,875

Table 14.5   Distribution of the Income Changes Generated by the Industrial Project, by Source and Use (In $)

Source	Use Consumption	Investment	Total
Investments	−7,229	−158,942	−166,171
• Financing	—	−156,600	−156,600
• Transfers to Workers	2,139	—	2,139
• Transfers to the Government	−9,368	−2,342	−11,710
Current Income & Costs	177,484	73,512	250,996
• Net Income of Firms	144,965	61,905	176,870
• Transfers to Workers	16,093	—	16,093
• Transfers to the Government	46,426	11,607	58,033
Total	170,255	−85,430	84,825

Source: Tables 14.2 and 14.3.

This shows that the project analyzed generates less direct consumption but uses more net investment funds. When valuing these investment funds with the $P^{finv} = 2.09$,

$$-2,830 + 2,780\ P^{finv} = 2,980$$

we can see that when the consumption generated by the differential effect of projects on investment funds is considered, the project analyzed generates more total consumption (direct and indirect) than the alternatives.

Table 14.6   Distribution of Income Changes Generated by the Alternative Projects by Source and Use (In $)

Source	Use Consumption	Investment	Total
Investments	−3,931	−162,244	−166,175
• Financing	—	−160,000	−160,000
• Transfers to Workers	5,045	—	5,045
• Transfers to the Government	−8,976	−2,244	−11,220
Current Income & Costs	177,016	74,034	251,050
• Net Income of Firms	123,630	66,570	190,200
• Transfers to Workers	23,530	—	23,530
• Transfers to the Government	29,856	7,464	37,320
Total	173,085	−88,210	84,875

Source: Tables 14.2 and 14.3.

CHAPTER 15

INTERPERSONAL DISTRIBUTIONAL WEIGHTS

Each time that the problem of the interpersonal aggregation of CVs has arisen so far, the efficiency analysis value judgment has been applied, i.e. the CVs of all those affected receive the same weight. This chapter briefly presents the implications of discarding this value judgment, and replacing it by another, which assigns different weights according to the consumption level of the person affected. The principles for calculating these weights will be dealt with in an introductory manner; the reader interested in more detailed discussions may consult Ray (1984) and Lal (1972). It should also be mentioned that discarding the interpersonal distributional value judgment of "efficiency" analysis has given rise to considerable controversy, which is outside the scope of the following presentation.[1]

---

1. In this regard, Balassa (1977), Harberger (1978 and 1980), Layard (1980), Little and Mirrlees (1974, Ch. 4), Mishan (1974 and 1982b), Ray (1984) and Schwartz and Berney (1977) can be consulted.

15.1 Introduction

If different people receive different weights, the value judgments on which these weights are based must be made explicit. The approaches summarized below are based on the following one: one additional unit of consumption is equally valuable for all people who have the same level of consumption, but one additional unit of consumption is more valuable (i.e. it receives a greater weight) the lower the consumption level of the recipient.

Thus, an additional unit of consumption for any individual i, whose level of consumption in year t is c_t^i, will receive a weight $w(c_t^i)$, while one for any individual j, whose consumption is greater $(c_t^j > c_t^i)$, will receive a smaller weight $[w(c_t^j) < w(c_t^i)]$. This value judgment may be represented, for example, in the form chosen in Figure 15.1, in which $\bar{c}_t$ indicates the per capita consumption level in year t. Now we have to select a consumption level per person for each year as a unit of account for that year. To facilitate comparison with the treatment of the discount rate in Section 8.4, per capita consumption each year will be chosen.[2] Thus, the weight for the CVs of individual i in year t will be

$$u_t^i = \frac{w(c_t^i)}{w(\bar{c}_t)}$$

which indicates how much more valuable an additional unit of consumption is in year t for a person with a consumption level c_t^i, in comparison with a person with the per capita consumption level.

Let us now consider a case in which total investment can be increased until all the projects are included whose rate of return (at the prices resulting from the interpersonal distributional value judgment being used) is higher than the discount rate. Consequently, an additional unit of consumption for the per capita level is as valuable as an additional unit of investment and the analysis does not require the use of an accounting price of investment. If a project affects person i in year t in CV_t^i, then $u_t^i CV_t^i$ expresses the CV of the person with consumption c_t^i in units *equivalent* to those for the person with the per capita level. Consequently,

$$B_t = \sum_i u_t^i CV_t^i$$

---

2. Some authors prefer to choose as the basis for comparison what they call the "critical income level" (Scott et al., 1976, Chapter 3) or "base consumption level" (Little and Mirrlees, 1974, Section 13.13).

Figure 15.1 Greater Weights Assigned to Lower Consumption Levels

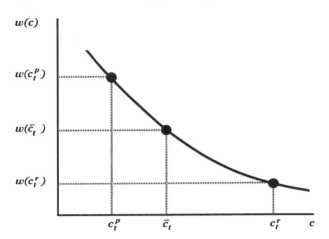

will be the benefits in year t expressed in *equivalent* units for the per capita level. In other words, increasing the consumption of individual i in year t by CV_t^i is, according to the interpersonal distributional value judgment, *equivalent* to increasing the consumption of a person with the per capita level by $u_t^i \, CV_t^i$.

It can now be seen clearly that as far as interpersonal distributional value judgments are concerned, efficiency analysis is a particular instance of what is presented here and implies a function $w(c)$ which, in Figure 15.1, would be a straight horizontal line. Consequently, the weights u_t^i are all equal to one and the benefits at efficiency prices in a year t can be calculated simply as follows:

$$B_t = \sum_i CV_t^i$$

15.2 Interpersonal and Intertemporal Weights

The discussion in Section 8.4 on a discount rate based on the principle of "diminishing marginal utility of consumption", included a reference to the fact that this approach was not consistent with equal interpersonal weights for all those affected. If an additional unit of future consumption is discounted in relation to one in the present because the future generation will have a higher per capita consumption level, by the same token, an additional unit of present consumption for a rich man should receive a lower interpersonal weight than one for a poor man. It is now possible to compare the expression for the

251

interpersonal weight u_t^i with that for the *discount factor* obtained in Section 8.4. These expressions are as follows:

$$u_t^i = \frac{w(c_t^i)}{w(\bar{c}_t)}$$

$$\frac{1}{(1 + d_t)} = \frac{w_t}{(1 + n)\, w_{t-1}} \qquad\qquad [8.2]$$

in which w_t in [8.2] is identical to $w(\bar{c}_t)$, i.e. the contribution to "total welfare" of an additional unit of consumption for the person with the per capita level. Consequently, both expressions compare in the same way the valuation of additional units of consumption for people with different levels of consumption. The first, u_t^i, does this between people with different levels of consumption at the same moment in time, expressing additional consumption in units that are equivalent for the per capita level at that time. The discount factor compares the increases in consumption, already expressed in equivalent units for the per capita level at each point in time, in order to take into account the changes in per capita consumption over time and to express annual increases in equivalent additional units for the per capita level of the year selected as the point of comparison, normally year zero. The discount factor also depends on the population growth rate because in a future year, a given additional consumption will be a smaller increase in the per capita consumption of that year, the greater the growth in population.

The reader should remember that when the formula for the discount rate was worked out, weights $w(c)$ were assumed to diminish at a constant rate and, assuming that the population growth rate was also constant, we arrived at the following expression:

$$1 + d = (1 - e\,\dot{c})(1 + n) \qquad\qquad [8.4]$$

that is, at a constant discount rate over time, which must be interpreted as a simplification of an operational nature. Now, since in practice the long-run growth rate of per capita consumption is also taken as being constant, this implies that parameter e is a constant. Consequently, the implicit $w(c)$ function will be one of constant elasticity, whose general form is

$$w(c) = Kc^e, \quad e < 0$$

On the basis of this function, weights u_t^i can be expressed as

$$u_t^i = \frac{w(c_t^i)}{w(\bar{c}_t)} = \left[\frac{c_t^i}{\bar{c}_t}\right]^e$$

and will depend on the *relation* between the consumption of person i in the without project situation in year t and the per capita level the same year. However, this creates the need to forecast the consumption level over time of those affected by a project. Since this is not feasible, in practice the *relation* between consumption levels in year zero is assumed to be constant over time,

$$\frac{c_0^i}{\bar{c}_0} = \frac{c_1^i}{\bar{c}_1} = \cdots = \frac{c_t^i}{\bar{c}_t}$$

which gives constant weights u^i over time. In this case, the weights u^i are calculated on the basis of the data for year zero and by making the distributional value judgment implicit in parameter e, numerically explicit.[3]

15.3 The Use of Interpersonal Weights

We begin discussion of the use of interpersonal weights on the simplifying assumption that the rate of return of marginally displaced investment, calculated using the weights, is equal to the discount rate, and that consequently, there is no need to be concerned with the distinction between consumption and investment. The step is merely illustrative, since the implausibility of this assumption will be discussed later.

Let the compensating variation of the project being analyzed for individual i in year t be denoted by CV_t^i and that for the marginally displaced project by CV_t^{mi}. As a result, the *net* benefits attributable to the project being analyzed in year t will be

$$\Delta B_t = \sum_i (CV_t^i - CV_t^{mi})\, u^i$$

in which u^i is the interpersonal weight of individual i. The present value of the flow of net benefits will then be

$$PV(\Delta B_t) = \sum_t \frac{\Delta B_t}{(1 + d)^t} = \sum_t \frac{\sum_i (CV_t^i - CV_t^{mi})\, u^i}{(1 + d)^t}$$

---

3. Note that the equal weights of efficiency analysis imply that $e = 0$.

and can be separated into the present value of costs and benefits from the project analyzed less that of the marginally displaced project. Thus we obtain:

$$PV(\Delta B_t) = \sum_t \frac{\sum_i CV_t^i u^i}{(1 + d)^t} - \sum_t \frac{\sum_i CV_t^{mi} u^i}{(1 + d)^t}$$

However, since the present value of benefits minus costs from the marginal project was assumed to be equal to zero (its rate of return is equal to the discount rate), the second term on the right is equal to zero and the present value of the *net* benefits of the project analyzed is simply

$$PV(\Delta B_t) = \sum_t \frac{\sum_i CV_t^i u^i}{(1 + d)^t}$$

the present value of its costs and benefits.

Now, how plausible is the assumption that the present value of the costs and benefits of the alternative project is nil? From a theoretical point of view, this would require subjecting *all* the investments to cost-benefit analysis, doing it with a single set of weights u^i and making the total investment budget big enough to include all the projects for which the present value of costs and benefits is positive. Thus, and as a hypothetical example, in societies where there is a public sector in which a single set of weights u^i could be used and the public investment budget could be of unrestricted size, together with a private sector which uses another set of weights, either explicitly or implicitly, the condition would not be met. In this hypothetical case, the condition could be met within the public sector but not in the private sector, so that the accounting price of private investment would not be equal to one. Consequently, to analyze public sector projects, we have to know the accounting price of investment corresponding to the private sector and, as discussed in the preceding chapter, the distribution of the income changes corresponding to the alternative use of the funds. This accounting price of investment will be different from the one worked out in Chapter 14 since the flow of consumption generated by reinvestment will have to be valued using weights u^i. Thus, this accounting price can be expressed as

$$P_u^{finv} = \frac{(1 - s) \, q' \bar{u}}{d - s \, q'}$$

in which $\bar{u}$ is the average weight derived from applying the u^i to the particular "average" distribution generated by the reinvestment. The above expression clearly results from a highly simplified example and attempts only to show the

254

lines along which the expressions deduced in the previous chapter have to be modified.

15.4 Changes in Government Revenue

Application of the analysis presented in the preceding sections runs into a particular difficulty when the issue of an interpersonal distribution weight for changes in Government revenue or expenditure arises. The system of Government revenue and expenditure functions in reality as a system of transfers between individuals, so that changes in Government revenue or expenditure have to be "translated" in terms of their effects on people according to the distributional effect of this system at the margin. This will allow for those changes in Government to be expressed in terms of changes in peoples' income. Thus, for example, a change ΔG_0 in Government expenditure in year zero will give rise to a set of compensating variations CV_t^i of the individuals affected and the interpersonal weight of Government funds in year zero (u_0^g) will be the one that satisfies

$$u_0^g \, \Delta G_0 = PV\left(\sum_i u^i \, CV_t^i\right)$$

Note that a change ΔG in one year gives rise to the present value of a flow of CVs, whenever part of those funds is used for investment. Clearly, in practice it would not be possible to calculate a weight u_t^g for each year t. It would be necessary to use a single weight u^g calculated taking into account the distributional effects of the variations ΔG_t for only a few years considered "representative" of Government activity.[4] The important thing is that this would require estimating the impact at the margin of Government revenue and expenditure, something about which very little is known, particularly in quantitative terms.

---

4. Although expressed in a different context, the reader may find some ideas in this connection in Londero and Morales Bayro (1982).

CHAPTER 16

THE EXPERIENCE OF THE
INTER-AMERICAN DEVELOPMENT
BANK

Since 1979, the Bank has been estimating the distribution of the income changes brought about by the projects it helps to finance. Beneficiaries are classified and results presented in a way similar to the one used in the analysis of alternative expansion plans for electricity generation (Chapter 10). Estimates proper are made according to methodological rules similar to those presented in Part I and Part II of this study. The Bank has thus accumulated practical experience in estimating the distribution of income changes generated by the type of projects it analyzes most frequently.

The first two sections of this chapter draw on the Bank's experience to summarize the different degrees of difficulty involved in these estimates. The presentation will be limited to projects whose costs and benefits correspond to goods and services that are the subject of commercial transactions. Consequently, we will exclude those such as environmental effects (noise, pollution) or public goods (recreational parks, public lighting), whose valuation could hardly be based on directly observable data on prices and quantities. In all cases, the presentation will be limited to the distribution by beneficiaries according to income levels.

Estimating the distributional effects made it clear that working methods had to be modified to meet the requirements of a more demanding project analysis. The last section of this chapter summarizes the experience acquired while implementing a new set of tasks, one never before undertaken on the scope implied by the operations of a multilateral financing organization.

16.1 Project Costs and Financing

Notwithstanding the risks inherent in generalizations, we can say that there are no serious problems in estimating the distribution of the main income changes brought about by project costs (in the financial sense), beyond those existing for their valuation at efficiency prices. As presented in Chapters 9, 10 and 12, the cash flow from the project is the point of departure for identifying the items that are mere financial transfers and allocating them according to those affected. Finally, the transfers that explain the difference between market and efficiency prices are recorded.

Difficulties may arise more from the availability of a set of "correctors" of market prices than from the identification and quantification of the main transfers. When the analyst uses accounting prices that have already been calculated, it is difficult for him to go beyond the identification and quantification of transfers that took place when they were estimated. For this reason, when the distribution of income changes generated by projects is sought, it is necessary to take the appropriate measures *at the time the accounting prices are estimated.* Thus, for example, when input-output techniques are used, particular attention has to be paid to the breakdown used when preparing the matrix for non-produced inputs and transfers (or matrix F in accordance with the notation used in Part II). When valuation is direct, as could be the case for imported inputs or regional labor, the income changes recorded will be limited by the level of detail with which the analyst may make the estimate. For example, if in order to approximate the efficiency price of labor, we assume that it is equal to wages in alternative employment, for distributional purposes no more income changes can be taken into account other than those resulting from the wage difference for the hired worker plus, if necessary, some additional effect due to contributions to the social security system.

The main difficulties in quantifying the amount of the transfers caused by financing, both long and short-term, have already been mentioned in Chapter 9. With regard to long-term financing, the main problem is expressing the loan repayment flow in real terms in those cases where there is no adjustment clause for inflation. Doing so will inevitably involve a margin of error that is unpredictable and always present in any financial analysis. The error will be bigger when fixed nominal interest rates are involved and smaller when they are variable, since the latter will at least reflect to some extent the prevailing rate of inflation, i.e. *a posteriori*, variable nominal interest rates will result in a real rate that changes less abruptly than a fixed nominal rate agreed on before the start of a period of change in the inflation rate.

Short-term loans will be less affected by this since inflation rates fluctuate less in the short-run, and the transfer per unit of loan amount will depend more on the policy for real interest rates. However, estimating total transfers resulting from these loans presents another problem whose origin lies in the way in which financial statements are often prepared. Short-term financing requirements are calculated on the basis of estimates for the sources and uses of funds. Not only do these already include possible errors originating in long-term financing but in addition, they normally assume that the financial balances of one year substitute for short-term credit the next. This normally results in estimates that after a certain moment show diminishing requirements for short-term funds over time. Conversely, experience shows that in response to low real interest rates in relation to the alternative private profitability of funds, firms will resort to more short-term borrowing and less use of their own funds than projected in the sources and uses of funds presented in the project document. In these cases, it may be preferable to derive short-term financing from firms' customary practices in the form of, for example, coefficients per unit of gross production value of the good in question.

Estimating the distribution of income changes originating in financing not only requires quantifying the *amount* of the transfer but also identifying who the *beneficiaries* are at both ends of it, i.e. who grants it and who receives it. One end will always be easy to identify because it will consist of a person or group of persons forming part of the project, for example, the industrial firm in the example of Chapter 9 or the farmers in the example in Chapter 12. The other end of the transfer will not be as easy to identify.

Let us assume first that the supply of funds is infinitely elastic at the prevailing interest rate and that, disregarding intermediary financial costs, the discount rate used is greater than this interest rate. Under these circumstances, all financing for the project will be additional, the transfer will be received by the project and granted by savers, and can be distributed by income sectors according to the respective marginal propensities to save. However, the real situation is usually the opposite. Supply is very inelastic to the interest rate, there are no financial markets in which the interest rate adjusts the supply and demand of funds, interest rates are regulated by the monetary authority and are lower than the private profitability of marginal investment, and credit is subject to a rationing mechanism. Consequently, any transfer implied in the financing will come from its alternative users. The final impact of the transfer will depend on the use which would have been made of these funds, and on its "degree of transferability" through prices, as opposed to retaining it as firms' profits. In this situation it is practically impossible to determine who grants the transfer.

Summing up, as far as project costs and financing are concerned, the main difficulties created by the estimation of distributional effects are found in estimating accounting prices and in identifying who grants the transfer that may accompany a loan. The remaining difficulties are well known and affect cost benefit and financial analyses in general. Estimating distributional effects only puts them on the spot. In the case of accounting prices, the difficulty has to be solved at the estimating level. This involves additional work to that required to obtain accounting price ratios at efficiency prices, due to the greater disaggregation required in the matrix of non-produced inputs and transfers.

16.2 Project "Output"

The topics mentioned so far affect, to a greater or lesser extent, all projects without distinction. Conversely, estimating the distribution of income changes originating in the "output" flow is more specific to the type of project, and depends on the nature of these "outputs" and on the procedure traditionally followed to estimate the respective CVs. The rest of this section briefly discusses, for some types of projects, specific aspects that affect estimating the distribution of income changes originating in the "output" flow.

A first group of projects is the one in which the main individuals affected are farmers and benefits are estimated on the basis of comparing "representative" farm budgets in situations with and without the project. Since the techniques used and the goods produced depend on the size of holdings, it is customary for such farm budgets to be prepared according to farm size and type of technique used. The latter are characteristics that determine the net income levels from farming activities, so that classification by size and technique also provides one for income yielded by *the farm*. Irrigation projects or those for rural access roads are examples of this type of project.

Two aspects which affect estimating the distributional effects are worth mentioning. The first is identifying the farm's net income with that of its owner, which may result in an estimation error whenever a person is, for example, the owner of a small farm affected by the project and of many others in or outside the project area. The second, already discussed in Section 7.3, has its origin in the lack of data on the marginal producers displaced by the additional supply. This leads to using the equality between price and average cost at efficiency prices for these producers, i.e. $p_0 = c^t$ in terms of the notation used in that section.

The first problem only affects the estimate of the distributional effect

259

through the classification of beneficiaries, while the second affects analysis at efficiency prices and through this the estimate of the distributional effect. When the project does not affect final prices by changing the technique that defines the production margin, and the error introduced by the two points mentioned above is not substantial, an estimate of the distributional effect based on comparing farm budgets in the situations with and without the project will be a good approximation. If the project does affect final prices in a significant manner, it will be necessary to estimate areas below the demand function, a complication affecting all types of projects and stemming from the measurement criterion (the CV). The problems that this may create for estimating the distributional effect will depend on whether we are dealing with consumer or intermediate goods. In the first case, it is necessary to have data on expenditure on such goods according to income brackets, which can normally be obtained from surveys on family income and expenditure. As for intermediate goods, the use of a range for the transfer through prices and estimating the effect of this transfer on consumption expenditure by income bracket, along with the errors involved, have already been discussed in Chapters 7 and 10.

A second set of projects consists of those for which the quantification of benefits at efficiency prices is effected mainly through willingness to pay for *additional* consumption of a single and relatively homogeneous good supplied by public or publicly-regulated monopolies, i.e. cases such as electricity and drinking water. Here, the main additional data required by the distributional analysis and specific to the type of project is residential consumption projections by income brackets, since this has a considerable effect on the final result. The importance of this information does not lie only, and sometimes not even principally, in the most general aspect of income elasticity of demand, but specifically in the supply policy that determines *access* to the service. Thus, projection of the quantity demanded by the medium and high-income sectors can be made, for example, on the basis of population and income growth rates and estimates of the income elasticity of demand.[1] Conversely, since a considerable proportion of lowest-income people do not have *access* to the good in question, projection of the quantity demanded by them depends also on the connection policy determining investment in distribution networks, and this is difficult, if at all possible, to forecast.

Road improvement projects in which the benefits are quantified by savings in time, vehicle operation and maintenance costs, have special characteristics beyond those regarding transfers and the incidence of firms' cost savings. Part of the savings in time and operating costs of light vehicles correspond to "pleasure trips" and it would be difficult to classify these savings according to

---

1. In reality, the problem is more complex. See Westley (1984b).

income brackets. In the case of passenger transportation, it would be necessary to classify the occupants according to income brackets, and their trips as business or pleasure. In both cases, data are required that are specific to the project (route of the road) and may be costly to gather, particularly if it is more than merely incorporating questions into an origin and destination survey. For these reasons, it is likely that many estimates will depend more on the analyst's criterion for reasonable assumptions to be made and less on data.

16.3 Some Implementation Issues

Estimating the distribution of income changes generated by a project has been and continues to be a learning process for the Bank, not only from the theoretical and methodological points of view, but also regarding implementation. This section deals with what the author considers the most important issues involved in executing a policy for estimating distributional effects. First we will consider the individual project and its analysis, and second, the issues concerning organization.

It is well known that project analysis begins during project preparation. Therefore, it is important to take into account the estimation of distributional effects right from the start of the project preparation, including the identification of alternatives and the gathering of specific data. Subsequently, this estimation should become an integral part of preparing financial flows by identifying the main effects by beneficiaries classified according to the same criteria that will be used in cost-benefit analysis. Only the allocation of transfers that explain the difference between market and efficiency prices should be left for the last step.

Concern for distributional effects of economic policy measures (part of which are investment decisions), should also be reflected in gathering basic data. Thus, censuses and surveys would include questions on income levels, questions would be formulated in a way that is compatible with existing complementary data, and surveys would be designed so as to avoid problems of low statistical significance that arise when processing data classified according to income levels. Many times, even though the analyst may try his best to consider the distributional aspects while preparing a project, he will find that the available data is insufficient. In that case, he has three alternatives: to ignore the distributional effects, to estimate them inadequately (with large margins of error), or to delay the formulation of the project in order to obtain the relevant data. It is unlikely for the last alternative to be chosen.

It may also be necessary to research subjects directly related to distributional effects. If, for example, when estimating the impact of an increase in the price of electricity purchased by industrial clients on consumer goods' prices (see sections 10.4 and 10.5), an input-output approach is used, at least two problems may arise:

(a) the transactions matrix is too aggregated for that purpose and/or electricity production has been assigned to a sector that also includes other services such as potable water, all of which could have been avoided; and
(b) household consumption is not disaggregated by income brackets.

To overcome these difficulties, partly due to inconsistency between the concern for distributional aspects and data collection, specific tasks may be required.

Another important issue to be considered is the margin of error involved in these estimates. All project analysts know that the results of a conventional cost-benefit analysis made on the basis of what we called here the operational version of efficiency analysis, are subject to error. Estimating the distribution of resulting income changes may uncover inconsistencies in the analysis and possibly help to reduce error. However, error may subsequently be increased by not estimating distributional effects as an integral part of project formulation, and by the consequences of using inadequate data. As a result, the estimate of distributional effects can only be considered indicative, rather than a precise calculation.

Organizational problems are to be expected when introducing the requirement for an estimation of distributional effects. The first one to be considered is the analyst's (and his supervisor's) reaction to change, as they will be forced to take a second look at their traditional approach and modify their work routines. This situation is made more serious by the fact that the traditional teaching of cost-benefit analysis is based on the criterion that transfers have a null value, all of which leads to an almost certain need for re-training and specialized supervision in order to facilitate "learning by doing". At the same time, there is extra work to be accounted for when estimating the effects of a project by groups affected. While most of this extra work should take place, as mentioned before, during the preparation of the project, it is more likely for it to be pushed forward to the appraisal stage, provoking the problems just described.

A second important point is how the analyst perceives the relevance of his estimation of distributional effects to the project's future. In the Bank, the estimates of distributional effects are not part of decision criteria. However, there is a cumulative goal for all projects analyzed over a four-year period. Consequently, the relation between an individual project and an accumulated four-year result is distant, a situation that may be aggravated when the analysts do not actively participate (or have responsibility) in selecting or preparing the projects to be analyzed. Under these circumstances, good communication between those with an overall view of goal achievement and those in charge of programming operations is essential. The analysts' participation in this process helps to highlight the importance of the project analysis level as well as to evaluate the expected results of alternative programs.

A third and last group of considerations is the potential for inconsistent goals. For example, in a case like the one at the Bank, where lending goals for broad economic sectors also exist, conflicts may arise between sector goals and the objective of reaching a certain distributional effect. In a multilateral financial organization, this conflict is intensified by the fact that the project universe is defined by the member country's investment policies. This situation becomes more difficult during "adjustment" periods dominated by fiscal considerations, during which the investment budget becomes a very important "adjustment" variable. Under any circumstances, when multiple goals are established, they must be consistent. Distributional goals are no exception to the rule.

APPENDICES

APPENDIX A

THE CHANGE IN CONSUMER SURPLUS AS AN APPROXIMATION OF THE COMPENSATING VARIATION

A.1 The Compensating Variation in Relation to Demand Functions*

Consider Figure A.1(a), which represents the consumer's indifference map between good q and all the remaining goods, and the consumer's budget constraint. Unlike Figure 2.1, and in order to simplify notation, the basket of the remaining goods m is represented by the equivalent monetary income for prices p_0^m,

$$Y = m\, p_0^m$$

so that the budget constraint will then be

$$Y_0 = Y + q\, p_0^q$$

---

* This section is based on the presentation by Morales Bayro (1981).

Initially, the consumer is situated at point A', consuming q_0 of good q given his monetary income Y_0 and the price p_0 of good q. The price of q relative to the prices of the remaining goods is implied in the slope of the straight line $Y_0 A'$. In this situation, the consumer spends $(Y_0 - Y_3)$ of his income on good q and Y_3 on other goods, obtaining a level of welfare represented by indifference curve U_0. Figure A.1(b) shows that point A, located on the individual demand curve D_y, follows from the selection of consumption q_0 for price $p_0 = (Y_0 - Y_3)/q_0$ and income Y_0. This demand curve D_y assumes that the consumer's monetary income is constant at Y_0.

Let us now suppose that a project increases the supply of q, reducing the price to the consumer. Figure A.1(a) shows that if his monetary income is not altered and the new price is implied in the slope of straight line $Y_0 D'$, the consumer will increase his consumption of q to q_3 in order to maximize his welfare at level U_2. Figure A.1(b) indicates that the new level of consumption q_3, associated with the new price $p_1 = (Y_1 - Y_3)/q_0$, corresponds to point D situated on demand D_y, which assumes that the consumer's monetary income is constant at Y_0.

Since the final impact of the reduction in the price of q is the possibility for the consumer to raise his level of welfare from U_0 to U_2, we want to obtain a monetary measure of his welfare increase $(U_2 - U_0)$. One of these measures is the compensating variation. This is defined as the reduction (increase) in the consumer's income needed, following the reduction (increase) in the price of a good, in order for the consumer to obtain his original level of welfare. In Figure A.1(a), the compensating variation of the reduction $p_0 - p_1$ in the price of q will be $Y_0 - Y_2$, since with this reduction in income, and at the new relative prices, the consumer can obtain the initial level of welfare U_0. However, as his equilibrium positions would only be observable from his market behavior, it is necessary to know the relation between the compensating variation and the demand functions.

The first approximation of the problem consists in estimating the maximum reduction in monetary income needed, after the reduction in the price of q, for the consumer to be able to purchase the original consumption basket corresponding to point A'. According to Figure A.1(a), if the consumer's monetary income is reduced by $(Y_0 - Y_1)$, he could if he wished consume the initial combination of q and other goods, since point A' is also located on the new budget line that starts at Y_1. Consequently, since in reality, monetary income continues to be Y_0, the individual could consume the same as before and even have the surplus monetary income $(Y_0 - Y_1)$. If applied to the additional consumption of q and other goods, this would enable him to raise his level of welfare from U_0 to U_2. As a result, the first approximation of the monetary measure of his "additional welfare" would be the "surplus" monetary income $(Y_0 - Y_1)$.

Figure A.1 The Compensating Variation of a Price Reduction and its Relation to the Demand Function

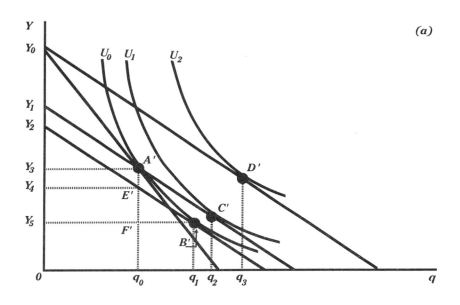

(a)

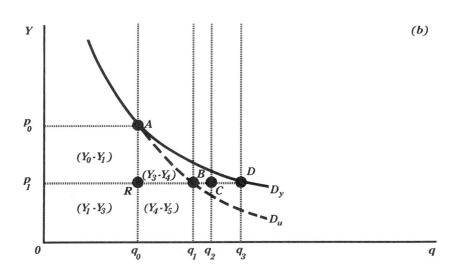

(b)

269

In Figure A.1(b), if the individual consumes the same quantity q_0 at the new price p_1, he would reduce his expenditure in an amount equal to the area $p_0 ARp_1$. In Figure A.1(a), this area can be expressed as follows:

$$p_0 ARp_1 = (p_0 - p_1) q_0$$

$$p_0 ARp_1 = \left[\frac{(Y_0 - Y_3)}{q_0} - \frac{(Y_1 - Y_3)}{q_0} \right] q_0$$

$$p_0 ARp_1 = (Y_0 - Y_1)$$

Consequently, the first approximation of the increase in the consumer's welfare corresponds to the area $p_0 ARp_1 = (Y_0 - Y_1)$ in Figure A.1(b).

However, if the consumer continues to react to changes in the conditions affecting him, he will not remain at point A' (Figure A.1(a)) when his monetary income is reduced to Y_1. As illustrated in this Figure, the consumer will decide that the best alternative within his reach is given by point C', since by spending part of his income Y_1 on consuming q_2 units of q (instead of only q_0), he can raise his level of welfare from U_0 to U_1. This means that if the consumer can freely choose his consumption basket, he will be at C' if his monetary income is Y_1 and at D' if his income increases to Y_0. As a result, additional income $(Y_0 - Y_1)$ is the equivalent in monetary units of additional welfare $(U_2 - U_1)$, which is less than the additional welfare $(U_2 - U_0)$ brought about by the reduction in the price of q.

In Figure A.1(a), the only way the consumer can be kept at the initial level of welfare U_0 through changes in his monetary income (given the new relative prices), is by reducing his monetary income by the additional amount $(Y_1 - Y_2)$. Thus, if the price reduction $(p_0 - p_1)$ is compensated by a reduction in income $(Y_0 - Y_2)$, the consumer will move from point A' to point B' located on the budget line that begins at Y_2. As B' implies the same level of welfare U_0 as A', this means that the price reduction has been exactly *compensated* by the reduction $(Y_0 - Y_2)$ in the consumer's monetary income, since he keeps exactly the same level of welfare U_0 once he has chosen the best combination of consumption (point B') within his reach, given the price and income constraints.

If his monetary income were only Y_2, the consumer would choose point B', consuming q_1 units of q and reaching a level of welfare U_0. Conversely, if his monetary income rises to Y_0, he will move to point D', consuming q_3 and raising his welfare level to U_2. Consequently, as his monetary income continues in reality to be Y_0, we can consider that the increase $(U_2 - U_0)$ in his welfare level (resulting from the reduction in the price of q) can be compensated by a reduction in his monetary income equal to

$$(Y_0 - Y_2) = (Y_0 - Y_1) + (Y_1 - Y_2)$$

Transferring the analysis to Figure A.1(b), we see that the first element $(Y_0 - Y_1)$ of the gain in welfare $(Y_0 - Y_2)$ is already implied in the area $p_0 A R p_1$. Consequently, only the element $(Y_1 - Y_2)$ needs to be identified. The first step is to observe that in Figure A.1(a) if the consumer's monetary income is only Y_2 and the price of q is p_1, he will consume q_1 units of q. This defines point B in Figure A.1(b) and implies that a demand function assuming that the consumer's welfare level is constant at U_0, and known as the compensated demand function, passes through points A and B.

In Figure A.1(a), the consumer does not alter his level of welfare U_0 when moving from point A' to point B' since the reduction in welfare due to the reduction $(Y_3 - Y_5)$ in the consumption of other goods is compensated exactly by the increase in his welfare from consuming $(q_1 - q_0)$ additional units of q. In other words, in order to consume $(q_1 - q_0)$ additional units of q, the consumer is willing to forgo up to $Y_3 - Y_5$ units of Y, called his *willingness to pay* for $(q_1 - q_0)$. Since the budget line which starts at Y_2 and goes through points E' and B' reflects his income and prevailing market prices, it follows that even if the consumer were willing to forgo up to $(Y_3 - Y_5)$ units of Y in order to consume $(q_1 - q_0)$ of q, in reality he only has to forgo $(Y_4 - Y_5)$. Consequently, the difference between his valuation of additional consumption $q_1 - q_0$ (his willingness to pay) and what he actually pays to obtain it can be expressed as

$$(Y_3 - Y_5) - (Y_4 - Y_5) = Y_3 - Y_4$$

As this magnitude is identical to the vertical distance $A'E'$ in Figure A.1(a), and this in turn is identical to $(Y_1 - Y_2)$, we conclude that in the expression

$$(Y_0 - Y_2) = (Y_0 - Y_1) + (Y_1 - Y_2)$$

$(Y_1 - Y_2)$ measures exactly the surplus that the consumer could obtain if he increased his consumption of q by $(q_1 - q_0)$ and to do so spent only income equivalent to $(Y_4 - Y_5)$ units of Y. Hence, if his monetary income were reduced by a magnitude $(Y_1 - Y_2)$, this would simply compensate that potential surplus and the consumer's welfare level would not change.

In Figure A.1(b), the area ABq_1q_0 below the demand function that assumes the consumer's welfare level is constant at U_0, represents the maximum amount that he would be willing to spend in order to consume $(q_1 - q_0)$ additional units of q, since in this way he would at least not change his welfare level. Similarly, the area RBq_1q_0 (defined by price p_1) expresses the actual expenditure required for additional consumption $(q_1 - q_0)$. Consequently, area ABq_1q_0 corresponds to income $(Y_3 - Y_5)$ and area RBq_1q_0 to income $(Y_4 - Y_5)$, and the difference between them (area ABR) is equivalent to income $(Y_3 - Y_4) = (Y_1 - Y_2)$. It can then be concluded that the increase in welfare $(U_2 - U_0)$ experienced by the individual due to the reduction in the price of q, can be compensated by a $(Y_0 - Y_2)$ reduction in his income, which in Figure A.1(b) is represented by the area p_0ABp_1. Thus, the compensating variation of the price reduction $p_0 - p_1$ will be:

$$(Y_0 - Y_2) = p_0ABp_1$$

or

$$(Y_0 - Y_1) + (Y_1 - Y_2) = p_0ARp_1 + ABR$$

Therefore the change in the consumer's surplus is not an exact measure of the compensating variation. In the example of Figure A.1(b), it overestimates the compensating variation in area ABD. The reader will note that BD is the change in the consumption of q resulting from a change in income $Y_0 - Y_2$ at the new relative prices. The further to the right point D' is from B' the greater the income elasticity of demand for q and the greater the ABD error will be for the same change in income. If the income elasticity of q were nil, point D' would be exactly above B', functions D_u and D_y would coincide in the interval $[q_0, q_e]$ and the change in the consumer's surplus would be an exact measure of the compensating variation. This situation is illustrated in Figures 2.1(a) and (b). Conversely, if income elasticity were negative, point D' would be to the left of B', D_u to the right of D_y and the change in consumer's surplus would underestimate the compensating variation. The situation is reversed when there is a price increase. The change in consumer's surplus will underestimate the compensating variation corresponding to a price increase when the income elasticity of q is positive, and will overestimate it when this elasticity is negative.[1]

A.2 The Significance of the Measurement Error

In the preceding section, we demonstrated that a change in the consumer's surplus caused by a price change is not an *exact* measure of the corresponding compensating variation (CV). Consequently, it is important to know how big the measurement error is that results from using the change in consumer surplus as an approximation of the CV. To do this the expression for the

---

1. Since the CV of a reduction $p_0 \rightarrow p_1$ is equal to the equivalent variation of the increase $p_1 \rightarrow p_0$, the equivalent variation is underestimated (overestimated) when the CV is overestimated (underestimated).

change in the consumer's surplus corresponding to a price change will be compared with that of the respective CV.

Starting from the elasticity of demand for q with respect to its own price,

$$E_{qq} = \frac{p}{q} \frac{\Delta q}{\Delta p}$$

the change in the quantity demanded for a change in price Δp will be

$$\Delta q = \frac{q \, \Delta p \, E_{qq}}{p} \qquad\qquad [A.1]$$

The change in the corresponding consumer's surplus (ΔCS) will be

$$\Delta CS = \Delta p \, q + \tfrac{1}{2} \Delta p \, \Delta q \qquad\qquad [A.2]$$

and substituting [A.1] in [A.2] finally yields

$$\Delta CS = \Delta p \, q + \tfrac{1}{2} \Delta p \, \frac{q \, \Delta p \, E_{qq}}{p}$$

$$\Delta CS = \Delta p \, q \, [1 + \frac{\tfrac{1}{2} \Delta p \, E_{qq}}{p}]$$

The corresponding compensating variation can be estimated by calculating Δq on the basis of the price elasticity of the compensated demand function (E^u_{qq}). This will be[2]

$$E^u_{qq} = E_{qq} + E_{qy} \, a \qquad\qquad [A.3]$$

in which

E_{qy} = income elasticity of demand for q

a = expenditure on q as a proportion of total expenditure

Using [A.3] and following a procedure similar to the preceding one results in

$$CV = \Delta p \, q \, [1 + \frac{\tfrac{1}{2} \Delta p \, (E_{qq} + E_{qy} \, a)}{p}]$$

---

2. See, for example, Henderson and Quandt (1971).

Table A.1   Ratios between the Change in Consumer's Surplus and the Respective Compensating Variation[a]

	$E_{qy} = 0.80$	$E_{qy} = 1.00$	$E_{qy} = 1.20$
$a = 0.02$			
$E_{qq} = 0.50$	1.0004	1.0005	1.0006
$E_{qq} = 0.90$	1.0004	1.0005	1.0006
$a = 0.04$			
$E_{qq} = 0.50$	1.0008	1.0010	1.0012
$E_{qq} = 0.90$	1.0008	1.0010	1.0012

a. Price reduction = 5%.

It is now possible to calculate the ratio between the change in consumer's surplus and the respective compensating variation for different values of E_{qy} and a. Table A.1 indicates that for acceptable values of these parameters, the error in estimating the CV of a price change is not significant. However, the ratios between the ΔCS and the CV to which Table A.1 refers, correspond to calculations of the ΔCS made on the basis of the real demand curve. In practice the economist will work, at best, with estimates of the demand function so that not even the sign of the error in estimating the CV will be known.

APPENDIX B

INTERPERSONAL AGGREGATION IN EFFICIENCY ANALYSIS

The objective of this Appendix is to show, from a different point of view than the one expressed in Chapters 1 and 2, that so-called efficiency analysis includes a distributional value judgment that is not always explicit.[1] Let $U^r(x_1, x_2, \ldots, x_n)$ be the utility function of consumer R and $U^p(x_1, x_2, \ldots, x_n)$ that of consumer P, in which x_i are the goods and services on which the utility level depends. The consumers maximize their utility function subject to their budgetary constraints (shown only for R)

$$Y^r - \sum_{i=1}^{n} x_i p_i = 0$$

---

1. Dasgupta and Pearce (1972, Chapters 1 & 2) gives a detailed discussion of the approach used in this Appendix. See also Pearce and Nash (1981, Chapter 3). The mathematical formulation of the consumer equilibrium model can be consulted in Henderson and Quandt (1971).

in which Y^r is the income of R, and p_i the market price of good or service x_i. This is equivalent to maximizing function

$$L^r = U^r(x_1, x_2, ..., x_n) - \lambda^r [Y^r - \sum_{i=1}^{n} x_i p_i]$$

The conditions necessary for this constrained maximum are

$$U_i^r - \lambda^r p_i = 0 \quad , \quad i = 1, 2, ..., n$$

[B.1]

$$Y^r - \sum_{i=1}^{n} x_i p_i = 0$$

in which U_i^r is the partial derivative of U^r with respect to x_i (i.e the change in U^r per unit of change in x_i, whereas all the other variables remain constant) and λ is the Lagrange multiplier. It can be shown that

$$\lambda = \frac{\partial U}{\partial Y}$$

i.e., that it is the marginal utility of income or change in the level of utility per unit of change in income when prices remain constant.

From equation [B.1] it follows that

$$U_i^r = \lambda^r p_i$$
$$U_i^p = \lambda^p p_i$$

and the increase in the utility level attributable to the consumption of an additional unit of x_i at (a constant) price p_i will be

$$dx_i^r U_i^r = \lambda^r dx_i^r p_i$$
$$dx_i^p U_i^p = \lambda^p dx_i^p p_i$$

When efficiency prices are used, the "willingness to pay" criterion indicates that the net increase in "total welfare" attributable to the increase in consumption $dx_i = dx_i^r + dx_i^p$ will be equal to

$$p_i dx_i = p_i dx_i^r + p_i dx_i^p$$

This assumes that the increase in "total welfare" ΔW will be

$$\Delta W = dx_i^r \, U_i^r + dx_i^p \, U_i^p = \lambda^r \, dx_i^r \, p_i + \lambda^p \, dx_i^p \, p_i$$

and that $\lambda^r = \lambda^p$. In other words, an additional unit of income is considered equally valuable for both consumers and the total welfare change is proportional to the sum of the individual welfare changes.

APPENDIX C

AGGREGATING AREAS BELOW ELECTRICITY DEMAND CURVES AND THE USE OF AN AVERAGE TARIFF

This Appendix presents a simple way of calculating an "average" tariff for consumers located in different consumption blocks that will allow us to obtain, using a pseudo aggregate demand curve, reasonable approximations of aggregates of areas below individual demand curves (willingness to pay and compensating variations).

If the variable tariff charge (p) increases by a proportion α for all consumers, and the change brought about in consumption does not change the block in which the consumer is, his willingness to pay for the energy that he no longer consumes can be expressed linearly as

$$WP_i = p_i^0 (g_i^0 - g_i^1) + \tfrac{1}{2}\alpha p_i^0 (g_i^0 - g_i^1)$$

in which

WP_i = willingness to pay of consumer i for energy $\Delta g_i = g_i^0 - g_i^1$
p_i^0 = variable tariff charge for consumer i before the tariff increase

278

α = proportion of increase in the tariff for consumer i, that is
$$p_i^1 = (1 + \alpha)\, p_i^0$$
g_i^0, g_i^1 = electricity consumption of i at prices p_i^0 and p_i^1, respectively

The willingness to pay for all the energy that is no longer consumed is

$$\sum_i WP_i = \sum_i p_i^0 \Delta g_i + \tfrac{1}{2} \sum_i \alpha\, p_i^0\, \Delta g_i \qquad [\text{C.1}]$$

This could be calculated by using an "average" tariff $\bar{p}$ complying with

$$\sum_i WP_i = \bar{p} \sum_i \Delta g_i + \tfrac{1}{2} \alpha \bar{p} \sum_i \Delta g_i \qquad [\text{C.2}]$$

From [C.1] = [C.2] we deduce that

$$\bar{p} = \frac{\displaystyle\sum_i p_i^0 \Delta g_i + \tfrac{1}{2} \alpha \sum_i p_i^0 \Delta g_i}{\displaystyle\sum_i \Delta g_i + \tfrac{1}{2} \alpha \sum_i \Delta g_i} = \frac{\displaystyle\sum_i p_i^0 \Delta g_i}{\displaystyle\sum_i \Delta g_i} \qquad [\text{C.3}]$$

is the correct formula for the average price $\bar{p}$ to be used for calculating the consumer's willingness to pay for energy $\Delta G = \Sigma_i\, \Delta g_i$. Since the price elasticity of demand of consumer i is

$$E_i = \frac{p_i^0}{g_i^0} \frac{\Delta g_i}{\Delta p_i}$$

Δg_i will be

$$\Delta g_i = \frac{E_i\, g_i^0\, \Delta p_i}{p_i^0}$$

$$\Delta g_i = \alpha\, E_i\, g_i^0 \qquad [\text{C.4}]$$

and substituting [C.4] in [C.3], the latter can be rewritten as

$$\bar{p} = \frac{\displaystyle\sum_i \alpha\, E_i\, p_i^0\, g_i^0}{\displaystyle\sum_i \alpha\, E_i\, g_i^0} \qquad [\text{C.5}]$$

279

If E_i is the same for all the consumers in the group, expression [C.5] is reduced to:

$$\bar{p} = \frac{\sum_i p_i^0 g_i^0}{\sum_i g_i^0} \qquad [C.6]$$

Expression [C.6] was the one used to calculate the average price in Table 10.2. This is valid for a uniform increase in the variable component of the tariff provided that:

(a) a linear approximation of the willingness to pay of each consumer is acceptable;
(b) the effect of a tariff increase does not change the block that the consumer is in; and
(c) all individual demand functions have the same price elasticity at prices p_i^0.

The average price $\bar{p}$ obtained with equation [C.5] also allows for sums of compensating variations to be calculated on the same set of assumptions. The compensating variation of the tariff increase to consumer i (CV_i) can be approximated as

$$CV_i = \alpha\, p_i^0\, g_i^0 - \tfrac{1}{2}\, \alpha\, p_i^0\, \Delta g_i$$

and the sum of the CV_i for an equal percentage increase α for all consumers will be

$$\sum_i CV_i = \alpha \left(\sum_i p_i^0 g_i^0 - \tfrac{1}{2} \sum_i p_i^0 \Delta g_i \right) \qquad [C.7]$$

The "average" tariff sought should verify

$$\sum_i CV_i = \alpha \left(\bar{p} \sum_i g_i^0 - \tfrac{1}{2} \bar{p} \sum_i \Delta g_i \right) \qquad [C.8]$$

From [C.7] = [C.8] it follows that

$$\bar{p} = \frac{\sum_i p_i^0 g_i^0 - \tfrac{1}{2} \sum_i p_i^0 \Delta g_i}{\sum_i g_i^0 - \tfrac{1}{2} \sum_i \Delta g_i} \qquad [C.9]$$

Substituting [C.4] in [C.9] we now obtain

$$\bar{p} = \frac{\sum\limits_{i} p_i^0 g_i^0 - \frac{1}{2} \alpha \sum\limits_{i} E_i p_i^0 g_i^0}{\sum\limits_{i} g_i^0 - \frac{1}{2} \alpha \sum\limits_{i} E_i g_i^0} \qquad [C.10]$$

and if E_i is equal for all the consumers in the group

$$\bar{p} = \frac{(1 - \frac{1}{2} \alpha E) \sum\limits_{i} p_i^0 g_i^0}{(1 - \frac{1}{2} \alpha E) \sum\limits_{i} g_i^0} \qquad [C.11]$$

$$\bar{p} = \frac{\sum\limits_{i} p_i^0 g_i^0}{\sum\limits_{i} g_i^0}$$

One problem arises when using expression [C.6] for the average tariff: new customers and "old" customers adjust differently to price increases. The new customers will adjust faster, since the price increase preceded their connection to the grid. In other words, it is logical to expect them to choose the electrical equipment after taking the new tariffs into account and, consequently, their adjustment will be closer to that indicated by the long-run price elasticity. Conversely, consumers connected to the grid prior to the tariff increase will only be able to adjust more slowly over time. Therefore connecting a consumer whose demand function is identical to that of an existing consumer will result in different Δg_i for the same price increase (see expression [C.3]) and the passage from equation [C.5] to [C.6] will not be possible.

One way of avoiding the problem raised by different speeds of adjustment is to treat the following components separately: (a) the consumption of "old" customers prior to the tariff increase, that adjusts slowly; (b) the change in consumption of those customers who adjust faster; and (c) the consumption of the new customers, who can probably make the long-run adjustment before being connected. Such a level of refinement has not been introduced in this work.

APPENDIX D

COMPARING EXPANSION PLANS
AND THE LONG-RUN
MARGINAL COST TARIFF

Determining tariff p, which maximizes the net benefits at efficiency prices B at time t, can be presented as a problem of maximizing the difference between willingness to pay WP_t for energy G_t and the cost of supplying it, C_t, i.e.

$$B_t(p) = WP_t[G_t(p)] - C_t[G_t(p)]$$

The necessary condition for this maximum will be

$$\frac{dWP_t}{dG_t}\frac{dG_t}{dp} = \frac{dC_t}{dG_t}\frac{dG_t}{dp}$$

equality between the price and marginal cost. However, when dealing with an investment plan, the problem can be presented as determining the *constant tariff over time p* that maximizes the present value of stream B_t, i.e.

$$max\ PV[B_t(p)] = max\ PV\{WP_t[G_t(p)] - C_t[G_t(p)]\}$$

The necessary condition for this maximum will be

$$\frac{dPV[B_t(p)]}{dp} = 0$$

which implies

$$PV\left[\frac{dWP_t}{dG_t}\frac{dG_t}{dp}\right] = PV\left[\frac{dC_t}{dG_t}\frac{dG_t}{dp}\right] \qquad [D.1]$$

The above condition can be interpreted as the equivalent in a dynamic context to equality between price and marginal cost, subject to the condition that p must be equal in each period t.[1]

Price p, which maximizes $PV[B_t]$, is the same as the one that maximizes

$$PV[\Delta B_t] = PV[B_t(p) - B_t(p_0)] \qquad [D.2]$$

the change in the present value of benefits on the basis of an initial price p_0 since the $B_t(p_0)$ are constant. Now, equation [D.2] can be written as

$$PV[\Delta B_t] = PV\{WP_t[G_t(p)] - WP_t[G_t(p_0)]\}$$
$$- PV\{C_t[G_t(p)] - C_t[G_t(p_0)]\}$$

that is,

$$PV[\Delta B_t] = PV\{\Delta WP_t[G_t(p)]\} - PV\{\Delta C_t[G_t(p)]\}$$

The procedure followed in Section 10.3 is an approximation of the maximum of $PV[\Delta B_t]$. Since a price increase was involved in those sections, the objective was to approximate the maximum difference between the present values of the cost saving and the value of the reduction in energy consumption. In addition, the analysis was carried out subject to the additional condition that the tariff *structure* was constant, since the percentage increases were the same for each type of tariff.

To find the tariff that maximizes $PV[B_t(p)]$, a similar procedure can be followed on the basis of [D.1]. The first step is to calculate the present value

---

1. The problem could also be expressed as that of finding vector $[p_t]$ that maximizes $PV[B_t]$, which would require a considerably more complicated algorithm for its solution. This approach would be made even more difficult by consideration of the difference between the short-run and long-run adjustments. Furthermore, the usefulness of a system of signals that changes each year is doubtful.

of the saving (increase) in costs corresponding to a certain initial $\overline{\Delta G}$ and to calculate the tariff $p_0 + \Delta p$ which verifies

$$p_0 \left(1 + \frac{\Delta p}{p_0}\right) \sum_t \frac{1}{(1 + d)^t} = \frac{\sum_t \frac{\Delta C_t}{(1 + d)^t}}{\overline{\Delta G}}$$

Then, knowing the price elasticity of the demand function(s), the $\Delta G(\Delta p)$ corresponding to this price change can be calculated and the preceding exercise repeated until $\overline{\Delta G} = \Delta G(\Delta p)$.

This procedure may be more effective for finding the tariff increase that maximizes the present value of benefits subject to the constraint of a constant price over time, in particular if the marginal cost is insensitive to different projections of demand $G_t - \Delta G$. However, the procedure used in Section 10.3 has an advantage: it can be used when there is a maximum acceptable tariff increase that is lower than that required for the condition [D.1] to be met.

APPENDIX E

THE CALCULATION OF PARAMETERS q AND q'

In Chapter 14, the formulas for P^{finv} were deduced by using a yield in perpetuity q', when in practice alternative investments will not generate a perpetual income stream. The problem is how to calculate a q' for the alternative project that yields an equivalent result. The present value of the changes in *income* generated by the marginally displaced project can be written as

$$PV(\Delta C^m) = - (I^m - T^m) + \sum_{t=k}^{n} \frac{B_t^m}{(1 + d)^t} \qquad [E.1]$$

in which $I^m - T^m$ is the present value of investment costs valued at efficiency prices. The hypothetical project that produces income in perpetuity q on the basis of an investment at efficiency prices equal to $I^m - T^m$, but which is carried out in year zero, and whose present value is $PV(\Delta C^m)$, will be

$$PV(\Delta C^m) = - (I_0^m - T_0^m) + \sum_{t=1}^{\infty} \frac{(I_0^m - T_0^m)\, q}{(1 + d)^t} \qquad [E.2]$$

Using expression [14.5], and recalling that by definition $I^m - T^m = I^m_0 - T^m_0$, expression [E.2] can also be written as

$$PV(\Delta C^m) = -(I^m - T^m) + \frac{(I^m_0 - T^m_0)\, q}{d}$$ [E.3]

Now, from [E.1] = [E.3] it follows that

$$\sum_{t=k}^{n} \frac{B^m_t}{(1 + d)^t} = \frac{(I^m - T^m)\, q}{d}$$

from which q can be found as

$$q = \frac{d}{(I^m - T^m)} \sum_{t=k}^{n} \frac{B^m_t}{(1 + d)^t}$$ [E.4]

Then, since

$$q'\, I^m = q\, (I^m - T^m)$$

we obtain

$$q' = \frac{q\, (I^m - T^m)}{I^m}$$

Now substituting [E.4] in the above expression we arrive at

$$q' = \frac{d}{I^m} \sum_{t=k}^{n} \frac{B^m_t}{(1 + d)^t}$$ [E.5]

It should be pointed out that the value of q obtained from [E.4] *is not* the internal rate of return (at efficiency prices) of the marginally displaced project. In Table E.1, the internal rate of return is 10.6% while the resulting value of q is 5.8% for a discount rate of 5%.

Table E.1 Flows of a Hypothetical Project

	Year						Present
Source	0	1	2	3	4	5	Value
$(I_t^m - T_t^m)$	-50	-70	—	—	—	—	-116.67
B_t^m	—	—	40	40	40	40	135.09
Total	-50	-70	40	40	40	40	18.42
		$d = 5\%$		$IRR = 10.6\%$		$q = 5.8\%$	

BIBLIOGRAPHY

Bacha, E. and Taylor L. (1971), Foreign Exchange Shadow Prices: A Critical Review of Current Theories. *Quarterly Journal of Economics.* Vol. 85, No. 2, pp. 197–224.

Balassa, B. (1977), The Income Distribution Parameter in Project Appraisal, in Balassa, B. and Nelson, R. *Economic Progress, Private Values, and Public Policy.* Amsterdam, North-Holland, pp. 217–232. World Bank Reprint Series. No. 41, Washington, D.C.: World Bank.

Bohi, D. (1981), *Analyzing Demand Behavior. A Study of Energy Elasticities.* Baltimore: The Johns Hopkins University Press.

Bruce, C. (1976), *Social Cost-Benefit Analysis: A Guide for Country and Project Economists to the Derivation and Application of Economic and Social Accounting Prices.* World Bank Staff Working Paper. No. 239, Washington, D.C.: World Bank.

Bulmer-Thomas, V. (1982), *Input-Output Analysis in Developing Countries. Sources, Methods and Applications.* New York: John Wiley.

Cargill, T. and Meyer, R. (1971), Estimating the Demand for Electricity by Time of Day. *Applied Economics.* Vol. 3, No. 4, pp. 233–246.

Castagnino, E. (1983), Guidelines for Estimating the Distributional Impact of Electricity Transmission and Distribution Projects. G-05, draft, Washington, D.C.: IDB.

Chase, S., ed. (1968), *Problems in Public Expenditure Analysis.* Washington, D.C.: The Brookings Institution.

289

Chenery, H. and Clark, P. (1963), *Interindustry Economics*. New York: Wiley.

Dasgupta, A. and Pearce, D. (1972), *Cost-Benefit Analysis: Theory and Practice*. London: The Macmillan Press.

Dasgupta, P. (1972), A Comparative Analysis of the UNIDO Guidelines and the OECD Manual. *Bulletin of the Oxford University Institute of Economics and Statistics*. Vol. 34, No. 1, pp. 33–51.

Dell, S. (1972), *The Inter-American Development Bank. A Study in Development Financing*. New York: Praeger.

Dobb, M. (1960), *An Essay on Economic Growth and Planning*. London: Routledge and Kegan.

Feldstein, M. (1973), The Inadequacy of Weighted Discount Rates, published in Layard (1972).

Ferguson, C. and Gould, J. (1975), *Microeconomic Theory*, 4th ed. Homewood: R. Irwin.

Fontaine, E. (1981), *Evaluación Social de Proyectos*. Santiago, Chile: Ediciones Universidad Católica.

Gittinger, J. (1982), *Economic Analysis of Agricultural Projects*, 2nd ed. Baltimore: The Johns Hopkins University Press.

Gutierrez, S. L. and Westley, G. (1979), *Economic Analysis of Electricity Supply Projects*. Washington, D.C.: IDB.

Hamilton, C. (1976), The Cost of Effort Expended: Examination of Some Arguments for Its Omission and an Illustration. *Oxford Economic Papers*. Vol. 28, No. 2, pp. 204–316.

———. (1977), On the Social Cost of Individual's Extra Effort. *Journal of Development Studies*. Vol. 13, No. 3, pp. 217–222.

Harberger, A. (1971a), On Measuring the Social Opportunity Cost of Labor. *International Labor Review*. Vol. 103, No. 6, pp. 559–579. Reprinted in Harberger (1973).

———. (1971b), Three Basic Postulates for Applied Welfare Economics. *Journal of Economic Literature*. Vol. IX, No. 3, pp. 785–797.

———. (1972), *Project Evaluation—Collected Papers*. London: The Macmillan Press.

———. (1973), On the UNIDO Guidelines for Social Project Evaluation. Proceedings and papers of the Symposium on the Use of Socioeconomic Investment Criteria in Project Evaluation. Washington, D.C.: IDB. Published in Schwartz and Berney (1977).

———. (1978), On the Use of Distributional Weights in Social Cost-Benefit Analysis. *Journal of Political Economy*. Vol. 86, No. 2 (Part II), pp. S87–S120.

———. (1980), Reply to Layard and Squire, *Journal of Political Economy*. Vol. 88, No. 5, pp. 1050–1052.

Harris, J. and Todaro, M. (1970), Migration, Unemployment and Development: A Two Sector Analysis. *American Economic Review*. Vol. 60, No. 1, pp. 126–142.

Helmers, F. (1979), *Project Planning and Income Distribution*. Boston, The Hague and London: Martinus Nijhoff.

Henderson, J. and Quandt, R. (1971), *Microeconomic Theory: A Mathematical Approach*. New York: McGraw-Hill.

Herrera, F. et al. (1970), *Una década de lucha por América Latina. La acción del Banco Interamericano de Desarrollo.* Mexico: Fondo de Cultura Económica.

Hicks, J. (1939), The Foundations of Welfare Economics. *Economic Journal.* Vol. 49, No. 196, pp. 696–712. Reprinted in Hicks (1981).

―――. (1975), The Scope and Status of Welfare Economics. *Oxford Economic Papers.* Vol. 27, No. 3, pp. 307–326. Reprinted in Hicks (1981).

―――. (1946), *Value and Capital.* 2nd ed. London: Oxford University Press.

―――. (1981), *Wealth and Welfare.* Cambridge, Mass.: Harvard University Press.

IAEA (1976), *WASP II User's Manual.* Vienna: International Atomic Energy Agency, Division of Nuclear Power Reactors.

―――. (1980), *WASP III User's Manual.* Vienna: International Atomic Energy Agency, Division of Nuclear Power Reactors.

IDB (1978), Proposal for an Increase in the Resources of the Inter-American Development Bank. Report to the Board of Governors. Document AB-648. Washington, D.C.: IDB.

Jenkins, R. and Joy, D. (1974), *Wien Automatic System Planning Package (WASP)— An Electric Utility Optimal Generation Expansion Planning Computer Code.* Tennessee: Oak Ridge National Laboratory.

Joshi, H. (1972), World Prices as Shadow Prices: A Critique. *Bulletin of the Oxford University Institute of Economics and Statistics.* Vol. 34, No. 1, pp. 53–73.

Joshi, V. (1972), The Rationale and Relevance of the Little-Mirrlees Criterion. *Bulletin of the Oxford University Institute of Economics and Statistics.* Vol. 34, No. 1, pp. 3–32.

Kornai, J. (1979), Appraisal of Project Appraisal, in M. Boskin, ed., *Economics and Human Welfare: Essays in Honor of Tibor Scitovsky.* New York: Academic Press.

Kumar, N. (1984), Social Cost-Benefit Analysis of an Export-Oriented Project with Foreign Collaboration in India. *Industry and Development.* No. 10, pp. 41–48, United Nations.

Lal, D. (1972), *On Estimating Income Distribution Weights for Project Analysis.* Economic Staff Working Paper No. 130, Washington, D.C.: World Bank.

―――. (1973), Disutility of Effort, Migration, and the Shadow Wage Rate. *Oxford Economic Papers.* Vol. 25, No. 1, pp. 112–126.

―――. (1980), *Prices for Planning: Towards the Reform of Indian* Planning. London: Heinemann.

Layard, R., ed. (1972), *Cost-Benefit Analysis.* Harmondsworth: Penguin Books.

―――. (1980), On the Use of Distributional Weights in Social Cost-Benefit Analysis. *Journal of Political Economy.* Vol. 88, No. 5, pp. 1041–1047.

Lekachman, R. (1982), *Greed is Not Enough.* New York: Pantheon.

Little, I. and Mirrlees, J. (1969), *Manual of Industrial Project Analysis in Developing Countries.* Vol. II, Social Cost-Benefit Analysis, Paris: OECD.

―――. (1974), *Project Appraisal and Planning in Developing Countries.* New York: Basic Books.

Londero, E. (1981), *El Salvador.* Published in Powers (1981).

_____. (1994), "Estimating the Accounting Price of Foreign Exchange: An Input-Output Approach", *Economic Systems Research*, Vol. 6, No. 4, pp. 415-434.

——— and Morales Bayro, L. (1982), *Sobre la estimación de la distribución de los beneficios económicos netos de un proyecto de inversión.* Paper on Project Analysis No. 20. Washington, D.C.: IDB.

Marglin, S. (1963), The Social Rate of Discount and the Optimal Rate of Investment. *Quarterly Journal of Economics.* Vol. 77, No. 1, pp. 95–111.

Mazumdar, D. (1976), The Rural-Urban Wage Gap, Migration, and the Shadow Wage. *Oxford Economic Papers.* Vol. 28, No. 3, pp. 406–425.

Meade, J. (1972), Review of *Cost-Benefit Analysis* by E. J. Mishan, *Economic Journal.* Vol. 82, No. 325, pp. 244–246.

Mishan, E. (1968), What is Producer's Surplus? *American Economic Review.* Vol. 58, No. 5 (Part I), pp. 1269–1282. Reprinted in Mishan (1981b).

———. (1974), Flexibility and Consistency in Project Evaluation. *Economica* (London). Vol. 41, No. 161, pp. 81–96. Reprinted in Mishan (1981b).

———. (1981a), *Introduction to Normative Economics.* New York and Oxford: Oxford University Press.

———. (1981b), *Economic Efficiency and Social Welfare. Selected Essays on Fundamental Aspects of the Economic Theory of Social Welfare.* London: Allen and Unwin.

———. (1981c), *The Difficulty in Evaluating Long-lived Projects.* Published in Mishan (1981b).

———. (1982), *Cost-Benefit Analysis,* 3rd ed. London: Allen and Unwin.

———. (1982b), The New Controversy about the Rationale of Economic Evaluation. *Journal of Economic Issues.* Vol. XVI, No. 1, pp. 29–47.

Morales Bayro, L. (1981), Guidelines for Measuring the Distributional Impact of Potable Water Supply Programs. G-08, draft, Washington, D.C.: IDB.

Munasinghe, M. (1979), *The Economics of Power System Reliability and Planning.* Baltimore: The John Hopkins University Press.

———, and Gellerson, M. (1979), Economic Criteria for Optimizing Power System Reliability Level. *The Bell Journal of Economics.* Vol. 10, No. 1, pp. 353–365.

Pearce, D. and Nash, C. (1981), *The Social Appraisal of Projects.* New York: John Wiley.

Powers, T., ed. (1981), *Estimating Accounting Prices for Project Appraisal.* Washington, D.C.: IDB.

———, and Valencia, C. (1978), *SIMOP Urban Water Model: A Model for Economic Appraisal of Potable Water Projects in Urban Areas—User Manual.* Paper on Project Analysis No. 5. Washington, D.C.: IDB.

PREALC (1977), *Situación y Perspectivas del Empleo en El Salvador.* Santiago, Chile: Programa Regional del Empleo para América Latina y el Caribe.

Ray, A. (1984), *Cost-Benefit Analysis. Issues and Methodologies.* Baltimore and London: The Johns Hopkins University Press.

Schwartz, H. and Berney, R., eds. (1977), *Social and Economic Dimension of Project Evaluation.* Washington, D.C.: IDB.

Scott, M.; MacArthur, J. and Newbery, D. (1976), *Project Appraisal in Practice.* London: Heinemann.

Sen, A. (1961), On Optimizing the Rate of Saving. *Economic Journal.* Vol. 71, No. 283, pp. 479–496. Reprinted in Sen (1984).

———. (1966), Peasants and Dualism with or without Surplus Labor. *The Journal of Political Economy.* Vol. 74, No. 5, pp. 425–450. Reprinted in Sen (1984).

———. (1970), *Collective Choice and Social Welfare.* San Francisco: Holden-Day.

———. (1971), The Flow of Financial Resources, Methods of Evaluating the Economic Effects of Private Foreign Investment. Document TD/B/C.3/94/Add.1. Geneva: UNCTAD.

———. (1972), Control Areas and Accounting Prices: An Approach to Economic Evaluation. *Economic Journal.* Vol. 82, No. 325S, pp. 486–501. Reprinted in Layard (1972) and Sen (1984).

———. (1982), Approaches to the Choice of Discount Rates for Social Benefit-Cost Analysis. In R. Lind, ed., *Discounting for Time and Risk in Energy Policy.* Washington, D.C.: Resources for the Future. Reprinted in Sen (1984).

———. (1984), *Resources, Values and Development.* Cambridge, Mass.: Harvard University Press.

Squire, L.; Little, I. and Durdag, M. (1979), *Application of Shadow Pricing to Country Economic Analysis with an Illustration from Pakistan.* World Bank Staff Working Paper No. 330. Washington, D.C.: World Bank.

——— and van der Tak, H. (1977), *Economic Analysis of Projects,* Baltimore: The Johns Hopkins University Press.

Stewart, F. (1975), A Note on Social Cost-Benefit Analysis and Class Conflict in LDCs. *World Development.* Vol. 3, No. 1, pp. 31–39.

Sylos-Labini, P. (1962), *Oligopoly and Technical Progress.* Cambridge Mass.: Harvard University Press.

Taylor, L. (1975), The Demand for Electricity: A Survey. *The Bell Journal of Economics.* Vol. 6, No. 1, pp. 74–110.

Turvey, R. and Anderson, D. (1977), *Electricity Economics.* Baltimore: The Johns Hopkins University Press.

UNIDO (1972), *Guidelines for Project Evaluation.* New York: United Nations. Prepared by P. Dasgupta, S. Marglin and A. K. Sen.

van der Tak, H. (1966), *The Economic Choice between Hydro-Electric and Thermal Power Developments.* World Bank Staff Occasional Paper No. 1. Washington, D.C.: World Bank.

Weisbrod, B. (1968), Income Redistribution Effects and Benefit-Cost Analysis. Published in Chase (1968) and reprinted in Layard (1972).

Weiss, J. (1980), Cost Benefit Analysis of Foreign Industrial Investments in Developing Countries. *Industry and Development.* No. 5, pp. 41–58.

Westley, G. (1981), *The Residential and Commercial Demand for Electricity in Paraguay.* Paper on Project Analysis No. 19. Washington, D.C.: IDB.

———. (1984a), *The Residential and Commercial Demand for Electricity in Costa Rica.* Paper on Project Analysis No. 24. Washington, D.C.: IDB.

———. (1984b), *Forecasting Electricity Demand: A General Approach and Case Study in the Dominican Republic.* Paper on Project Analysis No. 26. Washington, D.C.: IDB.

AUTHOR INDEX

296

SUBJECT INDEX

A

Accounting price: defined, 30–31; distribution of income changes and, 257, 259; for non-traded goods (input-output numerical example), 196–98; for non-traded goods (input-output technique formulas), 192–96; for non-traded goods (input-output techniques), 189–92; non-traded goods and long-run marginal cost structures and, 198–200. *See also* Foreign exchange (accounting prices of); Investment (accounting prices of); Labor (accounting price for); Prices

Agricultural credit project (project produces consumer goods) example, 103–5

B

Benefits figure: deriving the total (cost-benefit analysis), 3–8; Pareto's principle and, 9–15; reaction to efficiency analysis and, 15–19. *See also* Distributional *entries*

C

Capital costs (industrial project analysis), 132–33, 149

Charges (electricity). *See* Tariff's (electricity)

Compensated Pareto improvement, 17

Compensating variation (CV), 84, 117; accounting price of foreign exchange and, 31, 33, 35–38, 41, 42, 48–49; "average" tariff and estimating aggregates of, 278–81; change in consumer's surplus as an approximation of, 22, 267–74; defined, 4–5, 21; efficiency price of labor and, 75, 77; electricity expansion plans and, 172, 173, 174; equivalent variation and, 21–24; import substitution and, 63, 65; interpersonal distributional weights and,

D

299

Informal sector: electricity expansion plans and, 172; labor analysis and, 84, 85, 91, 95

Input-output techniques: accounting prices for non-traded goods and, 189–92; accounting prices for non-traded goods (cost structures) and, 198–200; accounting prices for nontraded goods formulas and, 192–96; accounting prices for non-traded goods (numerical example) and, 196–98; breakdown used in, 257; problems with, 262; unskilled labor and, 222–27

Inter-American Development Bank: estimating distributional effects and, 256–57; implementation issues and, 261–63; project costs and financing and distributional changes and, 257–59; project output and, 259–61

Interest rate: as discount rate, 119–23; financial analysis and, 257, 258; industrial project analysis (financial flows) and, 134, 135, 139, 149

Intermediate goods: accounting price of foreign exchange and imported, 42–43, 50, 54; non-traded goods accounting price analysis and, 193, 195, 196; non-traded goods valuation and, 110–15

Interpersonal welfare comparisons, 27–28; accounting price of foreign exchange and, 31; accounting prices of investment and, 233; cost-benefit analysis and, 6–7, 8, 11; import substitution and, 65; in efficiency analysis, 275–77; irrigation project analysis and, 221. See also Distributional value judgments; Interpersonal distributional weights

Interpersonal distributional weights: accounting price of skilled labor and, 84; changes in government revenue and expenditure and, 255; consumption and, 249, 250–53; disregarding, 249; use of, 253–55. See also Distributional value judgments; Interpersonal welfare comparisons

Intertemporal comparisons: cost-benefit analysis and, 4–5; deriving weights for, 117; discount rate and, 116–19, 121, 127

Intertemporal distributional weights, 251–53

Investment, 200; cost-benefit analysis and, 20; cost structure construction and, 199; discount rate and project for, 116–27; electricity expansion plans and, 151; foreign, 145–47; industrial project analysis (capital costs) and, 132–33, 139, 145, 147; industrial project analysis (stocks) and, 131; irrigation project analysis and, 202; project that increases foreign exchange by increasing exports and, 32–40

Investment (accounting prices of), 250; concept of, 232–33; correct formula for profitability and, 285–87; examples, 241–48; formulas for calculating, 234–37; public sector and, 254; reinvestment of benefits and, 237–41; UNIDO presentation and, 231, 235, 236, 238

Investment funds, 231, 238, 241, 248

Irrigation project cost-benefit analysis: analysis of project and, 201–7; income changes generated by project and, 216–21; value of inputs (broken down into non-produced inputs and transfers) and, 207–16

Irrigation project (project produces consumer goods) example, 105–10

L

Labor (accounting prices for): accounting prices of investment and, 245, 246; imported labor, 82, 83; income changes and, 257; industrial project analysis and, 129, 133, 141; industrial project example of, 93–96; irrigation project and, 220; non-traded goods accounting price analysis and, 190, 191–92, 193, 196; skilled labor, 81–84, 129, 133, 196, 222; social security contributions and, 92–93, 94, 95; unskilled labor, 84–92, 93, 129, 133, 141, 172, 174, 190, 191–92, 193, 196, 220, 245, 246; unskilled labor and input-output techniques and, 222–27

Labor (efficiency price), 75–81
Labor migration, 83, 86–91, 94, 95

Technical change (examples of non-traded goods valuation process), 103–10; irrigation projects as, 202

Trade costs: accounting price of foreign exchange and, 33, 47, 52–53, 54; import substitution and, 61, 65; industrial project analysis and, 132, 133; irrigation project and, 207, 208, 209, 210, 211; labor analysis and, 94; non-traded goods accounting price analysis and, 193; project increase in exports and, 66; traded goods valuation and, 58, 59; unskilled labor and, 224

Traded goods valuation: defining, 55–56, exported goods demand increases and, 58–60; imported goods demand increases and, 56–58; import substitution and, 60–66; project increases exports and, 66–67

Trade incentives and disincentives, 54, 55, 56, 60, 66

Transportation (passenger), 261

Transport costs: accounting price of foreign exchange and, 33, 47, 52–53, 54; import substitution and, 61, 65; industrial project analysis and, 129, 132, 133; irrigation project and, 207, 208, 209, 210, 211; labor analysis and, 94; non-traded goods accounting price analysis and, 193; project increase in exports and, 66; traded goods valuation and, 58, 59; unskilled labor analysis and, 224

U

"Uncommitted public income" numeraire, 71

Underemployment, 84, 89, 90, 91, 94, 95

Unskilled labor: accounting price of, 84–92; accounting price of non-traded goods and, 190, 191–92, 193; accounting prices of investment and, 245, 246; electricity expansion plans and, 172, 174; industrial project analysis and, 129, 133, 141; irrigation project and, 220. *See also* Labor *entries*

W

Wages: accounting price of non-traded goods and, 191, 192; accounting price of skilled labor and, 82, 83; accounting price of unskilled labor and, 84, 85, 88, 89; efficiency price of labor and, 75, 77, 79; electricity expansion plans and, 172; irrigation project analysis and, 220; supply of labor and, 72–74; "reservation," 89, 90

WASP II model (electricity generating system expansion plan analysis), 152, 154, 165, 172

Willingness to pay: accounting price of foreign exchange and, 35, 37–38, 41, 42, 43, 52; an "average" tariff to estimate, 278–81; as valuation criterion, 276; compensating variations and, 20, 24–29; defined, 271; electricity expansion plans and, 155–56, 168, 170, 173; import substitution and, 63, 65; marginal cost tariff and, 282–84; traded goods valuation and, 58

Without project concept, 30; accounting prices of investment and, 242; efficiency analysis example and, 15; industrial project analysis and, 139; irrigation project and, 207; project increases demand for exported goods (trade goods valuation) and, 59; project "output" and, 259; project produces consumer goods examples and, 103, 105, 108. *See also* Projects

DATE DUE

DEC 0 6 1998			
APR 2 6 2000			
MAR 0 9 2001			
6/25/01			
8/24/01			
			Printed in USA